D0761875

FREE TO JUDGE

Kang, Michael S., 1973-
Free to judge : the power of
campaign money in judicial ele
2023.
33305256903661
ca 09/08/23

Free to Judge

The Power of Campaign Money in Judicial Elections

MICHAEL S. KANG
AND JOANNA M. SHEPHERD

STANFORD UNIVERSITY PRESS
Stanford, California

Stanford University Press
Stanford, California

© 2023 by Michael S. Kang and Joanna M. Shepherd. All rights reserved.

No part of this book may be reproduced or transmitted in any form or by any means, electronic or mechanical, including photocopying and recording, or in any information storage or retrieval system, without the prior written permission of Stanford University Press.

Printed in the United States of America on acid-free, archival-quality paper
ISBN 9781503627611 (cloth)
ISBN 9781503636200 (electronic)

Library of Congress Control Number: 2022052468

Library of Congress Cataloging-in-Publication Data available upon request.

Cover design: George Kirkpatrick
Cover painting: Michele Rushworth, *Judge Wm. F Downes, 2012*, oil on canvas, 40″ × 30″, Cheyenne Federal Courthouse, Wyoming
Typeset by Newgen in Minion Pro 10/14.4

Table of Contents

Acknowledgments vii

1 The Modern Era of Big Money Judicial Elections 1

2 The Rise of Judicial Elections 19
How We Got Where We Are

3 The Crocodile in the Bathtub 57
How Elections and Money Influence Judges

4 Why Money Matters 96

5 How to Fix Judicial Elections and Campaign Finance 133

Appendix 163

Notes 173

Index 199

Acknowledgments

OUR COLLABORATION BEGAN MORE THAN a decade ago when one of us, Joanna, ran a brown bag presentation of her preliminary findings on campaign contributions to elected judges and subsequent judicial decisions by those judges. The most interesting pattern in her findings was a relationship to partisanship that might not have been obvious at first but jumped out to Michael, as a political scientist and election law specialist. It was clear to both of us that neither of us could write the best paper from her findings without the other, and so began a long scholarly partnership that perfectly marries our individual skills and expertise. We are thankful that our lasting partnership has been not only productive, but also bolstered by our even longer friendship since we both began our legal academic careers together, long ago at Emory Law School.

We have many people to thank for their support, love, and friendship. Foremost, we thank our families for all that they do and all that they mean to us. Michael would like to thank his wife, Julie Cho, and their daughter, Kate, who makes them proud every day. Joanna would like to thank her husband, Richard Fields, and her two children, Ted and Sophia Shepherd, who have endured many conversations about this research around the dinner table.

This book would not have been possible, and certainly would not have come to life, without the many current and retired judges who shared their career experiences with us. Of course, we thank Marsha Ternus, Penny White, Bridget McCormack, and Brent Benjamin for discussing their careers and allowing us to understand judicial elections and campaign finance from their perspective. And we have met so many other judges, too many to thank individually, who invested their time and energy into giving us insight into a career that depends on dodging the crocodile in the bathtub we discuss in the book.

The book and all our work together benefitted immensely from the insights of our professional colleagues, both at our home institutions and elsewhere, throughout our careers. We started together at Emory Law School, which mentored us into professionals and taught us how to conduct the type of research upon which the book is based. We thank Rafael Pardo, who gave us the idea for the book's title and many other insights, as well as Bobby Ahdieh, Tom Arthur, Bill Buzbee, Mary Dudziak, Tim Holbrook, Kay Levine, Jonathan Nash, Robert Schapiro, and Fred Smith, among others, for their tireless efforts to help us improve our work. We also thank Michael's colleagues at Northwestern Pritzker Law School, where he moved in 2018, including Steve Calabresi, Zach Clopton, Erin Delaney, Shari Seidman Diamond, Tonja Jacobi, Andy Koppelman, Alex Lee, Jide Nzelibe, Jim Pfander, Marty Redish, Nadav Shoked, Matt Spitzer, and Emerson Tiller, again among many others, who offered valuable suggestions and observations at various presentations of the book.

There are so many friends and fellow students of judicial elections outside our home institutions who have encouraged our efforts and made our work better in every way. At risk of omitting many important people, we would like to thank specifically Alicia Bannon, Richard Briffault, Lee Epstein, Nuno Garoupa, Tracey George, Mitu Gulati, Sam Issacharoff, Pam Karlan, Bert Kritzer, Nancy Leong, Lori Ringhand, and Albert Yoon. They have guided to us to better answers so many times, in so many ways, over the past decade. We similarly appreciate all the feedback we've received from workshops and conferences at Emory University School of Law, Northwestern Pritzker School of Law, DePaul Law School, Duke University Law School, Florida State Law School, Harvard Law School, Stanford Law School, University of Chicago Law School, University of Denver Law School, University of Florida Law School, University of Georgia Law School, University of Illinois Law School, University of Kansas Law School, University of North Carolina Law School, University of Texas Law School, University of Toronto Law School, University of Wisconsin Law School, University of Virginia Law School, USC Gould School of Law, Vanderbilt Law School, Washington University Law School, the Annual Midwest Political Science Association Conference, American Law & Economics Association Conference, and Canadian Law and Economics Association Conference, among others. All errors and misstatements are definitely ours alone.

A number of deans and institutions have supported our work over the years as well. David Partlett, Robert Schapiro, and Mary Anne Bobinski gave us institutional support as deans at Emory Law School, while Dan Rodriguez, Kim Yuracko, Jim Speta, and Hari Osofsky provided institutional support as deans of Northwestern Pritzker School of Law. The American Constitution Society also funded and featured part of our work, on television and attack ads, discussed in the book.

We thank Stanford University Press and the ever-patient Marcela Maxfield, who blessed us with their guidance and wisdom in the writing of this book. We were lucky to have found Marcela, who shepherded us to publication despite the challenges of COVID and various travails that popped up during the past three years. She patiently nudged us to the finish line, and we are ever grateful.

Last but not least, we thank our student research assistants over the many years who have contributed to the work that culminates with this book. At Emory, Michael worked with Elizabeth Accurso, Emily Bronstein, Will Bradbury, Sagiv Edelman, Madeline Gwyn, Amanda Hodgson, David Li, Sarah Owens, Amanda Parris, Matt Sinnott, Brian Saling, Ren Siqin, Katherine Sheriff, Christine Thomas, Brad Warner, Ella Vacca, and Steven Zuckerman, among others on this work, and at Northwestern, Sierra Anderson, Zachary Furlin, Jordan Krieger, Shannon Lemajeur, Ivan Parfenoff, Xukun Rendu, Eric Selzer, Amanda Wells, and Shuhan Zhang. Joanna's research assistants on this work include Thomas Archibald, Min Cho, Charli Davis, Kevin Duong, Angela Grate, Caroline Herion, Jon Leckerling, Aaron McWhirter, Roberto Ocon, Michael Scariano, Grayson Walker, and Claudia Yang. Many thanks as well to our faculty assistants Matt Bergin, Juana Haskin, Tonya Holmes, Brenda Huffman, Danny Kim, and Czarina Morgan for everything they do.

FREE TO JUDGE

1 THE MODERN ERA OF BIG MONEY JUDICIAL ELECTIONS

"WE COULD LOSE OUR JOBS over what we just did," Chief Justice Marsha Ternus heard a colleague whisper. She and the other justices of the Iowa Supreme Court had just unanimously upheld the right of same-sex couples to marry under their state constitution. It had been no secret that the case, *Varnum v. Brien*, was political dynamite. "We had demonstrations outside the building during oral argument. Groups were coming in from outside the state raising a lot of objections to same-sex marriage," Chief Justice Ternus remembers. "So, we had an inkling that there would be people outside the state, and in the state, interested in retention elections depending on how we rule." The following year, opposed by an unprecedented million-dollar opposition campaign financed by out-of-state groups, Chief Justice Ternus and two of her fellow justices became the first appellate judges ever in state history to lose their re-election bids. Big-money judicial elections had arrived in the state of Iowa.

Marsha Ternus's defeat sharply marked this new era. Before 2010, Iowa Supreme Court justices had faced retention elections to keep their jobs fifty times, including Chief Justice Ternus twice before. Every time, the justice running for retention had won back their job and received an average of more than 80 percent voter approval, never less than 72 percent.[1] As Justice Ternus remembers it, thoughts about running for re-election in Iowa never came up. "I don't even recall thinking about it at all," she says. In fact, the day after one of her earlier retention elections, someone at work asked her whether she had won. Only then, she says, did she even remember that she was on the ballot. "That's how much of a non-issue [re-elections] were for all judges." Only two trial judges had ever lost their retention bids under the Iowa judicial system, and in those instances, the judges lost based on perceived lack of judicial temperament or competence, not ideology. As Justice Ternus explains, "That's what retention elections are for."

But by 2010, judicial elections had already begun to change nationwide. "We saw elections being politicized in other states," Ternus recalls. "There was certainly some feeling by people thinking about how to push their agenda, and the courts were an untapped avenue for that." Campaigns, particularly for state supreme court, were becoming more intense, expensive, and ideological than ever. Judicial races had once been relatively quiet affairs with high re-election rates, but since the 1980s they have become more politicized, partisan, and expensive—basically more and more like elections for other elected offices. Indeed, 2010 was a watershed year for judicial elections nationwide, with record spending greater than the total for the entire previous decade.[2] "Well, I just knew that in other states a lot of money had been spent on trying to get rid of particular judges. So, the fact that it happened here in Iowa because of the *Varnum* decision wasn't a big shock."

After *Varnum,* Chief Justice Ternus and her colleagues faced a political campaign against them unprecedented in state history. Interest groups, mostly from out of state, spent an Iowa record of nearly $1 million on campaign spending and advertising against the trio, who themselves didn't engage in any fundraising or campaigning in their own defense. "Under our judicial ethics, we could have formed a campaign committee and done fundraising and campaigned. And we chose not to do that," Marsha Ternus explains now. "We weren't comfortable in that role. And we felt that if we did that, we were only confirming this characterization of the people who opposed our decision that we were just making decisions based on our personal preference and our ideology. That it wasn't based in the rule of law." So, Marsha Ternus and her colleagues faced the voters as judges, not politicians. "And so we just decided, let the chips fall where they may. We are *not* going to campaign, and we are *not* going to fundraise. So we did lose."

The irony was that *Varnum*, the same-sex marriage case, was a simple, straightforward decision in their view. As she remembers it, "The decision itself was hard in the sense we had a banker's box of briefing to read. But the legal analysis, the standard legal analysis, clearly took you to the decision that there was an equal protection violation. That wasn't hard. And that's why it was unanimous." Five Democrats and two Republicans agreed in the 7–0 decision, with Republican Mark Cady authoring the opinion. Their decision in *Varnum* was vindicated by the U.S. Supreme Court's decision only three years later in a similar case, *United States v. Windsor*,[3] and then again definitively confirmed in a 2015 decision, *Obergefell v. Hodges*.[4] Looking back on her election defeat today, Marsha Ternus explains that "there was no reason to come after us, any of us. I was actually a Republican appointee, and the justice who wrote the decision was a Republican appointee. And I think we were kind of regarded as the more conservative people on the court. So, I wouldn't have thought any of these groups would come to Iowa and campaign against us."

However, *Varnum v. Brien* was about same-sex marriage. The Iowa Supreme Court had decided that an Iowa law banning the marriage of same-sex couples violated equal protection under the Iowa Constitution. It was a hot-button issue at the time that drew the ire, and campaign financing, of wealthy conservative interests across the country. The National Organization for Marriage spent almost a half million dollars against the justices' retention, while AFA Action Inc. and the Campaign for Working Families, all out-of-state groups, added six-figure amounts to the opposition campaign.[5] Justice Ternus recalls that "the campaign against us was so filled with fear and hate. It was really sad. . . . People don't seem to have any conscience about being accurate or fair." The campaign against these justices who declined to campaign and fundraise as a matter of principle motivated a group of former Iowa governors, lawyers, and judges to campaign on their behalf. This group, named Fair Courts for Us, argued their defense of Marsha Ternus and her colleagues was necessary for Iowans "to know courts will be fair and impartial and decisions won't be based on fear and popularity."[6]

The *Varnum* justices would later be awarded the John F. Kennedy Profile in Courage Award recognizing their judicial independence and integrity. As Caroline Kennedy put it while bestowing the award, "When Justices Baker, Streit, and Ternus joined a unanimous decision to overturn a law denying same-sex couples the privileges of marriage, they sacrificed their own futures on the Court to honor Iowa's constitution and the rights of all its citizens." Nonetheless, the leaders of the opposition crowed after the 2010 election that "[t]he people of Iowa stood up in record numbers and sent a message . . . that it is 'We the people,' not 'We the courts.'"[7] And it was exactly this demonstrated pressure to decide as public opinion would demand, rather than how the rule of law indicates, that worries many about today's judicial elections and campaign finance. Erwin Chemerinsky, dean of UC Berkeley Law School and eminent constitutional law scholar, lamented at the time that "[w]hat is so disturbing about this is that it really might cause judges in the future to be less willing to protect minorities out of fear that they might be voted out of office. Something like this really does chill other judges."[8]

New-style judicial elections, with organized, well-financed pressure campaigns like the one that defeated Marsha Ternus, change the character of the job and those who seek it. Although there "was nothing political about retention prior to the 2010 election [in Iowa]," judicial elections had changed by and since 2010. "I would never have been a judge if I had to campaign to get it," Marsha Ternus observes in retrospect. The new, politicized system "screen[s] out a certain group of people. And I think that system pressures people who would prefer not to have to prejudge issues. . . . It's hard to remain principled."

Judicial elections *have* changed. So have judging, judges, and the law as a result. This book is about this transformation of judicial elections and the influx of big money and organization to influence judicial decisionmaking. This book is about how and why that happens. And what can be done about it.

BIG MONEY JUDICIAL ELECTIONS AND CAMPAIGN FINANCE

Marsha Ternus won't be the last judge to feel the accelerating pressures of campaign finance and the next election. Nine out of ten state judges in the United States must win election to earn or retain their judgeships. Running for judge requires money. As Justice Antonin Scalia once wrote, "One cannot have judicial elections without judicial campaigns, and judicial campaigns without funds for campaigning, and funds for campaigning without asking for them."[9]

Of course, the problem is that money buys things and creates dependence. For people with money to spend on elections, this is a big benefit of their campaign spending. They can invest campaign finance money to elect and re-elect lawmakers who do as they, the investors, prefer in government. As a consequence, state judges may need to behave like other elected politicians who must win re-election to keep their jobs. As a California Supreme Court justice once put it, the next election is like a crocodile in your bathtub when you go into the bathroom: "You know it's there, and you try not to think about it, but it's hard to think about much else while you're shaving."[10] We can't be assured that judges will handle this pressure as well as Marsha Ternus did and be willing to lose their jobs to decide cases as they believe the law demands. In a system like ours that elects state judges, it means campaign donors generally support and can elect judges who will do what the donors want.

We are reaching a crisis point in judicial elections, if we're not already there. The American Bar Association formally opposes the use of judicial elections because of what it sees as the "corrosive effect of money on judicial election campaigns" and the associated "attack advertising" funded by increasing fundraising.[11] Campaign spending on state supreme court elections in 2015–16 was the highest to date.[12] The 2015–16 campaign cycle had twenty-seven state supreme court races in which at least $1 million was spent, the most ever in American history, and today, a third of state supreme court justices were elected in campaigns where more than $1 million was spent. State supreme court races are also featuring record amounts of television spending and outside spending by interest groups. A shocking 82 percent of spending by interest groups in judicial races is subject to ineffective disclosure, where the individual source of funding is not publicly known. The result is that elections arguably become, in one scholar's words, "floating auctions" where campaign spenders vie for influence over judges and their decisions.[13]

Justice Sandra Day O'Connor, who made it her cause after retirement from the U.S. Supreme Court to champion judicial election reform, warns that "there are many who think of judges as politicians in robes" and agrees that "[i]n many states, that's what they are."[14] Most voters, more than three-quarters of the public, already conclude that campaign contributions have influence over elected judges' decisions. Worse, judges themselves generally agree that campaign money affects their decisions. Almost half agree that campaign contributions have at least "a little influence" on their decisions, and more than half of judges actually believe that they "should be prohibited from presiding over and ruling cases when one of the sides has given money to their campaign." A staggering 80 percent of judges believe that interest groups are using campaign contributions to try to shape legal decisions in their favor.

We began studying judicial elections more than a dozen years ago by looking at whether judges were affected by the electoral incentives to win and then keep their jobs. Judicial elections are an almost uniquely American practice. Almost no other country entrusts judicial selection to popular elections.[15] Even in the United States, only *state* judges are selected and retained through elections. Most people focus on federal judges and the system of presidential appointment and lifetime tenure, but seventeen out of eighteen judges in the United States are *state* judges—94 percent of all judges—almost all of whom face elections to win or keep their jobs.[16] And state judges decide most of the legal cases in our country.

Although federal courts hog public and media attention, state courts make most of the law that affects you on a daily basis. State courts handle more than 90 percent of judicial business in America.[17] While the U.S. Supreme Court decides fewer than one hundred cases per year, more than ninety million cases are brought in state trial courts per year, or roughly one case for every three people in the country.[18] State courts decide torts, property, and contracts cases. They decide family law, criminal law, and state constitutional law.

Arguably, state courts are becoming more important than ever as an increasingly conservative U.S. Supreme Court abdicates a federal constitutional role in critical policymaking areas like redistricting and abortion. State courts alone will decide whether partisan gerrymandering is permissible and what reproductive rights women have under state constitutions, among many other decisions—enormously important constitutional questions that federal courts once dominated. The state judges presiding over and deciding these cases are overwhelmingly likely to have won an election to get their job, or else they will need to win an election to keep it.

Judicial campaigns require campaign money, as Justice Scalia famously observed. We are law professors with statistical training and mounds of data on these judicial elections, campaign finance, and the judicial decisions that follow. We have spent the past decade poring over the data and writing about the subject. When we investigate the influence of campaign fundraising on judicial decisionmaking, we find campaign money profoundly affects how judges do their jobs and shape state law. Intuitively, some critics of the legal system already felt they knew that campaign finance affects elected judges. Given the amount of money increasing in judicial elections, that's a fair guess. But others pooh-pooh concerns about money in politics and think that it doesn't make much difference with such experienced, duty-bound lawyers as our judges. We go beyond mere intuition and anecdote in our work and here in the book. Intuition and anecdote are important clues to what's going on, but not always reliably so. Quantitative analysis of objective data often tells us more.

American society is increasingly turning toward data-driven study of everything from professional baseball to medical care and government administration. Twenty years ago, Michael Lewis wrote the book *Moneyball* about a revolution in the way that major-league baseball thought about its business.[19] Major-league baseball, like most industries, was driven by long-standing assumptions about how to find baseball talent that often were as much untested myth as reality. Major-league management started to turn to quantitative analytics to pierce the mythology and get to some objective truth about how to find and identify baseball players by using statistics. In the following years, there have been similar *Moneyball* trends for management virtually everywhere you look, from pro basketball and pro football to health care,[20] law schools,[21] and the federal government.[22] We now live in a *Moneyball* era for everything. Statistics sometimes reveal or confirm empirical reality that is difficult to pin down just with qualitative observation.

This book presents the best empirical evidence to date that campaign money biases judicial decisionmaking. Our earlier work established a robust relationship between judicial decisions by elected judges and the campaign contributions received from a wide range of donors: business groups, political parties, left- and right-leaning interest groups, among others. Elected judges demonstrably lean toward the interests and preferences of their campaign contributors across all types of cases.

This predictive relationship between campaign contributions and how judges decide cases is troubling enough. We will detail how campaign contributors appear to get what they want for their money. Judicial elections allow them to influence how judges ultimately decide cases that they care about and that affect their interests. Ideally, our judicial system should decide cases independent of the policy preferences and interests of wealthy donors. But election systems where campaign finance helps decide who wins judgeships almost inevitably allows money to matter more than most of us would like.

HOW CAMPAIGN MONEY MATTERS IN COURT

One of the most infamous cases of a wealthy donor using campaign donations to get what he wanted from the judicial system was *Caperton v. Massey.* The case eventually reached the U.S. Supreme Court and actually became the basis for a John Grisham novel! Don Blankenship, a wealthy mining magnate in West Virginia, lost a $50 million verdict to Hugh Caperton over a contract dispute. Blankenship knew the case would be appealed to the West Virginia Supreme Court and moved quickly, before the 2004 election, to improve his odds there. He spent more than $3 million to defeat incumbent Justice Warren McGraw and replace him with a new Republican candidate who Blankenship expected to be more sympathetic to his case. The Republican candidate, local lawyer Brent Benjamin, swept into office by defeating McGraw and, as Blankenship hoped, cast the deciding vote in Blankenship's appeal, overturning the $50 million verdict against Blankenship's company. The original plaintiff, Hugh Caperton, who lost that appeal, remembers "looking up at a judge who had just gotten $3 million . . . to be elected and thinking, 'How in the world is this fair?'"[23]

In a major upset, the United States Supreme Court actually agreed that it wasn't. Caperton appealed the case up to the U.S. Supreme Court and argued that the Constitution required Justice Benjamin to recuse himself from Blankenship's appeal based on Blankenship's immense financial support of his election. The Court, in a 5–4 decision, sided with Caperton and ruled that Benjamin was required by the Due Process Clause to remove himself from the decision in Caperton's case.[24] Although courts had never required recusal in such a case before, the Court's majority opinion explained that Blankenship's $3 million in campaign finance support for Benjamin meant that "Justice Benjamin would feel a debt of gratitude to Blankenship for his extraordinary efforts to get him elected."[25]

This temptation to reciprocate by deciding in Blankenship's favor in his case, which the Court called "strong and inherent in human nature," created a "serious risk of actual bias—based on objective and reasonable perceptions—when a person with a personal stake in a particular case had a significant and disproportionate influence in placing the judge on the case by raising funds or directing the judge's election campaign."[26] The Court thus reversed the West Virginia Supreme Court's decision that overturned the $50 million verdict against Blankenship. The amount of money Blankenship spent for Benjamin—more than both candidates' campaigns spent combined, indeed while Blankenship's case was already pending and its appeal foreseeable—came too close to Blankenship "choos[ing] the judge in his own cause."[27]

The Court's decision, in our view, was correct. We agree that campaign finance support can create indebtedness and judicial bias in favor of campaign finance contributors when judges are elected to the bench. This is what our book is about. The Court's decision here, though, was based on its intuition that a justice faces temptations that "lead him not to hold the balance nice, clear, and true" when deciding cases involving his financial supporters.[28] We push beyond mere intuition to the hard data that we think corroborates and clarifies the Court's sensibility. Unfortunately, the Court's decision in the *Caperton* case was very limited to the specific circumstances of the case and hasn't served as much corrective for judicial campaign finance in subsequent years. It really hasn't made much difference on the ground. As a result, we have plenty of campaign finance data and caselaw to study in our research on campaign finance influences on judges, the *Caperton* decision notwithstanding.

To be fair, the Court acknowledged that it couldn't prove any quid pro quo agreement between Blankenship and Benjamin about how Benjamin would decide Blankenship's case. In fact, there was never any legal allegation of any such quid pro quo in the case. Justice Benjamin claimed he was never biased in Blankenship's favor. He argued that Blankenship's support wasn't decisive in getting him elected, which was much more complicated than Blankenship's money. He claimed, as a judge, that he could remain independent from campaign finance incentives and decide the case fairly without needing to recuse himself. We'll hear more about Justice Benjamin later in the book. His views on campaign finance and judicial politics evolved with more experience in the system.

But the point was never that anyone needed to prove a quid pro quo agreement or that Benjamin was decisively biased in this particular case. Instead, the Court thought it was "strong and inherent in human nature" that judges would feel indebted under similar circumstances, whether or not Benjamin himself did. It was reasonable for Hugh Caperton to think the system wasn't treating him fairly to allow a judge so indebted to his opponent to decide his case. More importantly, as we will demonstrate, it would be rational for most judges to think about their next election in deciding cases involving their supporters' interests if they want continued support and to win re-election.

It is important to acknowledge that money isn't the only factor that affects judicial decisionmaking. Law matters because judges want to apply the substantive law as faithfully as they feel they can.[29] There are certainly many cases where basically all judges agree, regardless of party, ideology, and campaign money, that the law is clear about how the case should come out. Of course, many other cases are harder calls, and judges do disagree about how the law applies and how the case should be decided as a matter of law. Judges have varying jurisprudential philosophies about how to interpret and apply the law.[30] This is where party and ideology matter most.[31] What's more, scholars find a variety of other factors that seem to influence how judges decide cases, from judges' race,[32] perhaps their gender,[33] and even the fellow judges deciding the case with them.[34]

But campaign money matters too. When we look at the broader pattern of data on campaign finance money and judicial decisionmaking, we consistently find that money predicts judicial decisionmaking rather well. As we'll describe further, we study comprehensive data over three decades of state supreme court decisions, ranging over the 1990s to the 2010s, as well as all the campaign contributions given to the elected judges deciding those cases across the fifty states.

What we see is troubling: Money too frequently manages to buy what it wants from judges and judicial elections. We find a robust and statistically significant connection between campaign finance contributions and elected judges' decisions in favor of the contributors' preferences over a wide range

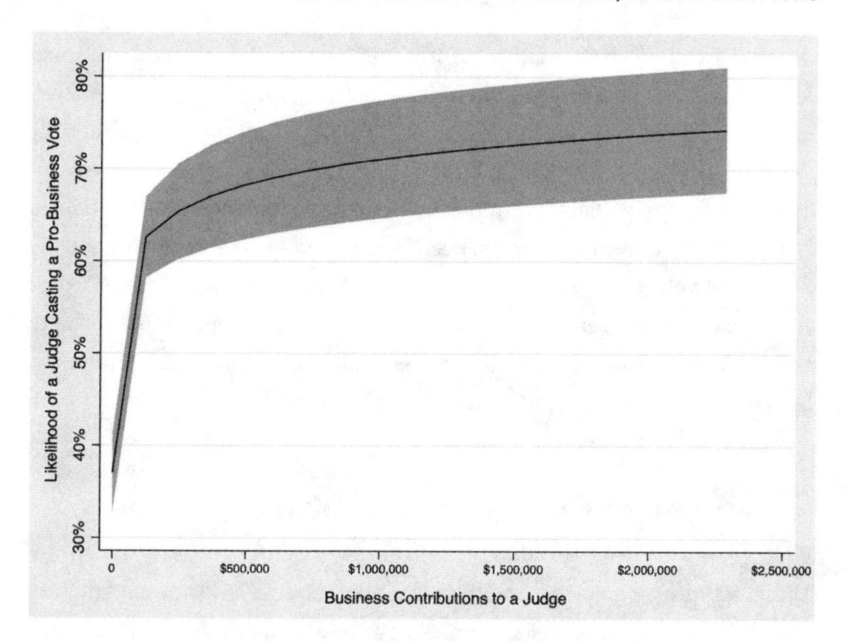

FIGURE 1.1 The Relationship Between Business Contributions and Pro-Business Votes by State Supreme Court Justices

of cases. Money generally gets its desired outcomes from the elected judges it supports. As Figure 1.1 illustrates, the likelihood that a judge casts a vote in favor of business goes up dramatically as the amount of money the judge receives from business groups goes up. Roughly speaking, averaged over all judges, each $10,000 contribution from a business increases the odds of a judge casting a pro-business vote by about 1 percent.

As we'll describe, money not only matters a lot, but even more money is pouring into judicial elections over time and making judicial elections more politicized, more partisan, and more like other kinds of state elections for non-judicial offices. We take you inside the numbers to understand how money influences judges, perhaps now more than ever.

Just as importantly, we think we have a new understanding about specifically *why* money matters so much to judicial decisionmaking. This is important because it not only clarifies the problem with money in judicial elections, but it also points to more promising, tailored solutions. It isn't simply that electing judges as a general matter consigns our judiciary to slavishly obeying their campaign donors once they are elevated to the bench. Instead, we argue from our findings that criticism should be aimed less at judicial elections, or judicial campaign finance as a general matter, and focus more on the specific problem of judicial *re-election*. Judges appear to be influenced by campaign money not simply to pay back or otherwise reciprocate campaign debts from the last election that put them on the bench. Rather, judges appear to be influenced by the need to raise campaign money for the *next* election that will allow them to keep their jobs. These prospective re-election concerns drive the biasing effects of campaign money and, therefore, point toward judicial reforms that limit or altogether remove the biasing effect of re-election, such as a single-term limit.

RE-ELECTION AS A KEY TO UNDERSTANDING CAMPAIGN MONEY'S INFLUENCE

Understanding our point about re-election requires a bit of explanation about the judicial election system. To figure out the cause of money's influence on judges, we need to realize first that there are really two parts to being a judge under a system of judicial elections. First, there's judicial selection—the process by which a candidate first attains judicial office. Second, there's judicial re-election—the process by which sitting judges either get to keep their jobs for another term or are replaced by someone else. Criticism of judicial elections, of which there's a lot, tends to focus on the first part, judicial selection, and neglect the second part, judicial re-election.

When we examine how money predicts judicial decisions, one puzzle is whether this happens simply because of a natural matching of campaign money with judicial candidates already predisposed toward their donors' preferences. That is, we know that judicial candidates are most likely to receive money from donors who already anticipate they will decide cases the way that the donors would like. Under this account, the pairing of money with subsequent judicial decisions occurs without judges being actively biased or otherwise distorting their decisions in favor of their donors. As Marsha Ternus once explained, "Do we really believe that special interest groups and corporations who support a judicial candidate do not expect that person once elected to vote a certain way on certain issues? Of course they do."[35] Under this account, wealthy donors simply may have picked well in choosing whom to support in the first place. This account we call a *selection* story. Judges are deciding cases the way that they think is correct, but donors have done a good job in selecting the judges who will decide cases as they want them to.

However, a different account of the relationship between campaign money and judicial decisions is that judges are actively biasing their decisions toward their donors' preferences and interests. Under this account, judges know that they need their donors' money to keep winning re-election and retain their jobs. Judges therefore may change how they decide cases to curry favor with these donors under the expectation that they must do so to keep receiving their support for the next election. Under this account, judges are bending toward their donors' preferences with re-election in mind and biasing their decisions from what they otherwise would decide if re-election wasn't a consideration. This account we call a *biasing* story. Judges actually are not necessarily deciding cases according to their best view of the law. Instead, they are adjusting their decisions, consciously or unconsciously, away from how they would rule if re-election wasn't a factor. They are biased toward their donors' financial support.

The reason it's hard to tell whether money matters because of selection or biasing is because the resulting statistical picture is the same either way—judicial decisions would follow campaign donors' interests and preferences. If judges who receive campaign money from business interests are more likely to vote in favor of businesses in business litigation, then it's hard to sort out whether they are doing so because business interests accurately selected them for support and helped get them elected, or because those supported judges are biased in favor of business in hopes of getting more money from them in the future. The money matches up with the donors in either case.

We solve this methodological puzzle by looking at a special category of judges: lame duck judges who can't run for another term. Most states impose an age limitation on state supreme court justices so that they can't run for re-election beyond a certain point. These judges are legally ineligible to run again, and importantly for our purposes, lame ducks know in advance that re-election is simply off the table for them.

For this reason, lame ducks were elected and received campaign money just like other elected judges, so *selection* still matters. We can assume that campaign donors still want and support judges who will decide cases as they prefer and did so in the past for these lame ducks. However, in their last term, these lame duck judges would not be *biased* by any re-election concerns. Since they're simply ineligible for re-election, continuing to curry favor with donors no longer makes sense.

We find that lame duck judges facing mandatory retirement no longer prefer their campaign finance donors in their decisionmaking in the same way. Of course, the effect of money doesn't totally go away for lame ducks. Selection matters enough that these judges still reflect their donors' interests to a degree, as we'd expect. But the effect of money greatly diminishes for lame ducks who no longer need to worry about re-election. In short, money still matters, but it doesn't matter anywhere close to the same way, shrinking by half or two-thirds in its influence on judges.

This result indicates that *re-election* concerns are largely responsible for biasing judicial decisionmaking, because the selection account would not predict this dramatic change in voting behavior during the final term. We present our evidence here using the best available data from decisions and elections since *Citizens United v. Federal Election Commission*, and we have sliced the data every plausible way to double-check our findings. No matter how we split or analyze the data, we find the same thing: Elected state supreme court justices are affected by business contributions, and this effect shrivels up for lame ducks. As we explain in greater detail later on, this rigorous battery of robustness checks convinces us against alternative explanations for our findings.

In other words, this book presents the strongest, most convincing evidence to date that elected supreme court justices are biased by re-election concerns and that the political pressures for campaign money explain the close relationship between money and decisions. When we explained our statistical findings to Justice Ternus, she summarized our conclusions nicely: "That's awful. It tells me that judges are impacted by the prospect of an election. And they make decisions in a way that will appease the masses. Or maybe not even the masses, maybe just again, they're bowing to people who shout the loudest. Or have the most money."

We think this is exactly right. Judges aren't inherently biased by the fact that campaign supporters have given them money in the past. In this sense, the U.S. Supreme Court in *Caperton* didn't have everything right. It isn't quite accurate to assume it's so "strong and inherent in human nature" that judges feel so indebted to past supporters they inevitably pay them back with favorable decisions. After all, we find that lame duck judges stop, to a really remarkable degree, paying back their past supporters when re-election is no longer a possibility. Once re-election is off the table, the influence of their supporters' money doesn't seem to matter nearly as much. Judges, at least non–lame ducks who are still eligible to run again, *are* motivated to please campaign finance supporters and attract their donations for the next election. When re-election is still a possibility, money seems to affect judges' decisions. Only when it is not does campaign money stop mattering so much to elected judges.

HOW TO FIX IT: JUDICIAL ELECTION REFORM AND THE WAY FORWARD

What our findings mean for institutional reforms to fix judicial elections and campaign finance is that we should be focused squarely on this re-election incentive as the main source of the problem. Our research suggests that judicial elections themselves are not the problem. Elected judges who have received money from campaign donors aren't inherently corrupt or biased as a result of the election process. If they were, then the lame duck judges would still decide cases in line with the interests of their donors, some of whom have supported them over a long career. Instead, the absence of the next re-election seems to liberate these judges from much of the influence of money. Money's influence is therefore mostly forward-looking, not backward-looking. Reforms that free judges from re-election concerns might allow all judges to act like lame ducks. Removing the possibility of re-election might, to a large extent, empower all judges to be free to judge.

This distinction between judicial elections and judicial re-elections is important because, as a practical matter, judicial elections aren't going away. Judicial elections are immensely popular with voters. Roughly two-thirds of the public favors electing judges, even though a similar percentage thinks that judges are affected by campaign contributions.[36] What's more, in most states judicial elections have been the method for selecting judges for more than a century. Although states may be willing to tinker with the process of their judicial elections, no state has done away with judicial elections altogether in more than forty years.[37] So, reforms that require getting rid of judicial elections wholesale are not realistically on the table. Instead, we need effective reform within the system of judicial elections, and our work points to the most promising ways to fix the problem of money in judicial elections along those lines.

In *Caperton,* the dissenting opinion by Chief Justice John Roberts asked a series of skeptical questions about how campaign finance influences judges, if it does at all. Roberts asked: "How long does the probability of bias last?"; "Does the probability of bias diminish over time as the election recedes?"; "Does it matter whether the judge plans to run for re-election?"; and "Is there likely to be a debt of gratitude?"[38] Roberts poses these questions as imponderables, obvious objections to any legal reform because they have no answers. In fact, these questions do have knowable answers. Indeed, we think this book has answers for Roberts. Looking at the quantitative data explains a lot about the process and politics of judicial elections. We chart the rise of big-money elections and new-style judicial campaigns for state supreme courts.

In Chapter 2, we start by describing the history of judicial elections and how money has played an increasing role in how judges get elected in the United States. The states didn't start with elections as the way to pick their judges, but judicial elections, ironically, were an attempt to remove judges from political corruption. Judicial elections themselves, however, eventually became politicized and subject to political forces that came to threaten judicial integrity.

More recently, judicial elections have become more political and competitive, with campaign money playing a bigger and bigger role. Judicial elections today, at least for many states' supreme courts, now resemble statewide elections for other offices in terms of partisanship, intensity, and campaign fundraising and spending. Some political scientists think this is a good thing. We don't. We explain why here.

In Chapter 3, we present what we have learned about the influence of campaign money on judges. With so much money spent on judicial elections, and so much at stake in state supreme court cases, many worry, per *Caperton,* that campaign money allows wealthy donors to buy the judiciary and judicial outcomes they want. We explain that our work and the rest of the empirical literature on judicial elections and decisionmaking substantiates this worry to a troubling extent. Judges, as we show, respond to electoral and other retention incentives. As a result, campaign money influences judges toward the preferences of campaign donors at the state supreme court. Worse, judges appear to anticipate competitive re-election fights and become more punitive in criminal cases just to protect themselves from accusations that they are "soft on crime." Judges, in short, behave in ways we'd expect from rational political actors. They want to keep their jobs and regularly do what they must to ensure this outcome.

In Chapter 4, we show that judges decide in favor of their campaign donors because they are biased by re-election concerns, not simply because they happen to be ideologically predisposed in their direction. We demonstrate this robust empirical finding with the most comprehensive dataset of campaign finance contributions and state supreme court decisionmaking available so far. That is, judges appear influenced by the forward-looking need for campaign money to get re-elected. Judges eligible for re-election reflect the interests of their campaign donors as a general matter. Judges no longer eligible for re-election, our lame duck judges, reflect the influence of campaign money far, far less. We rule out alternative explanations for our findings with a series of robustness checks that explore and ultimately confirm that age, last-term effects, and initial selection methods can't explain the biasing influence of money.

Finally, in Chapter 5, we endorse a reform approach that targets judicial *re-election* as the source of campaign money's influence on judges. The temptation of the next election, of re-election, causes judges to sway toward the interests of campaign contributors who might help them keep their jobs. As a consequence, legal reforms to address the problem of money in judicial elections should focus on removing altogether the possibility of re-election from the equation. We weigh the pros and cons of different mechanisms that remove re-election from judges' decisionmaking, from a single-term limit to longer terms or even lifetime tenure. No proposal is perfect in terms of insulating judges from political influence, and we underscore this point here. Some democratic input and political accountability can be valuable, but balancing these countervailing interests is very hard.

Although we are not dogmatic in any particular direction, we think a limitation of a single term best insulates judges from re-election worries and effectively removes the influence of money. Of course, this type of institutional choice implicates lots of other considerations, but from the standpoint of money's biasing effect, the possibility of re-election is the main problem. What we know is that the current system of big-money judicial elections isn't working. We need our judges to be free to judge.

2 THE RISE OF JUDICIAL ELECTIONS: HOW WE GOT WHERE WE ARE

THE SUCCESSFUL 1996 CAMPAIGN TO defeat Tennessee Supreme Court Justice Penny White's re-election was a critical bellwether foreshadowing the recent rise of big-money politics in state court elections. The well-funded, targeted campaign against Justice White came as a shock to both her and the Tennessee judiciary because, as she explained, "nobody had ever seen it happen" in Tennessee, or almost anywhere else at that time.

The 1990s were a turning point for judicial elections and judicial campaign finance. Although the shift happened at different times in different states, judicial races suddenly became more contested, more political, and more expensive in many states during the decade. Still, in Tennessee in 1996, Justice White and her colleagues admitted that they hadn't seen this new style of judicial election coming. She said, "This was back in the nineties. Money had not really hit [in Tennessee]." But then the state Republican Party organized and funded an unprecedented big-money campaign against Justice White to unfairly portray her vote in a single case and change the partisan composition of the Tennessee Supreme Court in the process.

Justice White originally went to law school to be a "small town lawyer." Growing up in rural Tennessee, she never considered the possibility of becoming a judge because she hadn't known many judges who looked like her: "I had never seen anything but a white male judge, with the exception of a juvenile court judge." However, during a fellowship at Georgetown University Law Center, Penny White found herself in courtrooms throughout Maryland. For the first time, she observed "judges of all genders and all races . . . who had certain attributes and traits, rather than people who had certain connections." It planted the seed in her head.

Penny White had a successful career in private practice during the 1980s, focusing on criminal defense, civil rights, and family law cases. She argued one case before the U.S. Supreme Court, impressing several of the justices. In a 1988 speech, Justice Harry Blackmun recalled how his colleague, Justice Antonin "Nino" Scalia, had grilled a then thirty-two-year-old Penny White. He "picked on her and picked on her and picked on her and she gave it back to him. . . . [F]inally at the end of the case we walked off and Nino said the only thing he could say: 'Wasn't she good? Wasn't she good?' The rest of us were completely silent. We knew she was *very* good."[1]

Penny White decided to run for a seat on Tennessee's First Judicial Circuit in 1990, following the retirement of a senior judge. At that time, as she remembers it, "[p]eople became judges and they served until they were ready to retire. There was never any competition for judgeships even though they were elected positions." Her first campaign for judge was a "grassroots" effort where she would "go every weekend door-to-door, knock on doors, ask for votes, spaghetti suppers, all those kind of things that you do in small-town judicial races." Back in the 1990s before big-money politics hit Tennessee judicial races, elections for judge were, as she remembers it, "very low dollar."

Not long after she was first elected as a judge on Tennessee's First Judicial Circuit, Governor Ned McWherter subsequently appointed Penny White to Tennessee's Court of Criminal Appeals in 1992. She was promoted with "the understanding that there was no way that [she] would be competitive, but that it would be a good opportunity to begin to get [her] name known in judicial circles." Governor McWherter promoted Penny White without ever meeting her or even calling her personally. And just two years later, the governor elevated her again to fill a vacancy on the Tennessee Supreme Court.

"This time, he did meet me and interview me. . . . So that's a long answer to how I became a judge."

Now on the state supreme court, Justice White almost immediately faced a retention election to keep her seat in 1996. The Tennessee legislature had just adopted a new method of selection and retention for the state's supreme court justices. Justice White was the first Tennessee Supreme Court justice to come up for retention under this new plan. Before then, Tennessee Supreme Court justices had to run for re-election in partisan races, but under the new law, Tennessee adopted the so-called "Missouri Plan." Under this reform, which we'll discuss in more detail later, the governor appoints justices from a list of potential nominees identified by a nominating commission. When the justice's appointed term is up, they then have to win retention by garnering majority approval in a contested yes-no retention election. Basically, the electorate has a chance either to grant the justice another term or to vote the justice out and create a vacancy for the governor to fill with a new appointee.

Although Justice White was the first Tennessee Supreme Court justice to face this new sort of retention election to keep her job, she actually had won a retention election while serving on the Court of Criminal Appeals. Immediately after Governor McWherter appointed her to that court, she faced a retention election and won the most votes of any judge in the state, just as she had in 1990 winning her First Judicial Circuit judgeship. Justice White was a winning judicial candidate with a track record of success.

So, when she faced another retention election, now as a state supreme court justice, Justice White didn't do anything differently. "I didn't campaign once, I didn't send one letter, ask one person to vote for me, nothing. And that was just the way things were in Tennessee." Early in the election year, she didn't anticipate a competitive race because, at least for the Tennessee Supreme Court, "nobody had ever seen it happen. And I can't say I had read anything or knew anything about it happening elsewhere."

But her 1996 retention election would be different, actually unprecedented, in the intensity of the campaign against her. As Justice White remembers it, she started to hear rumblings at a state judicial conference in June of that year hinting that this election would be different. "We got a call from the secretary, saying that something was brewing, that there was a 'Just Say No' campaign, and it was being orchestrated against me." If she lost, the newly elected Republican governor Don Sundquist, who had replaced Ned McWherter, would get to choose her replacement on the supreme court. Republicans therefore began organizing a well-funded opposition campaign against her retention. "Yeah, they just wanted the seat, and it was orchestrated by people in the governor's office. But, you know, it didn't look that way. They were smart enough to make it look more like a public uprising."

The opposition campaign rallied the public's fears about crime against Justice White's retention.[2] As one commentator later put it, conservative groups launched "a wildfire campaign that used a handful of rulings to cast her as an enemy of the death penalty and a coddler of criminals."[3] As Justice White would later say, using judges' decisions in death penalty cases against them is "the oldest trick in the book."[4] The Tennessee Republican Party declared that she "put the rights of criminals before the rights of victims."[5] The Tennessee Conservative Union distributed to voters a mailer, shown below in Figure 2.1, that claimed: "She wants you to vote 'Yes' for her in August. 'Yes' so she can free more and more criminals and laugh at their victims!"[6]

The opposition campaign focused especially on a single death penalty appeal, *State v. Odom*, decided by the Tennessee Supreme Court two months before the election.[7] The criminal defendant in the case appealed the death sentence he received for the rape and murder of a seventy-eight-year-old woman. The Supreme Court upheld his conviction but unanimously vacated the death sentence because the trial court had committed reversible technical errors during sentencing involving the exclusion of expert testimony and faulty instructions regarding mitigating factors raised by the defense. Penny White was one of five justices upholding the conviction but also holding that a procedural error by the trial court required that Odom receive a new sentencing hearing. She did not author the majority opinion or any opinion in the case. As she remembers it, "It was so correctly decided, it wasn't even close. . . . And we really did the least drastic reversal." The defendant was remanded for re-sentencing and ultimately received the death penalty again, this time without technical error.[8]

Nonetheless, the opposition lambasted Penny White for the court's decision to re-sentence the defendant. The Tennessee Conservative Fund fired off mailers and campaign ads with gruesome details of the defendant's crimes and falsely claimed that White had "voted to overturn his conviction . . . because Justice White said rape is not 'serious physical abuse.'"[9] The

Penny White is a justice of the Tennessee Supreme Court.

And she voted to overturn the death sentence of Miss Johnson's murderer.

Incredibly, she said 78 year-old Miss Johnson's rape was not "serious physical abuse.

Not serious! Not physical! Not abuse!

If the savage rape and bloody murder of a helpless 78 year-old woman is not "serious physical abuse" then what is???

This wasn't the first time her attacker had struck.

No indeed.

He was an escapee from a Mississippi prison where he was already serving a life sentence for another murder.

Yet Justice White voted to overturn his conviction.

Not on the evidence. Not because there was any doubt that he was the actual killer.

His`conviction was overturned because Justice White said rape is not "serious physical abuse."

Now, Justice White is asking for your vote.

She wants to remain on the State Supreme Court.

She wants you to vote "Yes" for her in August.

"Yes" so she can free more and more criminals and laugh at their victims!

That's just plain WRONG!

FIGURE 2.1 Mailer Distributed by Tennessee Conservative Union. Source: Stephen B. Bright, "Political Attacks on the Judiciary: Can Justice Be Done Amid Efforts to Intimidate and Remove Judges from Office for Unpopular Decisions?," *NYU Law Review* 72, no. 2 (May 1997): 331–333.

ads alleged that the "murderer won't be getting the punishment he deserves. Thanks to Penny White."[10] These influential ads asserted that Tennesseans should "stand up and vote NO . . . NO to judges who allow the rape and murder of 78-year-old women to go unpunished. NO to judges who re-write the law according to their personal views. And NO to Penny White."[11]

The state Republican Party campaigned against White, reinforcing that a vote against her retention sends a "message that law-abiding Tennesseans feel it is time to get tough on crime."[12] The party's ads, sensationalizing the *Odom* case, exclaimed that Tennessee law "provides for the death penalty; and we need judges that will not stand in its way when the criminal clearly deserves it."[13] A Republican Party mailer declared that "Richard Odom [the defendant in the *Odom* case] was convicted of repeatedly raping and stabbing to death a 78-year-old Memphis woman. However, Penny White felt the crime wasn't heinous enough for the death penalty—so she struck it down."[14] The ads were taking liberties with a line from Justice Birch's majority opinion in *Odom*, which emphasized the importance of reserving the death penalty for offenses that are the "worst of the worst" under Tennessee law.[15] But Justice White hadn't written the opinion, which didn't strike down the death penalty in any event. She simply agreed that the trial court made reversible errors in sentencing and that the defendant needed to be re-sentenced, as a result of which he later received the death penalty again.

Indeed, Justice White's record on the death penalty and criminal cases was far from what her opponents described. As her campaign supporters argued during the 1996 campaign, Justice White upheld convictions in 85 percent of the roughly two hundred criminal appeals she heard as an appellate judge.[16] *Odom* was actually the first and only death penalty case Justice White had heard during her nineteen months on the Tennessee Supreme Court and only her second death penalty appeal as an appellate judge. In that earlier case before *Odom,* as an appellate court judge, she and her colleagues had upheld the death sentence. As she later observed, "I think it is obvious that the tactic is used to instill fear in the public and to sort of try to create this false calculation that if a judge does not vote to affirm a death sentence in every single case, then the judge is doing something wrong."[17]

The intensity of the opposition campaign seemed to catch sitting Tennessee judges by surprise at the time. The situation was unique for the time "because nobody had ever seen it happen." She explained that "everybody had the same reaction: this is bad, but it'll blow right over. It's one-day news, you know just keep your head down, keep doing what you're doing." The story didn't blow over. In fact, the attacks on Justice White worsened, "and they began to just make it look like that's all I ever did was just free criminals." Justice White's short time on the bench meant "they had to mischaracterize me, because I hadn't had any real controversial cases."

The opposition blanketed the state with anti–Penny White mailers and postcards. One of the postcards included a gruesome quote about the murder of the victim from the death sentence case. Justice White remembers that the backlash against her was "pretty overwhelming [and] all people could unite over was [being] anti-Penny." The Tennessee Conservative Union pledged to run radio and print ads, mail 100,000 "fact kits," and print half a million postcards for mobilization against Penny White.[18] It argued that "people must make our stand" because Penny White had the support of "Big Labor Unions," "every trial lawyer," the ACLU, and "Liberal Newspapers."[19] The president of the Tennessee Conservative Union declared that he could not "sit back and do nothing while one of the most liberal judges in the entire country is given even more power!"[20]

Under the Tennessee Code of Judicial Conduct, Justice White was restricted from commenting on the case or stating her political views in general. Unable to defend herself, Justice White was removed from office by a 55 percent vote against her retention. Two days after her loss, U.S. Supreme Court Justice John Paul Stevens announced that judicial elections were "profoundly unwise" and said that judges campaigning on promises to be "tough on crime" established "evidence of bias that should disqualify the candidate from sitting in criminal cases."[21]

Justice White's election defeat presaged the changing tone and intensity of judicial elections from an earlier, quieter era to a new-style modern age of partisan politics, big money, and hardball campaigning. Her defeat was the result of "an unprecedented campaign by conservative activists and victim advocates who labeled her soft-on-crime."[22] Even her opponents were reportedly surprised by their success in the first-ever defeat of a sitting supreme court justice,[23] but their tactics and approach would be replicated over and over in the coming years, as we describe in this chapter.

Since her removal from the bench, Justice White—now a successful academic—has disdained judicial elections because of the "quid pro quo or motivation to rule in favor of parties that can help you get re-elected." She believes that opposition campaigns in judicial elections often target women and people of color. "If you look at the nature of the attacks . . . it's almost always crime and punishment and . . . all the stereotypes about women fit into the narrative, which is these women just can't be tough on crime." As she sees it, "people of color are subject to the same stereotypes promoting fear-based campaigns against them." At the core, Justice White believes "it's discrimination against women, and a belief that all women are a particular way that's not conducive to judging. And that all people of color are a particular way that isn't conducive to judging."

Moreover, Justice White contends that the nature of judicial elections attracts the wrong type of people to the bench. "I think what we will end up with are people on the bench who have more traits that enable them to stay in their positions than maybe those that enable them to be a good judge." More specifically, she explains that "that which makes one successful at getting votes and campaigning and backslapping is the opposite of that which makes people a good listener, a good neutral applier of the law, and a fair and honest arbitrator."

It seems that most of the world agrees with Justice White: Choosing judges by election is an almost uniquely American practice. In the United States, nearly nine out of ten state judges must win an election to gain or retain their seat on the bench.[24] Virtually no other country requires judicial candidates to win votes or campaign for office; judges are typically chosen by appointment, often with a long process of training and secure tenure.[25]

In France, for instance, judicial candidates are generally picked through an intense process that begins with competitive examinations for admission to the *École Nationale de la Magistrature*,[26] where as few as 5 percent of test takers will then begin their civil service career.[27] Once admitted, judicial candidates receive specialized training and take another set of competitive examinations to become *auditeurs de justice*, essentially entry-level judges. *Auditeurs de justice* then must undergo a thirty-one-month course of study through which they are ranked by academic standing and receive their initial posting as what we would consider a judge. This long process of selection and training is intended to ensure high quality of judicial performance and insulate judges from the political process.

Although not all countries have the same sort of system for judicial selection as France, most countries likewise remove judicial candidates and judges from electoral pressures. Only a handful of other countries use elections to initially select or retain judges. Switzerland uses elections to pick low-level local judges.[28] Japan uses a highly structured system of judicial selection similar to France's system, with competitive examinations and selection by merit-based appointment.[29] After their initial selection, Japanese Supreme Court justices must be periodically re-elected to keep their position, but retention is so routine that one scholar described the Japanese Supreme Court as "among the most autonomous constitutional or highest regular courts in the industrial world."[30] Bolivia, after a 2009 constitutional referendum, shifted to electing all its national judges through direct popular vote.[31] Candidates were, however, subject to a rigorous preselection procedure where they had to receive two-thirds approval by the national legislature to even reach the ballot.[32]

As a consequence, the American system of judicial elections to select and retain most state judges is an extreme international outlier. Mitchel Lasser, a law professor who has studied comparative judicial selection, explains that "the rest of the world is stunned and amazed at what we do, and vaguely aghast. They think the idea that judges with absolutely no judge-specific educational training are running political campaigns is both insane and characteristically American."[33]

Of course, it is only *state* judges who are selected and retained through elections in the United States. Federal judges, by contrast, do not ever run for election to obtain or keep their judgeships. Instead, federal judges are appointed by the president, subject to Senate confirmation,[34] and then enjoy lifetime tenure until they retire from office.[35] Federal judges never need to raise campaign money, stump for office, or win votes on election day to rise to the federal bench.

Federal judges, as a consequence, have a very different career profile than elected state judges. They generally have better professional qualifications, are more highly rated by bar associations, and are more highly esteemed in terms of their legal competence and professionalism, if only in comparison to state judges.[36] What's more, federal judges never need to worry about keeping their jobs, regardless of which litigants they decide for or against. Federal judges are, in this sense, immune from political pressure, free to decide as they see best under the applicable law. State judges, who face the prospect of losing their jobs if they do not win re-election, are not similarly free to judge.

In this chapter, we provide a brief introduction to judicial elections in the United States. First, we describe the evolution of the methods of judicial selection and retention, from the emergence of judicial elections during the nineteenth century to the wide range of partisan elections, nonpartisan elections, and variants of appointment and merit plans seen today. Second, we describe the increasing politicization of judicial campaigns in recent years and the growing importance of campaign contributions to candidates. Third, we explain that the rapid growth in campaign spending has ignited new worry about the influence of money on judges. However, most of the criticism and calls for reform have been aimed at a specific type of judicial election, and proposed reforms would simply replace one type of election with another. In contrast, we later argue that the threats to judicial impartiality may have less to do with the type of elections in which judges run, and more to do with the specific pressures for incumbent judges when they must run again for *re-election*.

A BRIEF HISTORY OF JUDICIAL ELECTIONS

Today, there is significant variation in the methods that states use to select and retain their judges. Many states use some form of election, while other states use different versions of appointment. This striking diversity results from a long historical evolution where states have reformed their legal systems in reaction to different concerns and crises. Regardless of the era, state reforms to judicial selection and retention were usually designed to insulate state courts from whatever political force seemed most problematic at that moment. However, judicial reform has tended to oscillate through a cat-and-mouse game where change leads to a new source of political influence on courts, which then requires further reform, and thereby repeats the cycle.

Prior to America's founding, judicial responsibilities in many colonies were carried out by elected officials. There weren't "elected judges" in the modern sense, because there was not a real separation of powers in the colonial era, but most American colonists wanted judicial duties carried out by elected local officials rather than those appointed by the Crown. However, once the states won their independence, they were no longer concerned about royal interference in the states' judicial business. State constitutional conventions explicitly endorsed a separation of powers and decided that judges under the new system would be appointed by either the state governor or legislature. These appointed judges, it was believed, would protect our fledgling democracy from democratic excess. Every state that joined the Union before 1845 did so with judicial appointments that mirrored the federal judiciary.[37]

However, over time it became increasingly apparent that these appointed judges did not have sufficient independence from the political branches that appointed them. In state after state, appointed judges who did not agree with the other branches were impeached, replaced, or otherwise weakened.[38] For example, when Pennsylvania Republicans defeated the Federalists in 1799, they set about impeaching judges appointed by their Federalist predecessors. In other states, such as Ohio, the new Republican majority in the state legislature replaced Federalist judges by abolishing judicial life tenure in favor of shorter, renewable terms and then forcing from office judges who had been appointed under the life tenure system. Other states weakened the judiciary by literally creating new courts. In Kentucky, for example, Republicans took away much of the jurisdiction of judges appointed earlier by the Federalists by creating new circuit courts and shifting jurisdiction to these new courts. The vulnerability of the appointed justices to the whims of the other branches significantly hindered their independence. Judges who were too politically independent were often replaced, so many never even bothered to maintain the appearance of independence.

Even so, most states in the early republic stuck with judicial appointments, and in only a few instances did states turn to judicial elections as their mode of judicial selection. As Jed Shugerman's historical work details, the few exceptions typically resulted from special political circumstances that made judicial elections particularly sensible. For example, when the Republic of Vermont wrote its constitution in 1777, its settlers were in open dispute with New York, which had been governing the Vermont territory. Vermonters decided to elect lower court judges as a reaction against New York's governing from a distance, believing that elected judges would be more responsive to local settler opinion.[39]

Georgia adopted elections for its lower court judges for similarly particular reasons in 1812.[40] The legislature had recently passed a law aimed at providing more relief to debtors, and elected judges were believed to be more pro-debtor than appointed judges. In addition, the state was still reeling from a large public scandal in which a series of corrupt Georgia governors and legislators had sold state land to friends and family for below market prices. Adoption of judicial elections responded to public concerns over this scandal and provided a means for shifting power away from government officials and to the public.[41]

Mississippi became the first state to adopt elections for not just lower court judges but for appellate judges, too, in 1832. Natchez, the state's major commercial center, had largely controlled the state legislature and, in turn, the state's legislatively appointed judges. However, at Mississippi's 1832 constitutional convention, the rural "Whole Hogs" outvoted the "Natchez Aristocrats" to adopt judicial elections that they believed would better represent local interests.[42] The Whole Hogs' case was helped by the U.S. Supreme Court's decision in *Worcester v. Georgia*, affirming the sovereignty of the Cherokee Nation and striking down Georgia's regulations regarding it.[43] With a large population of Choctaw and Chickasaw in Mississippi, removal of Native Americans was a significant issue to white settlers. The Court's unpopular decision, judicially striking down state law regarding Native American relations, convinced many Mississippi delegates that judicial accountability to voters through elections might keep state judges in line on these questions.

Mississippi's decision to elect all of its state judges didn't immediately influence other states to follow, but a decade later, the economic crisis of the 1840s and New York's adoption of judicial elections in 1846 had a cascading effect on state governments across the country. A severe economic depression in the early 1840s caused several states to default on their debts, while legislatures in other states, like New York, tried to spend their way out of the crisis. Fiscal irresponsibility and corruption on the part of many state legislatures during the crisis sparked a widespread movement against government by elites during the Jacksonian Era. When New York's constitutional convention met in 1846, it was considered so inevitable the state would adopt judicial elections that a formal vote on the question wasn't even held.

At the New York convention, a consensus of delegates contended that only judicial elections could properly promote judicial independence by insulating judges from the influence of the other political branches. This consideration was especially important given the perceived abuses of legislative power exercised during the economic crisis. Moreover, a complicated web of political parties competed for power in New York at this time. The parties denounced the appointment of judges by opposing parties, believing that party insiders were appointed rather than qualified judges. One delegate argued that the shift from appointed to elected judges would result in a bench full of "good men" instead of "politicians by trade."[44] The delegates argued that judicial elections offered the best protection of the people's individual rights. As one delegate explained: "Unless your judges are elected by the sovereign body, by the constituent, you will look in vain for judges

[who] can stand by the constitution of the State against the encroachments of power."[45]

While Mississippi's adoption of elections may have piqued the interest of other states considering reforms to judicial selection, New York's move to an elective judiciary gave the reform widespread acceptance and legitimated what had earlier seemed a risky experiment with judicial selection.[46] As state constitutional conventions during the era met to rewrite state constitutions and determine how to organize state governments, many relied heavily on New York's new constitution. And even in states that didn't directly borrow from New York's constitution, delegates were inspired and reassured by New York's move to a new form of judicial selection. In the five years after New York moved to judicial elections, seventeen states adopted elections for at least some courts, with twelve of those states choosing to elect all of their judges. By 1860, of the thirty-one states in the Union, twenty-three elected at least some judges, with eighteen electing all of their judges.[47]

As in New York, constitutional convention delegates across the country believed that judicial elections would produce more independent judges who would be free from the influence of the other branches of government. As a delegate at Indiana's constitutional convention explained, judges must be insulated from "the control of the other branches of the government" to be able to "protect the rights of the people and to preserve a proper equilibrium between the different departments."[48] Similarly, an Illinois delegate argued that he would "rather see judges the weather-cocks of public sentiment" than see them "the instruments of power . . . registering the mandates of the Legislature and the edicts of the Governor."[49] A Pennsylvania legislator agreed: "Election always has and always will give us better men and better officers than appointment—more independent men, sir, for I hold a man elected to office by the will of the people, and having the confidence of the people, is freer to act than the autocrat of Russia."[50]

In addition to protecting judicial independence from the other political branches, delegates also regularly affirmed that elections would ensure judges represent the voters and preserve the public good. For example, one delegate to the Kentucky convention in 1849 explained that a judge "is to look somewhere for his bread, and that is to come from the people. He is to look somewhere for approbation, and that is to come from the people."[51]

Ultimately, delegates frequently maintained that elected judges would improve the quality of the bench. As an Illinois convention delegate explained, "If only the federal judiciary had been made elective . . . the people 'would have chosen judges, instead of broken-down politicians.'"[52]

States that adopted judicial elections in the nineteenth century typically chose a particular type of election—partisan elections. In a partisan election, the judicial candidates are listed on the ballot with a partisan affiliation, and there is coordination between judicial candidates and political parties during the campaign. Parties play an important role in recruiting attractive candidates to run for judicial office. From the perspective of the parties, an attractive candidate is someone who can both get elected and who they believe will be loyal to the party's policy values once on the bench. After a candidate is recruited, parties assist the candidate's campaign with funding, advice, and connections. Parties generally provide direct funding to the candidate and help coordinate and channel the contributions of other campaign donors. Parties can also provide advice about how to run the campaign and mobilize endorsements from important political leaders.

One result of a judicial candidate affiliating with a political party is that the reputation of the judge and party become intertwined.[53] The party's image can be impacted by what the candidate says or does, both when they are running for election and when they are on the bench. As a result, parties have an incentive to monitor the decisions of judges to make sure that they continue to support the party's interests. Judges, for their part, continue to need the party's support to prevail in their next re-election. This reliance gives the judges a strong incentive to not decide cases in a way that conflicts with their party's interests.

The states adopting partisan elections in the mid-nineteenth century understood the connection that partisan elections would create between judicial candidates and political parties. However, they generally didn't worry about the influence that this role would give to the parties. Earlier forms of the judicial appointment process gave governors and legislators extensive power and opportunity to influence judges, resulting in cronyism and political patronage. Reformers believed that influence from political parties through partisan elections, by comparison, would be less problematic, because voters would serve as a critical check on cronyism and corruption.

Moreover, reformers assumed that only powerful institutions like political parties could counterbalance the concentration of wealth and power that had amassed in other institutions at this time, including banks, big corporations, and state legislatures. Organized political power in the form of popular parties was necessary to protect democracy from the corruption of such aristocratic institutions. Indeed, supporters of judicial elections were initially pleased with what they saw as signs of judicial independence after the adoption of judicial elections. Elected judges struck down more laws than their appointed predecessors, suggesting the courts were more independent from the legislatures that had passed these laws.

However, despite this initial success, Jacksonian acceptance of the role of political parties had dissipated by the early twentieth century. During the Progressive Era, reformers became alarmed by what they saw as a resurgence of political corruption and therefore grew increasingly distrustful of party involvement in judicial elections. Because judges had to rely on party connections to be elected, reformers perceived judges as beholden to their parties and the special interests they represented. Partisan elections, in their minds, had allowed political parties to capture the judiciary. As a Nebraska governor of the era explained, elected courts were "composed of lawyers who owe their position, not so much to legal attainment and profound learning, as they do to political services rendered."[54]

Suspicions about partisanship and organized party patronage were at a head when Ohio convened its constitutional convention in 1911.[55] Like many progressives of the day, convention delegates overwhelmingly agreed that the influence of party machines and special interests should be reduced, and they decided that nonpartisan elections were the best way to accomplish that goal.[56] In contrast to partisan elections, in which judicial candidates are nominated by political parties and listed on the ballot with their party affiliation, nonpartisan elections do not have party nominations and do not list candidates on the ballot by party affiliation. Ohio became one of the first states to adopt nonpartisan elections, but only for the general election. Judicial candidates still had to win their party nomination in a primary election to get on the general election ballot. Although the progressive delegates at Ohio's convention were critics of partisanship, they were products of that party system themselves and couldn't bring themselves to eliminate the role of parties altogether.

Spurred by similar progressive values, other states adopted nonpartisan elections around the time that Ohio did. Most went further than Ohio and adopted nonpartisan primary elections as well. Between 1910 and 1920, nine states made the switch from partisan to nonpartisan elections. By the end of the twentieth century, twice as many states would use nonpartisan elections over partisan elections.[57]

However, it didn't take long for some states to notice that their adoption of nonpartisan elections produced some negative consequences. Nonpartisan elections prevented party identification of the candidate for both voters and the parties themselves, thereby reducing excitement about judicial races. Fewer voters turned out to vote in nonpartisan elections, and those who did often voted in only the major races at the top of the ballot but then "rolled off" and didn't vote in the judicial races.[58] Moreover, eliminating the partisan affiliation on the ballot removed an important signal that voters used to select judges. Without that signal, they were less sure how to vote in judicial races. In addition, critics of nonpartisan elections, notably the Commonwealth Club of California, warned that removing political parties from judicial races made some judicial candidates turn toward organized crime for the fundraising and political connections that parties had once provided. Indeed, newspapers reported on the "underworld" connections of Chicago judges in the 1920s.[59]

During the 1930s, concerns about crime galvanized calls for an entirely new type of judicial selection. Crime increased dramatically during the twenties and thirties as a result of the economic desperation of the Great Depression and the boost that Prohibition gave to organized crime. In the middle of this crime wave, Earl Warren, then a young prosecutor in Oakland, California, targeted judicial elections as an obstacle to cleaning up the streets.[60] He argued that judicial elections produced judges who either had no incentive to get tough on crime, or who were corrupt themselves and trying to curry favor with organized crime. Judicial elections, he claimed, resulted in a localized, decentralized justice system that was bound to be ineffective in combating large-scale crime. Warren decided that reform was necessary to modernize and centralize California's legal system.

In 1934, Warren initiated a "Curb Crime" movement that proposed amendments to the state's constitution which would replace judicial elections with a new system of merit selection. Under this system, judicial candidates would first be nominated by a blue-ribbon nominating board, and then the governor would appoint a judge from among the board's nominees. At the next general election, the now-sitting judge would then run for retention. Instead of competing against other candidates running for their office, the judge's name would appear on the ballot alone with only a yes-or-no choice for voters regarding the judge's retention.

The business community immediately supported Warren's merit selection plan. As early as 1912, California businesses had been trying to replace judicial elections with judicial appointments because elections, as they saw it, generally produced more pro-labor, anti-business judges. The business community saw an opportunity in Warren's anti-crime campaign, realizing that voters cared more about crime than business interests. With businesses contributing both resources and organizational support to the Curb Crime campaign, California voters passed Warren's merit selection plan in 1934. Six years later, Warren was elected governor of California and reaffirmed his support for the merit system: "I am of the opinion that no man should aspire to the bench unless he can run the gauntlet of his own profession."[61]

Missouri became the next state to adopt a merit plan in 1940.[62] Like California, Missouri had just endured a crime wave that had involved historically notorious criminals, including Bonnie and Clyde and "Pretty Boy" Floyd. The deluge of criminal cases overwhelmed the elected judges on Missouri courts. Lawyers in the state saw an opportunity amid the public outcry over crime and joined together to propose a merit system for selecting judges in Missouri. Like Warren in California, Missouri lawyers advocating for merit selection believed that judicial appointments would produce judges with more competence, expertise, and efficiency. The more qualified the judges, they believed, the more powerful the bench. Missouri lawyers also had growing concerns about the types of voters who would choose judges in judicial elections, given the state's rapidly growing populations of racial and ethnic minorities. A merit selection system would make sure that the selection of the judiciary stayed with the white elite.

Interestingly, the merit selection plan today is widely known as the "Missouri Plan" rather than the "California Plan." At the last minute, California businesses convinced Earl Warren to switch the roles of the governor and the nominating board, with the governor choosing the nominees and the board appointing a judge from among the nominees. In contrast,

Missouri adopted a system that was faithful to Warren's original proposal and is still popular today in many states: A bipartisan commission, composed of judges and leaders of the state bar, nominates a slate of judicial candidates from which the governor chooses their appointee. At the next general election, the selected appointee faces an unopposed retention election in which voters can vote only to retain or unseat the sitting judge.

From the 1950s through the 1970s, similar merit plans were adopted by nineteen states, primarily in the South, Great Plains, and Rockies. As in California and Missouri, the bar and business community generally led campaigns for merit selection as they tried to professionalize the bench and replace pro-labor elected judges. However, advocates also took advantage of other factors to mobilize popular support.[63] They pointed to World War II and the history of fascist regimes as proof that the protection of individual rights required judges who were beholden to neither an executive with sole authority over their appointment nor the partisan politics of elections. They similarly argued that the Cold War reaffirmed the importance of the rule of law. In several southern states, including Alabama, Florida, and Tennessee, advocates appealed to Southern racism and further argued that merit selection plans would help retain white control of the courts as Black voting populations expanded.[64]

A new crime wave during the late 1960s and early 1970s gave the business and legal communities an additional opportunity to win public support for merit selection. Across the country, murders and rapes doubled and overall violent crime rates tripled. Business and legal elites used the public outcry over crime to build support for merit selection, arguing that selection based on merit would produce judges more qualified to handle the growing crime wave. This harnessing of anti-crime propaganda in the 1970s was reminiscent of the business community's support of Earl Warren's Curb Crime campaign in California in the 1930s. Later we'll discuss how the business community again turned to an anti-crime campaign strategy for its own purposes in the 1990s. In the 1990s, they used this strategy not to reform elections, but to win elections like Penny White's in Tennessee.

For over two centuries, states have experimented with different selection methods in their efforts to insulate the judiciary from political pressures, among other things. In the mid-nineteenth century, many states switched from appointments to elections to protect judges from the influence of legislatures and governors. Then, in the early twentieth century, several states made the shift from partisan to nonpartisan elections to shield judges from political parties. When nonpartisan elections didn't produce the independent, high-quality judges that reformers had hoped, many states adopted merit systems to professionalize the bench. This cycle of reform, political response and capture, followed by a new round of reform has repeated several times nationwide.

Not every state went through these cycles. Maine, New Jersey, and South Carolina never broke from gubernatorial or legislative selection of judges. Other states, including Florida, North Carolina, and Indiana, have jumped around several times among different methods of judicial selection. Many states use the same method to select judges for their lower courts as they do for their highest courts, while others have adopted different methods for different levels of courts.

This long historical evolution has led to a variety of methods by which states choose judges for their highest courts. Today, twenty-two states use elections to choose state supreme court justices: Eight use partisan elections, while fourteen use nonpartisan elections. In the twenty-eight remaining states, the governor or legislature appoints judges to the state supreme court, but twenty-one of those states use a form of merit selection where qualified judges are first identified by a commission. Figure 2.2 maps the methods states currently use to select state supreme court justices.

Separate from judicial selection is the question of judicial retention. States often use one method to initially select judges, but then use a different method to decide whether to keep the judges in their positions. For instance, the merit selection plans use a form of gubernatorial appointment for judicial selection, but they then use retention elections to decide whether those gubernatorial appointees get to keep their job longer than their initial term.

For this question of judicial retention, states initially borrowed the federal judiciary's provision of permanent tenure for their supreme court justices, just as they originally modeled their selection of supreme court justices on the appointive federal system. Of the twenty-three states that established a supreme court by 1820, only four did not originally grant their judges life tenure.[65]

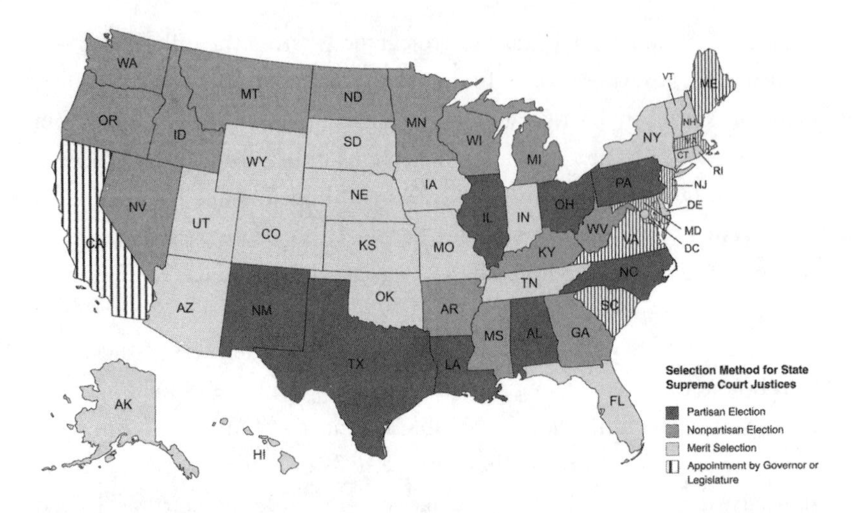

FIGURE 2.2 Method of Selection of State Supreme Court Justices. Source: Data collected from websites of individual state judicial systems and Brennan Center for Justice, "Judicial Selection: An Interactive Map," https://www.brennancenter.org/judicial-selection-map.

However, when states started to consider shifting from appointments for judicial selection to elections, they also reconsidered the desirability of permanent tenure and began to adopt different forms of judicial retention. At the state constitutional conventions that we previously mentioned, many delegates argued that elections should be used not just for judicial selection, but also for judicial retention.

Requiring judges to face voters in periodic elections, under this view, would maintain judicial independence, because voters would not tolerate judges who were anything other than fair and independent. A delegate to the Massachusetts Convention asserted that if judges facing re-election "were found to yield to their private political opinions, and carry out their judgments and decisions against their duty . . . I believe those judges would be hurled from their seats by the people more readily than if they had been guilty of a higher degree of corruption in any other direction; because, I believe the quality which the people most require in a judge is independence."[66] In the same convention, another delegate argued that "if you provide that [judges] shall come before the people for re-election, they will take care that their opinions reflect justice and right, because they cannot stand upon any other basis."[67]

Some delegates, though, recognized that requiring judges to face the voters for re-election could instead jeopardize judicial independence. When Mississippi became the first state to adopt judicial elections and re-election for all state judges, at least some delegates argued that "independence and freedom from the excitement of electioneering contests . . . [is] essential to the firmness, and impartiality of judgment."[68] Similarly, a decade later in New York, a delegate argued that re-elections would lead judges to "yield to the popular caprices, or prejudices, or passions of a particular period."[69]

Despite this recognition that popular opinion might pressure judges, most delegates believed re-election incentives would align with the public good because voters would support, and re-elect, independent judges. Seventeen of the nineteen states that had originally granted permanent tenure to supreme court justices moved instead to limited terms in the mid to late 1800s. Only two states, Massachusetts and New Hampshire, opted to retain permanent tenure for supreme court justices; Rhode Island would join them in 1842.

States that originally switched from appointments to elections generally also chose judicial elections as their method of judicial retention. However, as states eventually tried out even newer selection methods to insulate their judiciary, they didn't always update their methods for judicial retention. As a result, the states today display a hodgepodge of selection and retention method combinations. For the retention of their state supreme court judges, five states currently use partisan elections and fourteen states use nonpartisan elections. Nine states rely on reappointment by the governor, legislature, or a judicial nominating commission. In nineteen states, state supreme court judges face an unopposed retention election in which they are listed on the ballot with only a yes or no option for voters. Figure 2.3 displays the current retention methods states use for supreme court justices.

INCREASING COSTS AND POLITICIZATION OF JUDICIAL ELECTIONS: THE 1990S

As a result of this long evolution in judicial selection and retention methods, approximately 90 percent of current state judges must be elected or re-elected by voters. Unfortunately, the nature of judicial elections has fundamentally changed since the original supporters of elections heralded

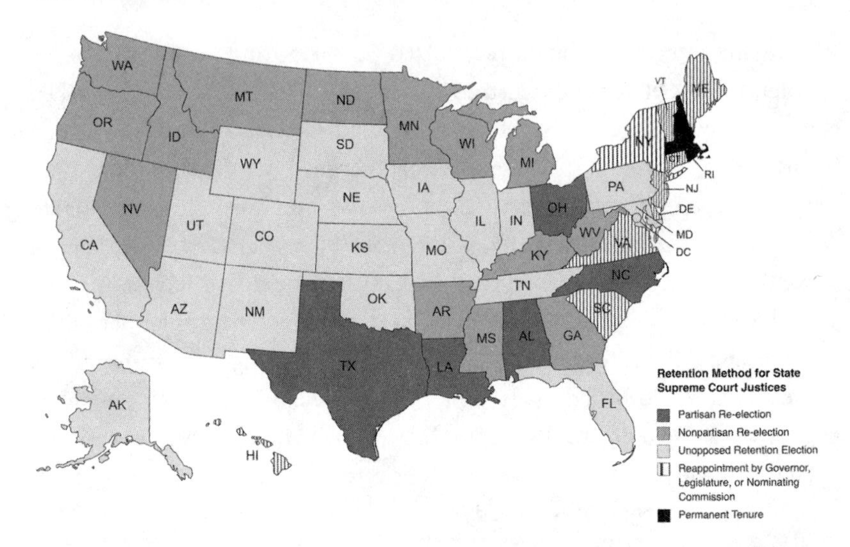

FIGURE 2.3 Method of Retention of State Supreme Court Justices. Source: Data collected from websites of individual state judicial systems and Brennan Center for Justice, "Judicial Selection: An Interactive Map," https://www.brennancenter.org/judicial-selection-map.

them as shields against partiality. Those original supporters could not have imagined that judges would one day run for office like other politicians, raising millions of dollars from groups with a financial stake in who sits on the bench.

This change in judicial campaigns is primarily a product of the last three decades. Until the early 1990s, state judicial elections were generally not very competitive. Campaigns spent little money and advertising was modest, if it happened at all. But this changed during the 1990s as elections became more competitive and political and campaign spending skyrocketed. At the beginning of the 1990s, state supreme court candidates across the United States raised roughly $10 million in aggregate for an election cycle, but by the end of the decade, the total had increased more than sixfold.[70] Figure 2.4 displays the candidate contributions raised during each cycle of the 1990s.

So, what happened in the 1990s that caused this dramatic increase in campaign contributions to state supreme court candidates? We believe that three primary forces combined to bring about this inevitable shift: (1) increased caseloads for state courts; (2) growing interest group involvement in judicial elections; and (3) relaxed restrictions on campaigning for judicial office.

First, there was more at stake in judicial elections as the influence of the state supreme courts grew. The number of cases filed in state appellate courts doubled every ten years between the 1960s and 1980s.[71] As the American Bar Association (ABA) described that period, "While federal and state courts both witnessed an upsurge in the controversial, policy-laden cases they were called upon to decide in the latter half of the twentieth century, this trend has become especially noticeable in state court systems." State supreme courts were not only hearing more cases; they also seemed to be hearing more important cases as the federal government increasingly devolved power to the states under the "new federalism" of the 1970s and 1980s. At the same time, state courts looked more to their own state constitutions to provide protections beyond the federal minimum guaranteed

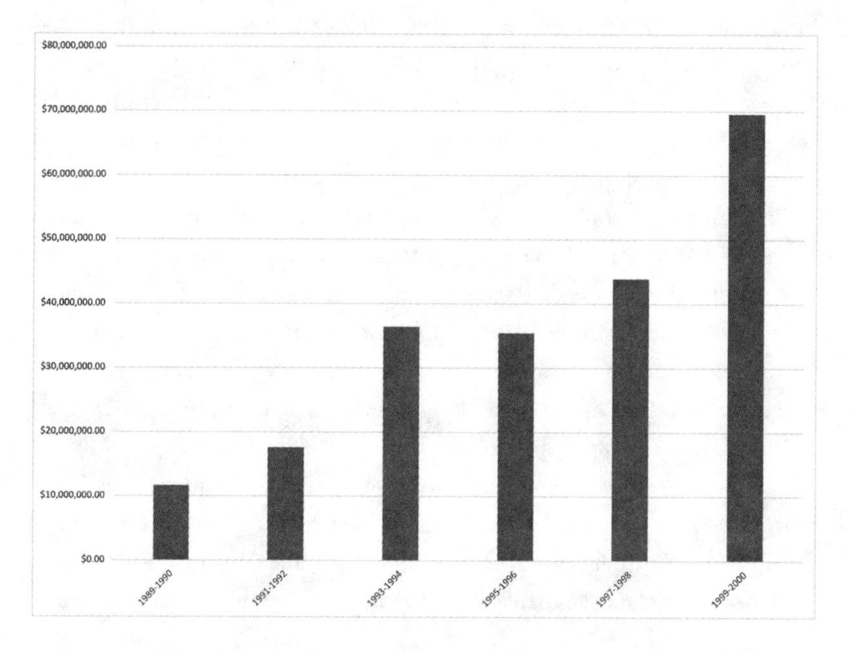

FIGURE 2.4 Total Contributions raised by State Supreme Court Candidates (in 2020 dollars). Source: James Sample, Charles Hall, and Linda Casey, "The New Politics of Judicial Elections 2000–2009: Decade of Change," *Judicature* 94, no. 2 (2010). Data for 1989–2000 is not inflation-adjusted in the "Decade of Change" report, so we adjusted the reported nominal dollars into 2016 dollars.

under the U.S. Constitution. The ABA explained that "state courts have become a new forum of choice for litigation of constitutional rights and responsibilities, which has placed them in the political spotlight with increasing frequency."[72]

Tort reform played a large role in increasing the politicization of judicial elections. During the 1980s and 1990s, several state legislatures were confronted with what they perceived to be an insurance and liability "crisis" characterized by increasing numbers of tort cases, higher damage awards, and rising insurance premiums.[73] Many state legislatures responded by enacting tort reform legislation that curtailed the civil liability or damage awards of tort defendants such as product manufacturers and doctors. These tort reform laws were regularly challenged later in state court, eventually reaching the dockets of the state supreme courts.

Tort reform contributed to the second force responsible for the dramatic increase in judicial campaign financing—the rise in interest group involvement in state judicial races. Between 1968 and 1988, the number of registered special interest groups in the United States doubled from 10,300 to 20,600.[74] Interest groups were initially focused primarily on the outcomes of legislative and executive elections, but they soon took an interest in state judicial elections as well. Judicial campaigns generally raised less money, meaning an interest group could influence the outcome of a state judicial election more cheaply than an election for governor or a state legislator. In addition, interest groups only needed to elect four or five tort-reform-friendly judges to attain a majority in the court, while it would have taken dozens of state legislators to form a legislative majority. As one interest group representative explained: "We figured out a long time ago that it's easier to elect seven judges than to elect 132 legislators."[75]

Texas was one of the first states to experience significant interest group involvement in judicial elections. In 1988, several business interest groups decided to inject themselves into the Texas Supreme Court races. The races soon became the most expensive in the state's history, with candidates raising over $10 million.[76] The effort paid off as business-friendly judges won several seats on the court. Texas appellate judge Phil Hardberger believed that that 1988 election remade the court and, in turn, transformed tort liability in the state. As he put it, "With this new Court, previous expansions of the law were stopped, then rolled backwards. Jury verdicts became highly suspect and were frequently overturned for a variety of ever-expanding reasons. . . . Damages, too, did not go unnoticed. Juries' assessments were wiped out by increasingly harsher standards."[77]

Although the expense of the Texas Supreme Court elections in the late 1980s was an anomaly for that decade, it was a harbinger of things to come. In the 1990s, many other states experienced an increase in interest group involvement in state supreme court races over tort reform issues. For example, the Alabama state legislature enacted several tort reforms in 1987 that were overturned by the Alabama Supreme Court in the early 1990s. Interest groups rallied to the cause, generating an over-sevenfold increase in Alabama Supreme Court candidate expenditures from 1986 to 1996.[78] The involvement of interest groups in state judicial elections quickly spread throughout the country. The U.S. Chamber of Commerce summarized the motivation behind many of the interest groups that were newly invested in state judicial elections: "Meaningful [tort] reform is unlikely unless and until the justices elected to the [state] Supreme Court by the plaintiffs' bar are replaced by the voters."[79]

The third cause of the increasing politicization and expense of state judicial races was legal change that allowed judges to become more explicitly political. The ABA previously enforced a canon of judicial conduct in its Model Code that forbade judges from announcing their views on legal or political issues.[80] In 1990, the ABA repealed this canon because of concerns that it might violate the First Amendment's protection of free speech. Twenty-five of the thirty-four states that had originally followed the ABA's canon also eventually eliminated it, and the U.S. Supreme Court in *Republican Party of Minnesota v. White* struck down enforcement of the canon in the remaining nine states.[81] Scholars have generally viewed *White*'s loosening of the restrictions on judicial campaigning in 2002 as a watershed event in escalating the politicization of judicial races.[82] However, *White* was only the first U.S. Supreme Court case to have a significant impact on state judicial elections. More were to come.

NEW-STYLE JUDICIAL ELECTIONS

The increasing spending in state supreme court races leveled off during the early 2000s, but judicial elections soon underwent a dramatic shift in the sources of campaign money. Traditionally, candidates' own campaign committees raised most of the campaign money in judicial elections, with outside spending by interest groups and political parties contributing very little by comparison. Beginning around 2010, however, more and more of the money raised in judicial campaigns has been outside spending by interest groups. These interest groups are less transparent about their donors and less accountable about their spending than the candidates themselves. Moreover, with their donors cloaked in secrecy, these groups often run more inflammatory and deceptive ads that degrade the tone and civility of judicial campaigns.

The flashpoint for this sudden growth in the outside spending by interest groups was the U.S. Supreme Court's 2010 decision in *Citizens United v. Federal Election Commission.*[83] *Citizens United* transformed campaign finance by striking down bans on corporate and union electioneering that had been in place for half a century. This ruling allowed corporations and unions to contribute unlimited amounts to outside groups such as Super PACs and 501(c) and 527 organizations, which can then spend unlimited amounts advocating for the election or defeat of candidates, so long as the spending is formally independent of candidates or parties. Too much of this outside spending occurs without disclosure about who is really funding it, which prevents voters from knowing who is behind the candidate and messaging. According to the Brennan Center for Justice, the underlying donor could be identified from campaign finance filings for only 18 percent of the outside spending by interest groups in the 2015–16 state supreme court elections.[84] As a result, campaign finance reformers and groups like the Brennan Center refer to contributions from secretive outside groups that don't disclose their donors as "dark money."

Following *Citizens United*, outside spending by interest groups in federal elections dramatically increased. According to the nonpartisan research organization OpenSecrets, spending by Super PACs was roughly $62 million in 2010, the year *Citizens United* was decided. By 2020, Super PAC spending had grown to over $2.1 billion.[85] This spending has also significantly increased relative to overall federal campaign spending. In 2010, outside spending by interest groups made up about 8 percent of total federal election spending, but just three cycles later, in 2016, it comprised approximately 21 percent.[86]

But *Citizens United*'s impact goes beyond federal elections; the decision has also unleashed a flood of outside money from interest groups in state

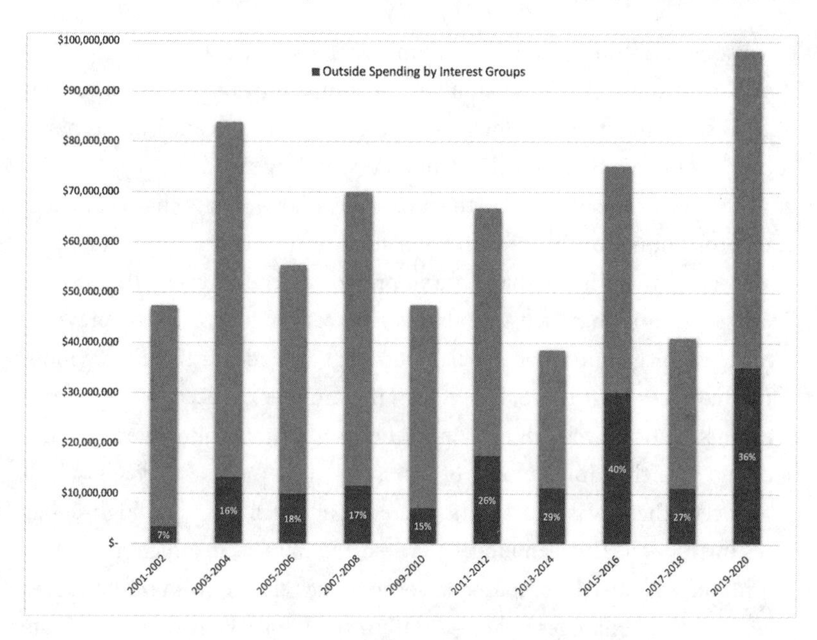

FIGURE 2.5 Total Spending and Outside Spending by Interest Groups in State Supreme Court Elections (in 2020 dollars). Source: Douglas Keith and Eric Velasco, "The Politics of Judicial Elections 2019–2020: Special Interests Are Spending More than Ever on State High Court Races. Here's Why," ***Brennan Center for Justice*****, January 25, 2022, 2.**

supreme court elections. In every state supreme court election since *Citizens United*, outside spending as a share of total spending has grown. Just before the decision, in the 2009–10 election cycle, outside spending by interest groups totaled just over $7 million (in 2020 dollars), accounting for approximately 15 percent of total spending on state supreme court races. In the election cycle just after *Citizens United*, interest groups spent over $17.5 million (in 2020 dollars), or 26 percent of the total.[87] Figure 2.5 reports the total spending on state supreme court elections and the portion of that total spending made up of outside spending by interest groups.[88]

Figure 2.5 reveals a standard pattern in campaign finance data: More money is generally spent in the cycles that coincide with presidential elections because there are more voters and, thus, more spending is needed to reach those voters. Looking past that oscillation, the trend in interest groups' share of total spending is obvious. Outside spending by interest groups never accounted for more than 18 percent of the total prior to *Citizens United.* After the decision, it has accounted for as much as 40 percent of total spending, roughly double the aforementioned peak, and has never accounted for less than 26 percent of total spending since.

The 2019–20 election cycle, the most recent for which we have complete data, broke numerous records in the history of state supreme court races.[89] Fundraising was higher than in any previous election cycle. In fact, the nearly $100 million raised was about 17 percent higher than the previous record set in the 2003–2004 cycle. One might wonder if there were more contested races in 2019–20, but in fact, the number of races was similar to previous election cycles. Simply put, there's a lot more money raised and spent now for the same number of races.

Indeed, there was a dramatic increase in the number of high-dollar races in 2019–20. Thirteen judges were elected in races in which more than $3 million was raised, compared to seven judges elected in $3 million races in 2015–16 and six judges in 2017–18 (all in 2020 dollars). Although no state had ever before raised more than $10 million for state supreme court races in a single cycle, five states raised more than this record amount in the 2019–20 cycle.[90]

Outside spending by interest groups also broke records in 2019–20. These groups spent over $35.2 million, which was 17 percent more than the previous record set in 2015–16 and more than double interest groups' outside spending in every other election cycle besides 2015–16. Moreover, outside spending by interest groups accounted for 36 percent of total spending, which was second only to the 40 percent share in 2015–16.[91]

The increase in both direct-to-candidate contributions beginning in the 1990s and interest groups' outside spending in the 2000s has transformed the way judicial campaigns are conducted. Campaigns increasingly rely on ads, both on TV and social media, to promote a preferred candidate or attack an opposing candidate. TV advertising in judicial campaigns was essentially nonexistent in the early 1990s, but by the 1999–2000 election cycle, more than $10.6 million was spent on 22,000 airings.[92] Even with this spending, TV advertising was still relatively rare in the early 2000s. Judicial elections featured TV ads in only four out of thirty-three states with state supreme court elections in 2000. TV advertising soon intensified and expanded across the country. By the 2015–16 cycle, more than $37 million was

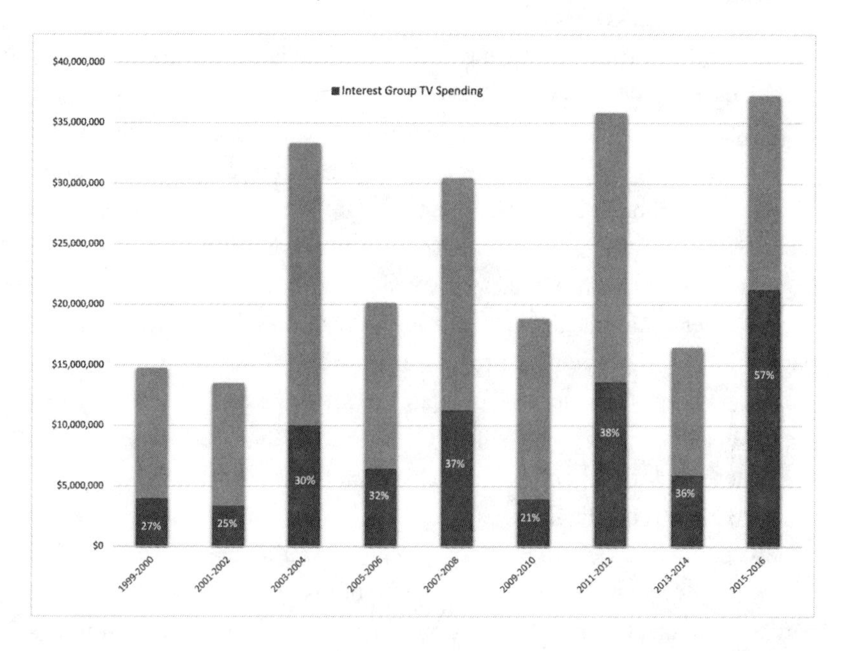

FIGURE 2.6 Spending on TV Advertising in State Supreme Court Elections and Interest Groups' Share of Spending (in 2016 dollars). Source: Alicia Bannon, Cathleen Lisk, and Peter Hardin, *The Politics of Judicial Elections 2015–2016: Who Pays for Judicial Races?* (New York: Brennan Center for Justice, 2017), 32.

spent on over 71,000 airings, and TV ads appeared in sixteen of thirty-three states with state supreme court elections.[93]

Interest groups, as distinct from the candidates' campaigns, have become the biggest players in TV advertising. As interest groups' outside spending has increased during the 2000s, so has the groups' focus on TV ads. In the 1999–2000 cycle, interest groups spent approximately $3.9 million on TV advertising, constituting just over a quarter of all dollars spent on TV ads during the two-year period.[94] However, in 2015–16, the last year for which data is available, interest groups spent a record $21.2 million on TV ads, accounting for 57 percent of all money spent on TV ads.[95] Figure 2.6 reports the total spending on TV ads and interest groups' share of that spending.

Although funders of TV advertising sometimes euphemistically refer to the ads as "voter education" efforts, the ads typically provide very little informational value.[96] Indeed, as early as 2004, a report reviewing the TV ads in that year's supreme court races concluded that "the judicial campaign ads of 2004 confirm that the days when judicial advertising focused primarily on candidate qualifications are gone, replaced by advertising that signals how candidates might decide cases and sometimes explicitly states their opinions on controversial issues that demand impartial adjudication in the courtroom."[97] Ads run by interest groups are especially likely to attack judges for their votes in a particular case, without providing details or nuance to explain why the judge voted how they did.[98] In the 1999–2000 cycle, 62 percent of such TV attack ads were financed by interest groups, but by the 2013–14 supreme court races, 100 percent of attack ads were purchased by interest groups.[99] Candidates and parties realize that they can maintain an image of respectability by refraining from attack ads and relying instead on interest groups to run them on their behalf.

Attack ads typically focus on judges' votes in criminal cases, even when sponsored by interest groups with no connection to criminal justice. Interest groups understand that portraying judges as "soft on crime" incites fear in viewers, especially if the crime is against children. For example, as we'll discuss further in Chapter 4, during the 2004 West Virginia Supreme Court election, Massey Coal Company CEO Don Blankenship funded a group named "And for the Sake of the Kids." This group ran an infamous TV ad alleging that an incumbent justice voted to release a "child rapist" and then "agreed to let this convicted child rapist work as a janitor in a West Virginia school."[100] In the 2020 Illinois Supreme Court election, trial lawyers funded a group called the "Clean Courts Committee" that ran a TV ad alleging that "a convicted felon, found guilty of predatory sexual assault of a child, is free on the streets. Why? Because Judge David Overstreet released this child rapist from Big Muddy prison."[101] Similarly, in 2020 Wisconsin Manufacturers and Commerce ran a series of ads alleging that a candidate "went easy on predators that committed unthinkable crimes" and "after a serial abuser and child predator shot a woman, [the candidate] went easy on him."[102] Screengrabs from some of these ads are shown in Figure 2.7.

Criminal justice has traditionally been the most common theme of state supreme court election ads, making up one-third to over one-half of all TV ads aired during supreme court races.[103] Inflammatory and deceptive ads, often funded by opaque and unaccountable interest groups, can distort voters' perceptions of a candidate and swing an election. Penny White argues that female judges are easy targets for such ads because "a woman

FIGURE 2.7 TV Ads Attacking Supreme Court Judicial Candidates. Source: Brennan Center for Justice, "Buying Time" (2018 and 2020), https://www.brennancenter.org/issues/strengthen-our-courts/promote-fair-courts/buying-time.

is more vulnerable to being viewed as soft on crime, maternal, you know, easily misled, all the stereotypes about women fit into the narrative, which is these women just can't be tough on crime."

Although data on social media advertising in judicial elections is more limited, the existing data shows that ever greater sums of money are also being spent on social media ads. During a six-month period in 2018, as much as $2 million was spent on Facebook ads supporting or opposing state supreme court candidates.[104] With social media's broader reach, these ads were viewed as many as 113 million times. Similarly, judicial campaign ads can now be found on Instagram, Twitter, and even TikTok.

Like TV ads, social media ads often rely on misleading and incendiary themes and provide little information about a judicial candidate's credentials or voting record. In fact, several features of social media make posting deceptive campaign ads on social media platforms *easier* than on TV. First, unlike running an ad on a TV network, almost anyone can post to social media, and the platforms are generally less willing to disclose the source of ad funding. This opacity allows funders to almost completely distance themselves from inflammatory ads.[105] In addition, social media content is generally not subject to meaningful content moderation or editorial filtering. Moreover, the echo-chamber nature of social media means it's unlikely that a deceptive ad making the rounds among viewers who are already inclined to agree with it will receive any backlash.

Perhaps most importantly, social media algorithms are programmed to boost content that receives substantial user engagement.[106] Incendiary content, such as posts accusing a judge of being lenient on criminals, is more likely to generate high engagement—more comments, more likes, and more shares—so algorithmic engineering disseminates it to more viewers. This widespread dissemination, in turn, increases the incentive to post more incendiary content in the future.

Social media has already become one of America's favorite pastimes and, with the public's growing distrust of traditional media, is also becoming one of the primary sources of news. Social media's broad reach means that interest groups, candidates, and political parties can reach a wider audience for a lower cost than is possible with TV ads. For an example of social media advertising's extreme efficiency, less than $16,000 was spent in total on the following three Facebook ads (see Figure 2.8) that were viewed as many as 2 million times.[107]

Justice Daniel Kelly
Sponsored • Paid for by **Friends of Justice Daniel Kelly**

Jill Karofsky is Eric Holder's hand-picked candidate. Vote AGAINST Karofsky on Tuesday!

FIGURE 2.8 Facebook Ads Attacking Supreme Court Judicial Candidates. Source: "Facebook Ad Library," https://www.facebook.com/ads/library/?active_status=all&ad_type=political_and_issue_ads&country=US.

ProgressOhio
Sponsored · Paid for by **ProgressOhio**

Ohio Supreme Court Justices Judith French and Sharon Kennedy should return the money they received from corrupt energy companies.

Dirty money has no place in our courts. Learn more.

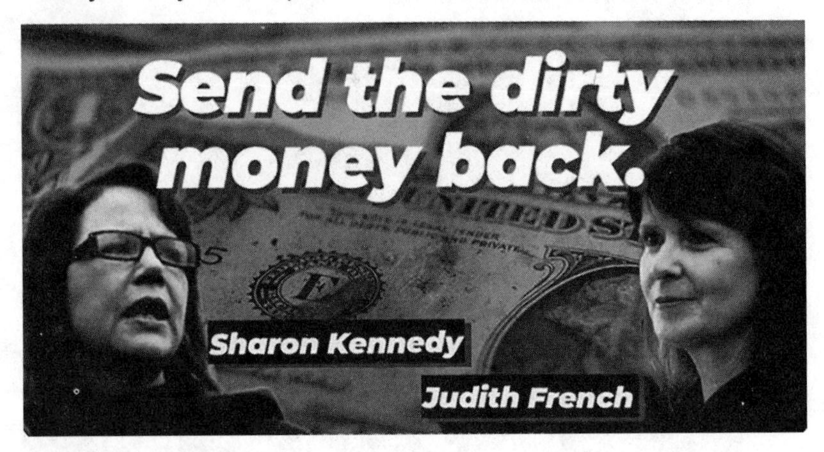

Progress Michigan
Sponsored · Paid for by **PROGRESS MICHIGAN**

A quick search of Mary Kelly's history shows questions about nepotism. And she wants to be on the MI Supreme Court?

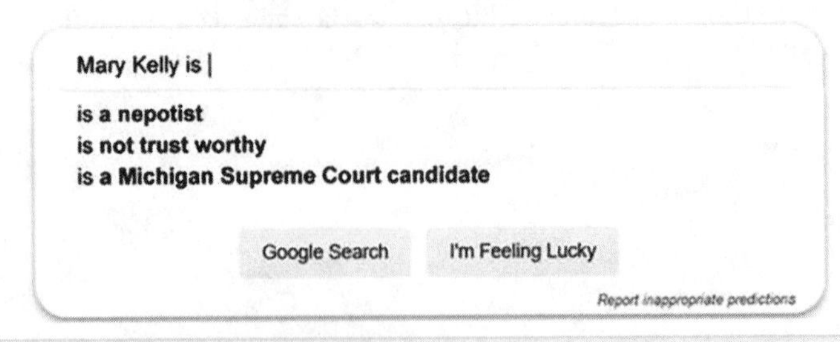

FIGURE 2.8 (*continued*)

So, who are the donors spending tens of millions of dollars in judicial races? Since at least 2000, business groups, lawyers, and lobbyists have been the largest contributors directly to supreme court candidates' campaigns. These donors generally are responsible for roughly half the money contributed directly to judicial candidates' campaigns, with lawyers and lobbyists usually contributing slightly more than business groups. However, in recent years, candidate fundraising has accounted for less than 60 percent of total spending in state supreme court races, while outside spending by interest groups has made up the other 40 percent. Business groups dominate this outside interest group spending and fund as much as 90 percent of the interest group spending on TV ads.[108] Although every state and each election is different, business groups are typically the largest overall spenders in state supreme court races, accounting for around 25 percent of direct contributions to candidates (which makes up 60 percent of total spending) and making up the majority of outside spending (which accounts for the other 40 percent of total spending).[109]

GROWING ALARM ABOUT JUDICIAL ELECTIONS

The picture of judicial campaign finance that emerges from our work is simple but striking. Campaign contributions have transformed judicial races so that they now more or less resemble competitive elections for other political offices. In fact, spending in most state supreme court races has surpassed spending for state legislative seats. In the 2015–16 cycle, twenty-seven judges in thirteen states were elected in races in which at least $1 million was spent.[110] In many states, spending was even higher. For example, over $21.4 million was spent on just three open supreme court seats in Pennsylvania.[111] In contrast, the average raised by candidates for state legislative seats in 2015–16 was over $1 million in only two states—California and Illinois.[112]

As a result, state supreme court justices face many of the same political pressures as elected politicians in other government offices. They worry about how voters and other politicians will respond to their judicial decisions, always with an eye toward the next election. They need to raise campaign money and curry favor with donors to win or keep office. In fact, over 90 percent of supreme court judicial races are won by the candidate who raised the most money.[113] In short, if an elected judge wants to keep the job, then re-election looms over even the best, most principled judges in the country. To reiterate how a California Supreme Court justice once described it, the next election is like a crocodile in your bathtub when you go into the bathroom: "You know it's there, and you try not to think about it, but it's hard to think about much else while you're shaving."[114] Penny White, who still speaks with many judges at judicial conferences, says that judges regularly tell her that they are "just trying to avoid a Penny White episode" where voters get "riled against them about the outcome of a case." As she puts it, "Every election cycle, there is a reminder in some state or many states that this can happen to you."

In the next chapter, we will describe the extensive empirical literature on the influence of money on judicial decisions, but it is not only judges and academics who have recognized the worrisome incentives created by judicial campaign finance. Polls find that the public also believes judges are influenced by their campaign contributions and need to satisfy donors. For instance, one poll reported that 60 percent of surveyed Americans averred that campaign contributions had "a great deal of influence" on judicial decisions, with a total of 90 percent agreeing that campaign contributions had at least "some" influence on judges.[115] Likewise, 70 percent of polled Americans felt it was a "very serious problem" that an elected judge may have received contributions from litigants with a pending case before the judge, with only 6 percent believing it is "not that serious a problem or no problem at all."[116]

More troubling is that even judges seem to agree that campaign fundraising influences judicial decisionmaking. A famous survey of state judges found that roughly 60 percent of state supreme court justices felt a "great deal" of pressure to raise money for campaigning during election years.[117] Eighty-five percent of state judges felt that interest groups are trying to use their campaign contributions to affect public policy.[118] And almost half of state supreme court justices felt that campaign contributions to judges had at least a little influence on decisions, with more than a third agreeing money had some or a great deal of influence on decisions.[119] As a former chief justice for the Tennessee Supreme Court put it, "Whether subtle or unintentional or not, there may be a tendency in the future for appellate judges to have one eye looking over their shoulder."[120]

Many in the legal community are alarmed about the growing influence of money in judicial elections. Justice Sandra Day O'Connor, a champion of judicial-election reform since retiring from the Supreme Court, warned that "there are many who think of judges as politicians in robes" and agrees "in many states, that's what they are."[121] Similarly, she has explained that because "elected judges in many states are compelled to solicit money for their election campaigns . . . [t]he crisis of confidence in the impartiality of the judiciary is real and growing."[122] For these reasons, the ABA endorses the elimination of competitive judicial elections in favor of merit selection plans or retention elections, arguing that "judges have a responsibility to know and impartially apply the law to the facts of the case at hand. In important ways, today's judicial elections often undermine judges' ability to perform this essential role."[123]

Sitting justices on the U.S. Supreme Court have also articulated this perspective. In *N.Y. State Board of Elections v. Lopez Torres*, the Court reluctantly upheld on First Amendment grounds New York's system for electing judges.[124] However, in their concurring opinion, Justices Anthony Kennedy and Stephen Breyer noted:

> When one considers that elections require candidates to conduct campaigns and to raise funds in a system designed to allow for competition among interest groups and political parties, the persisting question is whether that process is consistent with the perception and the reality of judicial independence and judicial excellence.[125]

They concluded:

> The rule of law, which is a foundation of freedom, presupposes a functioning judiciary respected for its independence, its professional attainments, and the absolute probity of its judges. And it may seem difficult to reconcile these aspirations with elections.[126]

In a separate concurrence, Justices John Paul Stevens and David Souter agreed with "the broader proposition that the very practice of electing judges is unwise."[127] But, they regretfully concluded, "The Constitution does not prohibit legislatures from enacting stupid laws."[128]

Most criticism has been aimed at specific types of judicial elections, and proposed reforms generally call for changing the kind of election used to select judges. In fact, of the only five states that have reformed their judicial selection methods since 1990, four simply traded in one type of election for another. Arkansas (2000), Mississippi (1994), and North Carolina (2002) simply switched from partisan to nonpartisan elections, though North Carolina switched back to partisan elections in 2016.[129] Tennessee (1994) switched from partisan elections to a merit selection system under which the governor appoints judges from a list of nominees identified by a judicial nominating commission. However, for retention, the Tennessee judges must run in elections to keep their seats.

Thus, both past and present critics of judicial races are generally focused on altering the specific type of election used to select judges. Most reformers do not call for an end to judicial elections altogether. Even proposals to adopt a merit selection system would require judges to face voters in retention elections to keep their seats on the bench.

In contrast, we argue that the best way to reform judicial races depends on how you think elections and the money raised in elections are affecting judicial outcomes. As we explain in detail later on, one possibility is that elections lead to the selection of judges who are already predisposed to favor campaign contributors' interests, and, as a result, judicial outcomes reflect those predispositions. If you think that this explanation is the root of the problem, then the best approach is likely to adopt other non-elective methods of selecting judges. In other words, get rid of judicial elections altogether.

However, another possibility is that pressure on sitting judges to ingratiate themselves with potential campaign donors for their future re-elections causes judges to adjust their decisions in favor of the donors' interests. So, if the need to raise future campaign money biases judicial outcomes, then we may not need to get rid of judicial elections but perhaps just judicial *re-elections*. We'll build to this point in the following chapters.

3 THE CROCODILE IN THE BATHTUB: HOW ELECTIONS AND MONEY INFLUENCE JUDGES

MICHIGAN SUPREME COURT CHIEF JUSTICE Bridget Mary McCormack is different from the other judges we meet in this book. Unlike the others we feature here, Bridget McCormack never lost a re-election bid and retired voluntarily from the bench at the end of 2022 with years remaining on her term. The specifics that make Chief Justice McCormack's career so exceptional highlight some important and worrisome aspects of our judicial election system.

Before first running for state supreme court in 2012, Bridget McCormack was an academic—a clinical professor of law at the University of Michigan Law School, one of the most prestigious law schools in the country. As she put it, "I had the greatest job in the world and taught whatever I wanted. I had all these students and resources, job security, and I was well-compensated with lots of autonomy. Very few better jobs in law." By contrast, running for statewide office, at least initially, seemed daunting. "It's a lot, and I would take a big pay cut, and public officials, mostly somebody's mad at you most of the time. It just seemed that I would need to give up a lot of privacy, and given the lucky professional position I was in, it seemed like

I would be giving up a lot." When her husband first suggested that she run for Michigan Supreme Court justice, she initially thought it was a "stupid idea, but then he kept talking about it." She eventually started to consider it seriously and remembers thinking that "before I knew it, I was running for a statewide office."

So, the process of running for judge was unfamiliar and, in her words, "just weird" to her. She had to compete in Michigan's hybrid judicial election system, where judicial candidates must win party nominations to qualify for the ballot but actually run in the general election as nonpartisan candidates. To win party support and campaign contributions, she had to campaign. "You go to these events, and people would say 'Well, what can you do for me?' which is a fair question to ask of most politicians running for office. They are supposed to be able, in the other branches, to deliver something. If you vote for me, I would deliver you this set of policies, right?"

But the role of a judge, in Bridget McCormack's view, and ours, is different. Judges aren't simply representatives of voters. They are required to attend impartially to the facts and law in cases before them, not vote as Republicans or Democrats in support of outcomes that their supporters desire. The U.S. Supreme Court has been clear about a judge's special role, even elected judges. As it once declared, "Public opinion should be irrelevant to the judge's role because the judge is often called upon to disregard, or even to defy, popular sentiment."[1] As a consequence, the Court has explained that judges are "not politicians, even when they come to the bench by way of the ballot."[2] Indeed, judges and courts are historically and traditionally understood as a counter-majoritarian bulwark in our American government structure, protecting individual rights and minorities against majority overreach.[3]

How do judicial candidates handle this challenge? They need to win voter support, often win party nomination, and actively campaign if they are to win election and become judges in the first place. However, once in office they are also expected to rule neutrally without regard to the voters, political party, and campaign donors who put them there. Bridget McCormack captures the dilemma judges find themselves in, remembering how she would have to say, "Oh, I can't promise you much. I'll work really hard. I won't cheat, but I can't promise you this or that policy. So it's a weird job to run for, obviously."

A persistent problem is that even the best candidates must raise campaign money in today's competitive supreme court races. Bridget McCormack didn't run television advertisements herself, but she raised around $650,000. As she puts it, "It's pretty crazy. . . . The pressure to raise money does feel, you know, complicated." Even when the money doesn't affect a judge's decisions, it still appears transactional with judges who ideally should be above it. "What's complicated is what the public thinks about it. I have lots of examples of having disappointed friends, including friends who wrote me a check." Typical donors, and voters in general, may not understand the distinctively impartial role of the judiciary, and instead assume judges should serve their interests the way that many legislative and executive candidates might once in office. "The public thinks, 'Why are these people spending money for this judge? It must be because she's going to favor these interests or those other interests, or not these interests, right?'"

Chief Justice McCormack, though, considers herself fortunate. First, she was a strong candidate who was the only nominee to win the endorsement of every newspaper in the state. Second, although she ran virtually no TV ads in 2012, she ran an effective digital campaign with a lot of volunteer support. "I had a bunch of interns, because Ann Arbor has lots of smart kids looking for work. And we had a lot more staff maybe than most supreme court campaigns do." Third, the party convention process worked out for her, eventually. "I was not the party chair's first choice. In fact, the party chair did not want me to run. So that was sort of step one of what was I thought difficult about running for the election." By the time of the convention, though, the UAW president, an important figure in Michigan politics, decided to support her and helped her win the nomination. "He made the determination that I was exactly the kind of judge who a party should support, so he told the party chair to sit down."

Still, the 2012 election cycle in Michigan was fiercely contested between the parties. Estimated campaign spending on the state's supreme court races that year was a record $18.4 million.[4] This is an estimated total, because most of that total was dark money spent on so-called "issue ads" whose funding went largely unreported and is difficult to track, according to the Michigan Campaign Finance Network, a nonprofit that tries to document state campaign spending.[5] Although McCormack hardly bought any TV advertisements herself, the Democratic Party spent more than $6 million for ads on behalf of the party nominees for state supreme court. But even the ads on her behalf were, in her words, "discouraging." As she put it in retrospect, "You know I appreciate that they were working to promote my name and candidacy, but I have no control over how they do that. It wasn't for me to say. And I don't mean to sound not grateful for their help. I just wouldn't have described myself [the way the party's ads did]." The realities of big-money judicial campaign finance don't always allow judicial candidates to speak for themselves.

Of course, the Republican Party and its allied groups spent plenty of money in opposition. Almost $7 million in ads was spent by the Republican Party, and notably, D.C.-based Judicial Crisis Network sponsored a million-dollar statewide ad blitz targeting Bridget McCormack just one week before the election. One of these ads accused her of "volunteer[ing] to free a terrorist" while at the University of Michigan.[6] This particular ad ran 416 times over eight days and featured the mother of military casualty in Afghanistan asking McCormack, "How could you?"[7] The ad was, as Bridget McCormack characterizes it, a "pretty traditional hit job." The law school's law reform clinic had accepted representation in a case, but Bridget McCormack had hardly been involved, and the clinic never even litigated the case because the detainee in question was actually released by the Bush Administration.[8] Like many of the negative ads run by outside groups, the ad was misleading and inflammatory.

Fortunately for her, Bridget McCormack had an ace in the hole that helped her rise above the partisan fray surrounding her election. Her sister Mary played Deputy National Security Adviser Kate Harper on the former hit TV show *The West Wing*. When Bridget McCormack and her sister spoke about low voting rates in judicial elections, her sister had the idea to rally her former *West Wing* castmates to film an advertisement in support of Bridget McCormack's candidacy. Mary McCormack and eight other actors from *The West Wing* volunteered to shoot a four-minute ad on this problem of ballot roll-off and promote Bridget McCormack's candidacy.[9] The ad was hilarious, went viral on YouTube within hours, and racked up more than a million views, giving Bridget McCormack's candidacy a valuable boost.[10] "Obviously I think it was incredibly helpful especially with the earned media." What's more, 2012 turned out to be a banner year for Democrats, with President Barack Obama winning more than 54 percent of the Michigan vote in that year's presidential election and Michigan Senator Debbie Stabenow retaining her seat by a landslide 21-percent margin. Bridget McCormack rounded out this victory on the judicial front, getting the most votes among several supreme court candidates and winning 24 percent of the general election vote, enough to secure one of two available seats on the Michigan Supreme Court.

Bridget McCormack is a success story who survived the challenges of judicial elections and campaign finance to become a widely respected judge. She was subsequently selected by her fellow justices as chief justice, unanimously as a Democrat on a court with a 4–3 Republican advantage, and then won re-election easily in 2020 to another eight-year term. She is a great example of how a good judge can rise above the politicization of judicial politics when blessed with the right advantages. Her fellow justice, Republican Elizabeth Clement, explained McCormack's selection as chief justice matter-of-factly: "Four Republican-nominated justices, three Democrat-nominated justices, and a Democrat is now chief. How did that happen? I'll be frank; it happened because we picked the best person for the job."

Justice Elizabeth Clement's judicial career tells a somewhat parallel but different story. Elizabeth Clement was appointed to the Michigan Supreme Court in 2017 by Governor Rick Snyder, a Republican for whom she formerly worked as Chief Legal Counsel, among other roles. But from the start, Justice Clement voted independently from her former boss and the Republican Party. She voted with the majority to allow a redistricting measure to be added to the 2018 general-election ballot despite her party strongly opposing it, and she upheld school policies that banned guns on school property, which upset pro-gun Republicans. As she put it, "I took an oath to the constitution of the State of Michigan, and the Constitution of the United States. Not to a political party. Not to any special interest groups."

However, in a judicial election system where judicial candidates depend on their party sponsors for support, there are electoral consequences for judicial independence. Clement had to run for re-election in 2018 and faced what she called "absolutely . . . an effort at bullying and intimidation." Now unpopular among party activists, she was booed at the party nominating convention and faced an effort at replacement as the party nominee.[11] She was omitted from Republican door hangers that listed every other party candidate on the ballot and was actually fired by her Republican fundraiser just months before the election.[12] Still, Justice Clement won re-election despite these efforts.

How do judges respond to these political pressures? Other elected politicians outside the judiciary are expected to bend toward the voters' preferences and satisfy public opinion to some meaningful extent—that's usually the point of requiring officials to run for re-election. But the U.S. Supreme Court insists that "public opinion should be irrelevant to the judge's role," even when they are elected to office. Of course, judges know certain decisions have electoral consequences because they will either please or anger their party and voters. Chief Justice McCormack explains, "I do think that's true. Not always. I think sometimes there are some sleepers that you never even knew and then people will focus on them, and then you're like, whoa! But other times, yes. The particular case Justice Clement ended up having difficulty resolving was a litigation brought by her party to the court. So you know, that one was on the nose." Instances like this illustrate the immense pressures judges are under to conform, both to their supporters and to the court of public opinion.

When we select and retain judges by judicial elections, judicial politics and campaign finance influence how judges make decisions and do their jobs. The public certainly thinks so.[13] Even worse, judges themselves think political pressures and campaign finance concerns affect how they decide cases.[14] Judges, as we've mentioned, describe the next election as "a crocodile in [their] bathtub," posing a potential threat to their job and casting a shadow over every judicial decision.

So far, we have discussed mainly what we call qualitative or anecdotal evidence of campaign finance pressures on judges. We hear what individual judges have gone through and what they and the public think about the system and process. This type of qualitative evidence has enormous value, which is why we describe it here in such detail. But qualitative evidence is subject to its own criticism as well. Perhaps the public perceives campaign finance to affect judicial decisions, but really they're wrong. Public opinion, after all, seems to be wrong about a lot of things based on anecdotal instinct. The public, for instance, believes that a penny dropped from the Empire State Building will kill someone,[15] that a coin flip is always a 50–50 chance,[16] and that eating too much sugar can cause a "sugar rush" in children.[17] Judges' beliefs about their own profession are harder to discount. We assume that judges wouldn't impugn their own or their colleagues' collective integrity without legitimate cause. We imagine that judges tell the unattractive truth about their own profession along these lines because they are concerned about these political pressures that make it harder for them and their colleagues to do the good job they want to do.

In this chapter, we present hard quantitative data and research on the influence of campaign money on judges. We have spent our careers compiling data on judges, law, and politics to better understand what influences judicial decisionmaking and how our system of judicial elections affects the dispensation of the law. And as we will explain, we're not the only ones. There are economists, political scientists, and other law professors who share our interest, training, and background. Still, these issues have not received the academic attention they deserve. Despite the diversity of scholars who study judicial elections and judicial campaign finance, the number of scholars actively researching these issues is too small.

We have, nonetheless, learned a lot in our work, and from the work of others, about important questions that we discuss in this chapter. Are judges, for example, affected by worries about getting re-elected and keeping their jobs? Does it matter who decides whether they keep their job or what kind of election they face? Does campaign finance influence how they decide their cases?

In this chapter, we explain what we think we have learned and what we know from our work, as well as others'. Most importantly, we find that judges are affected by worries about keeping their job. The type of election they face matters in a number of interesting ways. And perhaps most significantly for our book, along the same lines, campaign finance money does influence how judges decide cases. Re-election appears to weigh heavily on elected judges and biases their decisions in marked ways that we describe here.

DISTINGUISHING JUDICIAL SELECTION AND RETENTION

Recall the history of judicial selection and retention we described in the last chapter and why the states select and retain their judges through popular elections. Judicial elections were originally a response to public distaste for judicial appointments during the nineteenth century.[18] Jacksonian reformers in early America thought that judges appointed by elected officials, whether the governor or legislature, were beholden to politicians rather than the people.[19] From around the 1840s onward, states began adopting judicial elections as a way of circumventing politicians and letting the people select their judges. Up through the modern day, the argument for judicial elections has been based on accountability to the public. As defenders of judicial elections put it, "Like other public officials, judges have considerable discretion and should be held accountable for their choices, at least at the state level where we would expect a close connection between public preferences and public policy."[20]

The consequence of elections, then, is that elected judges are accountable to the voters. They therefore have to behave much like other elected politicians who must win re-election to keep their jobs. They need to raise campaign money and curry some favor with donors to win or keep office. They worry about how voters and other politicians will respond to their judicial decisions, with an eye toward the next election. In short, they must respond to re-election incentives. If an elected judge wants to keep the job, then re-election looms over even the best, most principled judges in the country. Again, as a California Supreme Court justice once said, the next election is like a crocodile in your bathtub when you go into the bathroom: "You know it's there, and you try not to think about it, but it's hard to think about much else while you're shaving."[21]

We began studying judicial elections more than a dozen years ago by looking at whether judges were affected by the desire to keep their jobs. There are actually two parts to satisfying the voters and becoming a judge.

First, there's judicial selection—the process by which a candidate *first* attains their judicial office. Federal judges are appointed by the president, while about half of state supreme court justices are appointed by either the state's governor or legislature.[22] Some states constrain this choice to candidates on a list prepared by a commission,[23] but the crux of the matter is that elected officials are entitled to decide who becomes a judge. As you know by now, state supreme court justices are elected to office by the voters in about half the states. As you also know, the details of the election process vary from state to state; sometimes they are partisan elections, sometimes they are nonpartisan, and a few states have a weird blend of partisan and nonpartisan.[24] This process of judicial selection, whether appointment or election, and in either case, what kind, receives most of the attention in public and scholarly debates about judges.

That said, there's the second part to holding a judgeship—judicial retention. Judicial retention is the process by which sitting judges either get to keep their jobs for another term or are ousted from office and replaced. Although it often gets lumped in with judicial selection, judicial retention is sometimes quite different, even within a given state. Most states that appoint their judges require them to run for re-election in what are aptly called retention elections.[25] Voters either vote to retain the judge or fire them in a yes-or-no decision. (If the voters vote the judge out, it triggers a new, separate process of judicial selection and another appointment in those states to pick any losing judge's replacement.) Other states, however, require judges to run for office in a competitive election against other candidates in order to keep their jobs.[26] Incumbent judges therefore have to campaign, raise money, and win votes to keep their jobs, just like many of them did to get their jobs in the first place.

Critics of judicial elections tend to focus on judicial selection and neglect the second part, judicial retention. Most judicial elections are actually matters of judicial retention one way or another, because most judicial elections involve incumbents trying to keep their job rather than all new candidates trying to win a vacant seat. A theme of our book is to highlight the difference between judicial selection and judicial retention. We want to reverse the usual focus on judicial selection and shift it to judicial retention. It's judicial *re-election* that is driving the crisis in judicial politics, not judicial *election*.

Once you think about the difference between judicial election and re-election, we think it's easy to see why re-election is more worrisome for judicial integrity and democratic equality. The process of judicial selection typically involves new candidates who aren't currently judges. Now, to be sure, this process can be too partisan, ideological, and money driven. These are common criticisms of judicial selection that resonate with common experiences in new-style judicial elections. But judicial retention typically involves all the same partisanship, ideology, and money, but it actually involves sitting judges as the central candidates running for another term of office. As an ABA commission on the judiciary observed, the worst election-related challenges to judicial integrity arise with judicial retention and re-election because they subject sitting judges, who decide difficult cases on a daily basis, to "the greatest pressure to do what is politically popular rather than what the law requires."[27]

The special problem with judicial retention and re-election is that sitting judges are sorely tempted to bias their decisions in ways that help them keep their jobs. Sitting judges aren't dumb. They know their record will be judged politically by voters, campaign donors, and politicians, among many others. Judges, for instance, know that criminal cases are highlighted in judicial campaign ads, and many won't want to risk being portrayed by opponents as soft on crime in the upcoming election, as we saw happen to Penny White.[28] Judges know that they'll need campaign money to win re-election and may be tempted to favor campaign donors' interests, or at least not decide too strongly against them. None of this guarantees that judges will make different or worse decisions because of re-election concerns. Some judges are so trustworthy and principled that they won't be consciously affected by these concerns. In fact, most judges probably are trustworthy and principled, and certainly most judges claim they are.

However, the specter of retention and re-election is still the crocodile in the bathtub for judges who want to keep their jobs. There is enough of a temptation for bias, when re-election is in the offing, that we should worry about it. Even the best people are subconsciously affected by professional incentives despite their best efforts. The problem is that it may not matter very much whether judges are good people or not. There's so much pressure in a system that incentivizes judges to think about re-election that it's no surprise when they do.

In fact, the point of judicial re-election *is* to make judges think about their re-election. The re-election incentive is supposed to be a touchstone for elected representatives. Political scientist David Mayhew once wrote that members of Congress, incentivized by the need to keep their jobs, should be assumed to be "single-minded seekers of re-election."[29] That is, officeholders who need to be re-elected to keep their jobs are intentionally directed to focus on what they need to do for re-election as a matter of institutional design. Indeed, in explaining the logic of periodic elections, James Madison argued that elections impress upon elected officeholders "an habitual recollection of their dependence on the people."[30] Officeholders, by design, are "compelled to anticipate the moment . . . when their exercise of [power] is to be reviewed" and contemplate their removal from office unless they satisfy public opinion.[31] We make officeholders run for re-election because we want them to do what voters and other actors want them to do. It shouldn't be a surprise, then, when they do.

Again, none of this means judges as a category of people are necessarily corrupt or dishonest. Rather, those facing re-election and retention encounter systemic pressures and incentives that impact decisionmaking, consciously or not. Law professor Lawrence Lessig describes this systemic pressure as an incentives problem—one based on money.[32] Monetary contributions create a bond and implicit pressure to reciprocate by responding to those donors. When fundraising is ingrained as a part of one's job, those who are better at soliciting these dollars will be rewarded because successful fundraisers are seen as more credible and having more support. When those funds are predominately from the wealthy and influential, office seekers will spend a disproportionate amount of time responding to a select few and thus cannot be "dependent on the people alone." Anecdotally, these observations are recognized by political actors who rely on fundraising to be elected and re-elected. Former Congressman Barney Frank aptly noted that "people say, 'Oh, it doesn't have any effect on me.' Well, if that were the case, we'd be the only human beings in the history of the world who on a regular basis took significant amounts of money from perfect strangers and made sure that it had no effect on our behavior."[33]

Most importantly and beyond anecdotal conjecture, we find empirical evidence that judges *do* seem affected by retention and re-election pressures. We can show that judicial decisions are impacted by the fact that judges need to win retention to keep their jobs. This is true for all different types of retention methods, whether competitive re-election, retention election, reappointment by the governor, or reappointment by the legislature. Judges who know they'll need to win someone's favor to keep their jobs decide cases differently, at least on average. The type of retention method matters too, but overall, across all methods, the need to win retention influences how cases are decided by judges. What's more, as we'll show later on, campaign money matters too. Money spent on judicial campaigning, on average, yields results for campaign donors.

HOW TO KEEP YOUR JOB AS A JUDGE IN THE UNITED STATES

Most judges, it seems, want to keep their jobs.[34] Judges generally have very nice jobs. They are paid reasonably well with steady hours and lots of public prestige from their position. More importantly, their work is interesting and challenging. Judges can dispense justice, shape the law from the bench, and serve the public interest as they see it. For all these reasons, federal judges regularly remain in their positions past the retirement age when they can receive their full salary without doing any work.[35] Many judges like their job so much they effectively do it for free. Former federal judge and law professor Richard Posner notes that a judge's "utility function must in short contain something besides leisure and the judicial salary" because many judges work "quite hard—often at an age when their counterparts in private practice have retired and are living in Scottsdale or La Jolla."[36]

To keep their jobs, virtually all state judges must win retention. Judges in states where retention is done by executive or legislative reappointment have a clear audience to satisfy. The governor or the legislature decides whether to return incumbent judges for additional terms in these states. These judges don't need to face the voters again, but they need the governor or legislature to agree that they're doing a good job and not feel the need to replace them with someone else.[37]

Judges facing yes-or-no retention elections answer to a different master. Incumbent judges in retention elections have no opponent challenging their seat. Voters will either return them to office for another term or remove them in a yes-or-no vote. Consequently, these incumbents mainly need to avoid controversial decisions that will provoke voters to remove them from office. Incumbent judges do not always get re-elected, as we've already seen for Justices Ternus and White, but they typically do.[38]

Judges facing competitive re-election have a more difficult task. Incumbents in states where retention is based on competitive re-election need to attract more votes than any other ambitious candidates who gun for their seats. Challengers will criticize their record and campaign aggressively against the incumbents' decisions, especially on matters such as criminal law. Incumbents therefore hope to build a record that voters will like, or at least not dislike, so that voters will elect them again.

The intensity of the re-election fight is especially great for the state supreme court compared to lower courts. More and more, supreme court justices have to buy TV advertising, raise money to pay for everything, and defend themselves from hostile attack advertising against their record.[39] All of this tends to intensify in states where state supreme court races have partisan elections, where the major parties pour more resources into the fight. As a result, for state supreme court elections between 2008 and 2020, incumbents running in partisan elections won re-election 90 percent of the time.[40] In that same period, incumbents in nonpartisan races won re-election 94 percent of the time.[41] This rate is similar to the re-election rate for Congress and state legislature. State supreme court judges should be expected to worry about their job security as much as your typical congressperson or state representative.

So, how does the specter of the retention decision affect judges? The most important way is that they should be mindful of the opinions, preferences, and interests of whoever decides whether they keep their job for another term. Where the governor will decide whether a judge gets another term, the judge might want to know how the governor wants judges to decide their cases. The governor is more likely to keep judges who do what the governor themselves wants them to do in their capacities as judges. The same holds for legislative appointment. Where the legislature decides whether the judge gets another term, the judge might want to know how the legislature wants judges to decide cases. Indeed, the whole point of requiring judges to win the governor's or legislature's support for another term is to make them responsive to the governor's or legislature's preferences. This is arguably all by design.

We gathered data to study systematically whether judges are actually attentive to the wishes of the decisionmaker who chooses if they get reappointed to another term. We looked at more than 28,000 judicial decisions involving almost 500 state supreme court justices across all fifty states over four years.[42] We wanted to find out, using advanced statistical methods, whether justices appeared to cater to the preferences of whoever controlled their reappointment.

To figure this out, we first looked at cases where the governor or the legislature (represented by state government) were actual litigants in cases and also would control the later reappointment of the judges in the case.

The theory is that the governor would want judges to decide cases in the governor's favor when that person's administration is involved in the case. Judges who decide these cases in the governor's favor therefore might curry favor with the governor by doing so. Conversely, judges who decide these cases against the governor might hurt their standing with the governor, at least at the margin. All the same holds true for judges whose reappointment is decided by the legislature. These judges probably help their standing with the legislature by deciding in the government's favor when it is involved in a case, and perhaps they hurt their standing by deciding against it.

Of course, judges are constrained by the merits of the individual cases and can't decide whatever they want, regardless of where their political self-interest lies. But judges do have a certain amount of discretion in deciding cases, and individual judges decide significant numbers of cases differently. That's why judicial selection matters and why the parties battle over judicial appointments and elections.

We simply wanted to know if judges exercised their discretion in ways that favored their reappointment. Namely, did judges curry favor with whoever controlled their reappointment when they had a chance to decide a case in that decisionmaker's favor? Along these lines, we looked to see if there was any statistical difference in the governor's and legislature's success rate in cases with judges whose reappointment they control compared to cases with judges whose reappointment was out of their hands. Controlling for other factors, we suspected judges whose reappointment by the governor or legislature lingered over them would probably be likely to favor the governor or legislature in these cases.

As we expected, when we analyzed the data we found that judges favored the government when their reappointment was controlled by the governor or legislature. Of course, judges subject to reappointment did not decide in favor of the governor or legislature in every case. Judges are too constrained by law and other considerations to be so blatant. But judges up for reappointment did favor the government at a disproportionately higher rate than judges not requiring reappointment by a statistically significant margin. For example, judges up for gubernatorial reappointment favored the governor's executive branch in cases by roughly 7 percentage points more than judges facing a retention election. This makes sense because these judges benefit from currying favor with the governor who will decide their reappointment, while judges up for retention election don't need to consider this.

Similarly, judges up for legislative reappointment tend to favor the state government in cases litigated by some government agent. They favor the executive branch by 8 percentage points and favor a legislative branch litigant by a whopping 40 percentage points more than judges facing only retention elections. By contrast, judges who must run for nonpartisan re-election or have lifetime tenure display no favoritism for government litigants, compared to retention election judges.

In other words, judges tend to vote according to their professional self-interest in cases involving government litigants. Judges who depend on the governor or legislature for reappointment favor the government in cases involving a government litigant by a statistically significant margin more than judges who don't depend on reappointment. Again, this is consistent with the incentives that reappointment systems put to judges. Indeed, the original nineteenth-century arguments for judicial elections in place of judicial appointment fell precisely along these lines. As one critic of judicial appointments claimed, the "appointed judiciary's 'connection with the legislative branch of government' was a great fault because in 'all cases in which the constitutionality of an act of the legislature was drawn in question . . . the point in dispute must necessarily have been prejudged in passing the law.'"[43] For this reason, another critic of judicial reappointment contended that judges dependent on reappointment become mere instruments of the government, simply "registering the mandates of the Legislature and the edicts of the Governor."[44] Our results empirically bear out these suspicions about judicial reappointment.

One question about our findings might be whether this is really about appointment, not reappointment. Put another way, could it be that appointed judges are different from elected judges, and this difference accounts for why they decide cases involving the government in the way they do? Perhaps, for instance, appointed judges are more loyal to their political party and compatriots in the governorship and legislature, while judges subject to nonpartisan elections or lifetime tenure are not. By this theory, judges up for reappointment favor the government in cases not because they want to seek favor with the governor or legislature, but because they are more partisan and would favor their governor or legislature out of political loyalty.

We tested this alternative theory by comparing (i) appointed judges who need periodic reappointment to retain their jobs, with (ii) appointed judges who face retention elections to keep their jobs. Both sets of judges were appointed by the governor, but the latter set comprises judges in California and New Hampshire whose retention decision switches to voters rather than being up to the governor. This comparison gives us a nice way of seeing whether it's really appointment that drives our results, or whether the explanation is *re*appointment. If judges in sets (i) and (ii) behave similarly, then we would infer that gubernatorial appointment selects judges who may be particularly loyal to the government and favors government litigants in cases. Both sets of judges were appointed by their governor, but if the judges behave differently, then it would indicate that the *retention* method (i.e., whether judges face reappointment or face re-election) drives our results. Although both sets of judges were initially appointed, the need to win reappointment influences judges to curry favor with the governor or legislature.

Indeed, we found that reappointment seems to drive favoritism for government litigants. Judges who were originally appointed by the governor but are subsequently subject to retention elections to keep their jobs do not favor the government in cases.[45] With no need to curry favor with the governor anymore, they do not seem partial to the executive branch or the government as a general matter in cases before them. By contrast, appointed judges who depend on the governor for reappointment favor the executive branch and government litigants as a general matter by statistically significant margins. It's control of their reappointment that matters in whether judges favor the government.

Even more tellingly, it seems that favoritism for government litigants increases as the reappointment decision looms larger. We analyzed our data with one new consideration in the mix: the amount of time until the reappointment will be decided. As this verdict approaches, we assume that judges are likely to become more conscious of the looming decision over whether they will keep their jobs. The governor or legislature deciding reappointment will consider a judge's entire term before making the decision, but it's natural to assume that the judge definitely doesn't want to cross the governor or legislature when reappointment is on the table in the near future. We find that judicial favoritism for the government increases by 1.6 percent for each year closer to a judge's gubernatorial reappointment.

Judicial favoritism for legislative branch litigants increases by 5 percent for each year closer to a judge's legislative reappointment.

In short, the data indicate that reappointment incentives significantly affect how judges decide cases involving the government. More importantly, the data suggest that judges behave strategically when voting in the cases they decide. Our results make sense because judges appear to be acting as you would expect them to act if they wanted to keep their jobs. You could argue that this is exactly what states with reappointment systems presumably want from their judges, because it is the direct result of institutional design.

We have shown so far that appointed judges vote on the bench in ways that curry favor with whoever decides whether they keep their job. We next move on to our main focus—elected judges. It turns out that elected judges have a more complicated challenge to keep their jobs. Of course, we would also expect retention incentives to matter for judges who need to win re-election instead of reappointment.

For judges facing re-election, their most important audience is the electorate, the voters of the state, rather than the state governor or legislature. These judges, who include more than half of state supreme court justices, need the voters to support their retention for another term. These judges therefore might want to anticipate how the voters will feel about the cases they are asked to decide. As an ultimate matter, they need to please the voters enough to win re-election.

THE PRESSURES OF RE-ELECTION: TV ADS AND CRIME

Judges know that voters are not paying attention to the details of every case they decide, but they also know that any controversial case is potential fodder for inflammatory campaign ads or angry newspaper editorials that could complicate their re-election. Judges aren't safe simply because regular voters aren't following what they're doing in the moment, even if most voters aren't. Judges need to be mindful of voters' *potential* opinion later on, if the judges' political opponents and election challengers publicize certain decisions or attack them based on their record.[46] Just as congresspeople worry about their voting record even if voters aren't reading the *Congressional Record* every day or following every vote in Congress on a regular basis, elected judges worry about their decisions when they could be weaponized against them in a future re-election campaign.

We shouldn't underestimate how informed voters are about judges, especially state supreme court justices. Political scientists have shown that voters take into account judicial experience when assessing judicial candidates and distinguish among qualified and less qualified challengers in deciding how to vote.[47] Voters seem to pay attention to campaign advertising and news coverage of judicial elections, at least enough to be influenced by the messaging.[48] Voters, for instance, are significantly more likely to vote in state supreme court elections when campaign spending is higher.[49] There is also scholarly evidence beyond anecdotal observation that voters actually understand issues relevant to judicial elections and vote based on judges' records as they perceive them.[50] As a consequence, incumbent judges would be right to consider how voters will assess their record and how political opponents might portray them in campaign advertising against them. We'll discuss how these concerns about voter reaction and public opinion affect judges, as well as what empirical work has shown us.

The Influence of Television Ads

We studied the re-election worries of supreme court justices by exploring how the number of television advertisements in state supreme court elections affects them.[51] Our theory was that an increase in television advertisements for supreme court elections in a state was likely to raise justices' anxiety about re-election.

Television advertisements are costly and require well-funded candidates with a stable of willing and wealthy donors. As a consequence, more advertisements in a state's supreme court races means that these elections, including any particular justice's next re-election contest, are more likely to be competitive, fiercely fought, and expensive in the future as well. Justices who see lots of television ads in supreme court elections know that they may need to worry about their next election and that victory is far from assured.

We used data on television advertisements in state supreme court elections from 2008 to 2013 and combined them with a dataset of almost 3100 criminal appeals decided over the same period by state supreme court cases in thirty-two states. We wanted to see if the number of television ads in a state's supreme court elections affected how its justices decided criminal appeals in the years that followed. Our belief was that the volume of television advertising signals to the justices how difficult their next re-election might be. As the number of ads increases, the more likely it is that justices will feel uncertain about keeping their positions and worry about their re-election prospects as they currently do their jobs.

Why focus on criminal cases? First, criminal law is really important in its own right. No subject of judicial decisionmaking more profoundly affects individual litigants and their alleged victims as criminal adjudication. Judges regularly decide matters of criminal guilt or innocence, the length of criminal sentences, and the application of the death penalty to criminal defendants.

Second, voters and judicial candidates focus a great deal of attention on criminal law in their campaign advertising, especially attack ads. It turns out that re-election for incumbent judges depends significantly on the prevailing crime rate,[52] and judges' criminal law decisions are the most frequent targets of television advertising and "new-style" negative advertising in particular.[53] Attack ads often highlight a judge's vote in criminal cases, asserting that the judge "fought to protect sexual predators," is "sympathetic to rapists," or agreed to release "child rapists" and other convicted offenders.[54]

Third, empirical studies suggest that these reasons lead to judges becoming more punitive as re-election approaches and gains salience. One study by Carlos Berdejo and Noam Yuchtman finds that judges handed down longer sentences as the next election approached such that the average sentence decided just before the next election was more than half a year longer than a sentence for the same crime decided at the beginning of the term.[55] In other words, the same criminal defendant convicted of the same crime faces more than six extra months in prison if they happen to be sentenced right before the judge's election rather than right afterward. In addition, Berdejo and Yuchtman find that the influence of election proximity disappears for retiring judges in their final term.[56] Again, the absence of a significant effect for lame duck judges cements the inference that judges in Berdejo and Yuchtman's study were influenced by re-election concerns.

A study by Gregory Huber and Sanford Gordon likewise finds that Pennsylvania trial judges imposed longer sentences, controlling for other factors, when a judge's next retention election was imminent, accounting for roughly 6 percent of total sentenced time during the period of study.[57] Huber and Gordon also report similar results for Kansas judges, with judges elected in partisan elections even more punitive than judges who face only retention elections.[58] Paul Brace and Melinda Gann Hall find that judges facing re-election also are more likely to uphold death sentences on appeal.[59] Indeed, a host of studies indicate that judges are influenced by re-election concerns in all different ways.[60]

Criminal law lends itself to a clearer inference of judicial bias than other areas of law. Not only do judges adjust their criminal law decisions as re-election looms over them, but they also adjust their decisions almost exclusively in a punitive direction against criminal defendants. Voters will rarely punish judges for being too tough on convicted criminals, but lenient decisions are subject to subsequent campaign attacks and potential voter anger. As Gordon and Huber explain, "In the context of criminal justice, fire alarms when sounded will almost always correspond to perceived instances of underpunishment, not overpunishment."[61] Judicial candidates are perpetually attacked for being soft on crime but never really for being too tough on crime.

For this reason, most judges become significantly more punitive when re-election concerns grow salient, but few judges become more lenient, even in very liberal jurisdictions.[62] As Huber and Gordon summarize, "All judges, even the most punitive, increase their sentences as reelection nears."[63] This unidirectional bias toward more punitiveness suggests that judges, consciously or not, adjust their decisions from what they would otherwise hold as correct outcomes under the law to preempt campaign attacks against them.

Returning to our own study, if judges are so influenced by the specter of the next election, judges might similarly be affected by the prospect of television and attack advertising against them in the next campaign. Judges might reasonably believe that television advertisements targeting them will hurt their re-election chances, or at least make re-election more costly even if they eventually prevail. Judges who are already worried about their re-election prospects as a general matter therefore might be worried about heavy television advertising that makes their re-election prospects less certain. Concerns about attacks in the future might motivate judges to be wary about making controversial decisions that could be targeted in ads.

In a report for the American Constitution Society (ACS), we found that overall levels of campaign advertising on television for earlier state supreme court elections appeared to have just such an effect on judicial decision-making in criminal cases.[64] We focused on cases from our 2008–13 state supreme court database involving violent crimes as defined by the FBI's Uniform Crime Reporting Program: Murder, Robbery, Violent Aggravated Assault, and Rape and other Sex Crimes. Our database, combining supreme court decisions and campaign advertisements over the same period, allows us to investigate the empirical relationship between campaign advertising and judicial voting by state supreme court justices in criminal cases they decided.

This ACS study found that justices became less likely to vote in favor of defendants in criminal cases as the amount of campaign advertising in a state's supreme court races increased, controlling for other considerations. In other words, as the intensity and volume of campaigning in a state's supreme court elections went up, state supreme court justices were less sympathetic to criminal defendants by a statistically significant margin even controlling for ideology, party, and other predictors of judicial decisionmaking.

Basically, as Figure 3.1 shows, in a state with 2000 total ads to start, sympathy for criminal defendants, as measured by voting for the defendant in a supreme court appeal, goes down by 2 percent on average as the number of television ads doubles. In other words, if a justice expects the next election to have twice the number of ads as the past election, then they become 2 percent less likely on average to vote in favor of a criminal defendant's appeal. This effect increases further as the baseline number of ads goes up. For example, in a state with 10,000 ads, sympathy for criminal defendants goes down by 8 percent on average as the number of ads doubles.

We believe that the reason for this effect is that state justices are more fearful of being cast as soft on crime when the campaign environment is fiercer and more competitive for a state's supreme court races. Justices effectively protect their flanks from campaign attacks by becoming more hostile to criminal defendants, knowing they are far less likely to be criticized for being hard on crime than soft on crime. We therefore estimate the independent effect of campaign ads by itself, as best as we can, as a proxy for the justices' re-election incentives. Our analysis controls for other variables,

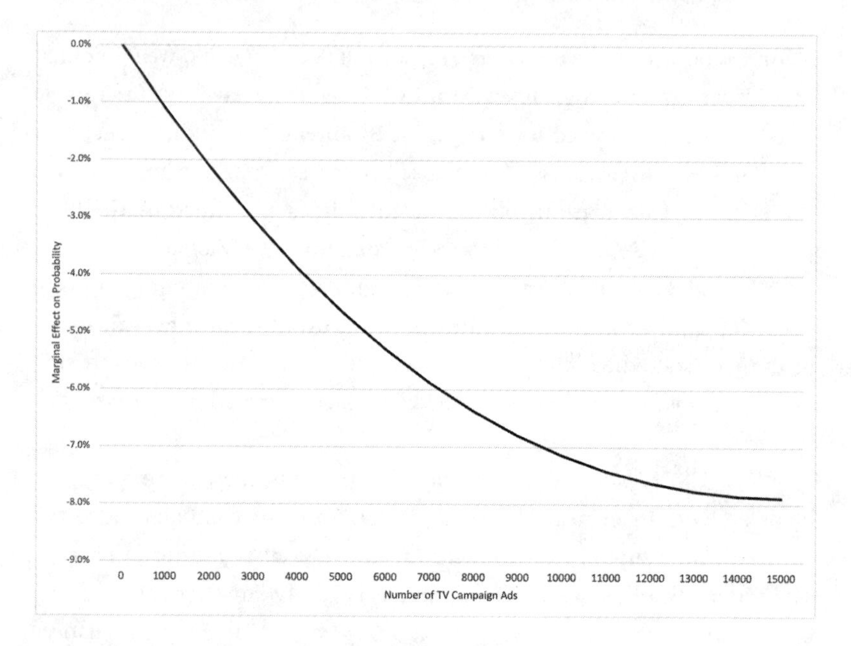

FIGURE 3.1 **The Relationship between Televised Campaign Ads and Voting in Favor of Criminal Defendants. Source: Re-created from analysis in Joanna Shepherd and Michael S. Kang, "Skewed Justice: Citizens United, Television Advertising and State Supreme Court Justices' Decisions in Criminal Cases,"** ***American Constitution Society*** **(2014), https://www.acslaw.org/analysis/reports/skewed-justice/.**

including the strength of the criminal defendant's case. Our study, and the others we've described, indicate that the re-election prospects of justices are thus having an important effect on many criminal defendants, even controlling for the merits of the cases and the ideology of justices, among other things. Re-election weighs heavily on justices' minds and significantly affects how they dispense people's fates.

Tellingly, we also found that the effect of television campaign ads in criminal cases was greater in states that were most affected by *Citizens United v. Federal Election Commission* and featured the greatest changes with respect to campaign advertising.[65] To summarize briefly, the U.S. Supreme Court 2010 decision in *Citizens United* dramatically changed campaign finance law and declared effectively unconstitutional state prohibitions on corporate and union electioneering in twenty-three states. In those states, corporate and union-funded campaign ads had basically been prohibited by law, and suddenly, after *Citizens United* in 2010, those prohibitions were lifted. As a result, in the twenty-three states formerly with bans, corporations and unions became newly free to spend on campaign ads in state supreme court races, among other elections. However, in the other twenty-seven states, no such prohibitions had existed in the first place, so *Citizens United* had less impact on corporate and union campaigning. In short, justices in these twenty-seven states could expect *Citizens United* to have less effect on their re-election races than the justices in the other twenty-three states that had previous prohibitions on corporate and union spending.

We found that the sudden likelihood of greater spending in supreme court races made justices significantly more hostile to criminal defendants. By unleashing corporate and union electioneering in twenty-three states, *Citizens United* made campaigning in those states more competitive and expensive. Justices appeared to adjust by adopting more conservative attitudes in criminal cases and becoming significantly more hostile to criminal defendants. This particular finding underscores how campaigns and campaign finance affect judicial behavior. As justices become less secure in re-election, judicial voting becomes unidirectionally more conservative in criminal cases. This additional finding emphasizes how these effects seem to be re-election incentives, driven by the campaign environment and its bearing on whether a justice keeps their job.

The Influence of Attack Ads

Of course, not all TV ads are negative or threaten a justice's re-election prospects. TV ads are just a statistical proxy that generalizes the larger electoral trend and effect of re-election anxiety. Still, we follow up the previous study of TV ads by refining our measure of campaign intensity just a bit more. In this analysis, we look specifically at "attack advertisements" rather than all television ads.

Attack ads on television seem to drive judicial anxiety about campaigns and re-election more than positive ads or spending as a general matter. Particularly for criminal decisions, justices worry about being criticized unfairly for being soft on crime in inflammatory, provocative ads. We therefore looked at data on attack ads in state supreme court cases from 2002 to 2008, coded and compiled by Campaign Media Analysis Group in conjunction with the Brennan Center for Justice, Justice at Stake, and the National

Institute on Money in State Politics. Over that period of study, attack ads surged to today's current levels. Television ads became more common in contested judicial races, jumping from appearing in 42.9 percent of races in 2002 to 72.4 percent in 2008.[66] Attack ads also increased from appearing in 17.9 percent of contested races in 2002 to 20.7 percent in 2008.[67] Altogether, more judicial races featured television and attack ads from 2002 onward, and the proportion of all TV ads that were attack ads increased from 7.6 percent in 2002 to 22.9 percent of ads in 2008.[68]

When we shift focus from TV ads specifically to attack ads, we find even *bigger* effects on judicial behavior than for TV ads in general.[69] We find that the more attack ads air during a state's supreme court elections, the less likely the state's justices are to vote in favor of criminal defendants by a statistically significant margin. One way of expressing the magnitude of these effects is to explain what would happen if the number of attack ads doubled, holding everything else constant. As Figure 3.2 shows, in a state that aired

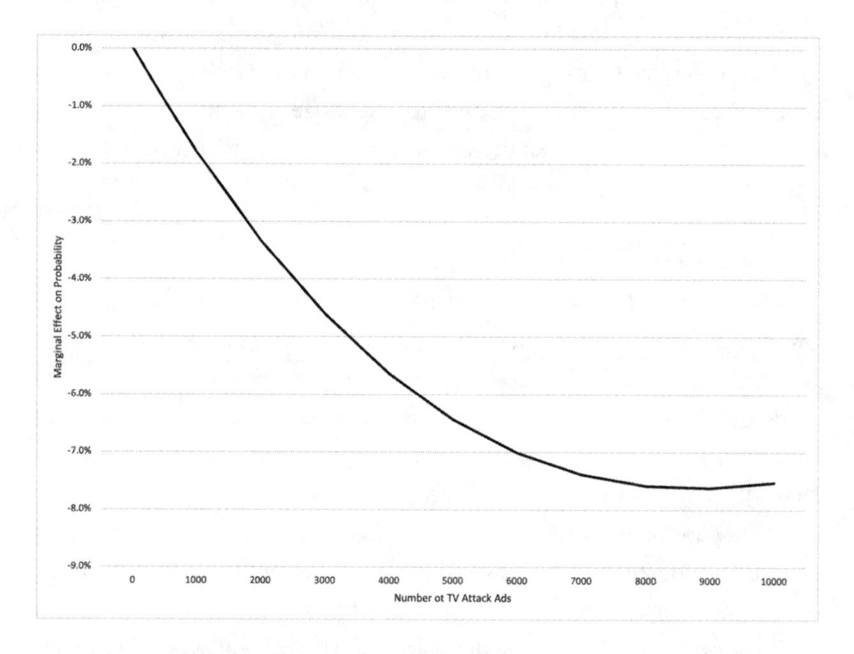

FIGURE 3.2 **The Relationship between Televised Attack Ads and Voting in Favor of Criminal Defendants. Source: Re-created from analysis in Michael S. Kang and Joanna M. Shepherd, "Judging Judicial Elections,"** ***Michigan Law Review*** **114, no. 6 (2016): 946.**

only 2000 ads, doubling the number of attack ads leads to a 3.3 percent drop on average in judicial voting in favor of criminal defendants. The effect for attack ads, in other words, is nearly two-thirds larger than the effect when the number of all TV ads doubles in such a state.

This larger effect for increases in attack ads tells us that the influence of TV ads that we previously discussed is driven largely by attack ads, just as we suspected. It is really the increase in attack ads that is responsible for the shift in judicial behavior, which makes sense, because attack ads have increased dramatically and threaten incumbent justices' re-election more than generic TV ads overall or positive ads by challengers.

Furthermore, just as for TV ads, the effect of doubling the number of attack ads is larger in states with a lot of attack ads in the first place. For a state with 10,000 attack ads to start, doubling the number leads to a decrease of 8 percent in voting in favor of criminal defendants in their appeals. In addition, we found that this effect was stronger for Republican justices than for Democratic and Independent justices, despite the fact that Republicans were already less sympathetic to criminal defendants in the first place, thus further increasing the partisan differential. In other words, this effect of attack ads seems not to have much to do with the ideological preferences of the justices. Republicans, who are more conservative in criminal cases than Democrats and Independents, also became more conservative as the number of attack ads increased.

The effect on Republican voting suggests that attack ads are not just forcing wayward justices to be more faithful to a conservative electorate. If it were wayward justices being brought under control as elections become more competitive, we would expect the liberal Democratic and Independent justices to move the most in a conservative direction back toward voters. And if it were wayward justices in both conservative and liberal directions brought back to the middle by electoral pressure, then we might expect conservative Republican justices to shift in liberal direction, while only liberal Democratic and Independent justices shifted in a conservative direction.

Instead, all categories of justices—Democrats, Independents, and Republicans—shift in a conservative direction, with the conservative Republican justices exhibiting the *biggest* shift of all. This pattern reflects that all supreme court justices are worrying more about re-election as TV and attack ads increase in their state, and consequently they are covering their flanks by becoming more conservative in criminal cases.

But even to mount an effective campaign and reach the voters in the first place, elected judges need to build support among campaign donors and raise campaign financing. Building up campaign fundraising may be the best way to protect their jobs and increase their chances of re-election. This is particularly true for state supreme court justices who now must fight hard in increasingly expensive and competitive elections that look a lot like elections for statewide office.

HOW DO ELECTED JUDGES KEEP THEIR JOBS? THE ROLE OF CAMPAIGN FINANCE

Judges running for re-election must worry about how to win over voters in today's competitive judicial elections and media politics. And the most important resource in politics is campaign money. As nineteenth-century Republican titan Mark Hanna once put it, "There are two things that are important in politics. The first is money, and I can't remember what the second one is."[70]

Judges who won an election to attain office in the first place also know the importance of campaign fundraising for winning an important office like state judge or state supreme court justice. Sue Bell Cobb, former chief justice of the Alabama Supreme Court, raised $2.6 million to win her seat in what was then the most expensive judicial election ever in 2006.[71] She explained that she raised so much money, "much of it from lawyers and interests with issues likely to come before the court," for "one simple reason: I had to."[72] Her opponent in that race, in fact, had raised almost $5 million to run against her, nearly double her total.[73]

Polls find that the public believes judges are influenced by their campaign contributions and the need to satisfy donors. For instance, one poll reported that 60 percent of surveyed Americans believed that campaign contributions had "a great deal of influence" on judicial decisions, with a total of 90 percent agreeing that campaign contributions had at least "some" influence on judges.[74] Likewise, 70 percent of Americans felt it was a "very serious problem" that an elected judge may have received contributions from litigants with a pending case before that judge, with only

6 percent believing that it is "not that serious a problem or no problem at all."[75]

More troubling is that even judges seem to agree that campaign fundraising influences judicial decisionmaking. A famous survey of state judges found that roughly 60 percent of state supreme court justices felt a "great deal" of pressure to raise money for campaigning during election years.[76] Eighty-five percent of state judges felt that interest groups are trying to use their campaign contributions to affect public policy.[77] And almost half of state supreme court justices felt that campaign contributions to judges had at least a little influence on decisions, with more than a third agreeing money had some or a great deal of influence.[78]

Do campaign contributions influence judges? This is the question that we have spent a great deal of our careers trying to figure out. We know that judges and the public harbor concerns about the influence of money, but are they right to be suspicious? After all, almost half of state judges feel money has an influence on decisions, but the other half disagrees. Rare is the judge who would publicly admit that campaign fundraising affected their own judicial decisions. Even Sue Bell Cobb claims that despite the fundraising pressures she encountered, she "dispensed impartial justice to the best of [her] ability" and "turned [her] mind against any form of bias with all [her] strength, and never consciously let politics intrude on the judicial process."[79] She acknowledges only the possibility of unconscious bias, and "[she]'ll never know for sure about that."[80] The best-intentioned judge may be biased by campaign finance pressures in ways that even they may not be able or willing to recognize.

We use quantitative methods and data to answer this challenging empirical question. We start with a large dataset of more than 28,000 state supreme court decisions over a four-year period, including votes from more than 470 justices from 1995 to 1998. Although these decisions date back two decades, the period likely understates the relationship between money and judicial decisionmaking, if anything. This period predates an acceleration in so-called "new-style" judicial campaigning that took off during the 2000s and the overall growth in judicial campaign spending since then. In other words, if we find an effect of money during this period, it is likely to be at least as great today. We then combine this dataset of decisions with campaign contribution data from 1989 to 2010, including donation amounts and the identities of the contributors. Together, along with various control variables, we can trace out statistically the relationship between campaign contributions and judicial decisionmaking by the judges who collected them.

Business Money and Business Cases

First, let's focus on money from business groups to supreme court judges and candidates. Business groups contribute a large percentage of the money spent on judicial campaigns, certainly for state supreme courts. Business groups accounted for the largest share of money given directly to judicial candidates, for instance, in the 2005–2006 election cycle, when they gave 44 percent of all money contributed to state supreme court candidates.[81] This share has decreased particularly since *Citizens United* but remained significant at 31.3 percent in the 2013–14 cycle, still second by industry sector only slightly to lawyers and lobbyists at 32.2 percent.[82] Business groups again remained the second-most generous group in state supreme court elections in 2015–16, giving 24.1 percent of donations,[83] but seem to be channeling more money through outside groups in the changing campaign finance environment since *Citizens United*.[84] In any event, business groups are some of the most important donors to state supreme candidates, and particularly so around our period of study.

We employ multivariate probit regression models to analyze the relationship between campaign contributions from business groups to state supreme court justices and subsequent decisions by those justices involving business interests.[85] This is technical speak for saying that we used state-of-the-art statistical techniques to isolate the effect of money on justices' decisions by controlling for other factors that might also affect decisions and laying bare how campaign money relates to what justices decide. We control for other factors like case histories, case participants, a proxy for political ideology of the justices, individual characteristics of the justices, and institutional variables describing aspects of the judicial system of each state. All these things also probably affect justices' decisions because some cases are strong, others are weaker, and additional factors like partisanship (as we'll discuss) influence how justices think about cases too. And we want to be sure that any connection between money and judicial decisions isn't the result of some other important factor we didn't consider.

We had data only on direct contributions from donors to candidates and do not include spending through issue advocacy or independent expenditures. Exclusion of this data, though, biases the results against finding a relationship of business group influence. If anything, business groups exert even more overall campaign finance influence when issue advocacy and independent expenditures are also included. So, we can be reasonably confident if we discover a positive finding of business group influence here because our study underestimates the overall influence of business groups.

We find a statistically significant connection between campaign finance contributions from business groups to state supreme court justices and subsequent decisions by those justices involving business interests.[86] On average, controlling for other things, we find that each $1,000 in contributions from business groups increases the likelihood that a judge would vote in favor of a business litigant by 0.03 percent. Although that seems like a small difference, it quickly balloons once the amount of money spent in state supreme court races is factored in.

A different way of stating our empirical finding is that $100,000 in business money is associated with a 3 percent greater likelihood that a justice votes in favor of business interests, which is a lot when one expects most supreme court cases to be roughly 50–50 to go either way.[87] If you increase the business contribution to $1 million, then the average likelihood is estimated at an increase of 30 percent probability of voting in favor of business interests. It is important to note that campaign spending for elected state supreme court seats routinely extends into millions of dollars. Total campaign spending for seventy-six state supreme court seats in 2015–16 reached a record $69.3 million, an average of almost $1 million per seat, and spending in Pennsylvania reached a total of $21.4 million for just three state supreme court seats.[88]

Alternatively, we also look at the proportion of a candidate's total contributions that come from business groups.[89] Rather than determine how favorable a candidate becomes toward business interests based on the aggregate amount of the contributions they receive from business groups, we check how the candidate's voting is based on the proportion of their campaign money that comes from business groups.

Again, state supreme court candidates vote more favorably for business interests in proportion to an increasing percentage of their money coming

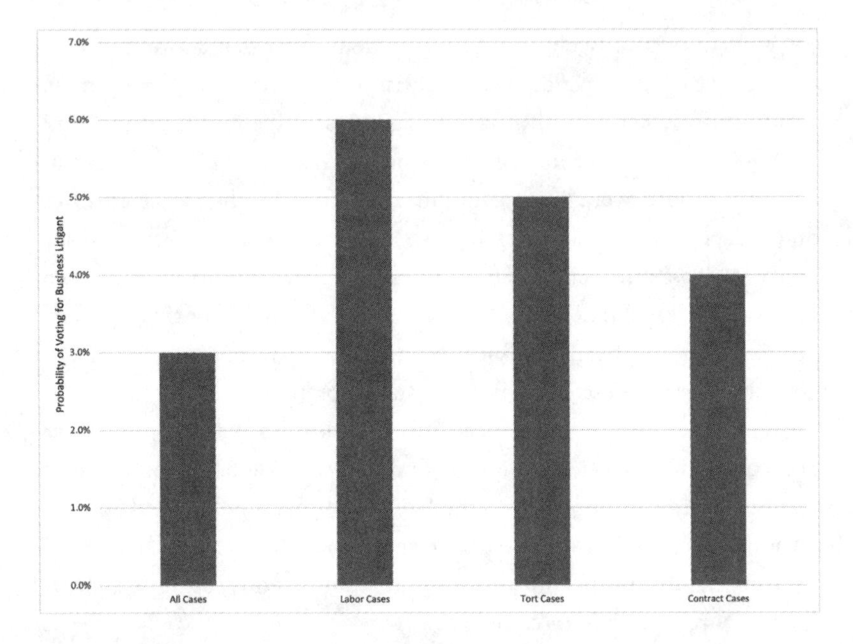

FIGURE 3.3 **Contributions from Business Groups and Voting for Business Litigants. Source: Re-created from analysis in Michael S. Kang and Joanna M. Shepherd, "The Partisan Price of Justice: An Empirical Analysis of Campaign Contributions and Judicial Decisions,"** ***NYU Law Review*** **86, no. 1 (April 2011): 100.**

from business groups. As Figure 3.3 shows, we find that, on average, as contributions from business groups make up an additional 10 percentage points of a justice's total fundraising, the justice become roughly 6 percent more likely to vote in favor of business litigants in labor cases, 5 percent more likely to vote in favor of business litigants in tort cases, 4 percent more likely to vote in favor of business litigants in contract cases, and roughly 3 percent more likely to vote in favor of business litigants in any case.

One additional result from this data was that campaign contributions from business groups were significantly associated with decisions in favor of business for partisan elected judges, but not necessarily for judges elected under nonpartisan elections. Nonpartisan elected judges behaved a lot like judges facing only retention elections when it came to business money, even though they raised more campaign money and faced more competitive elections with active challengers running against them.[90] This result intrigued us and made us wonder if the major parties, the Republican and

Democratic Parties, were critical to understanding judicial campaign finance. Perhaps the political parties were driving the relationship between campaign contributions and subsequent judicial decisionmaking by linking up and bonding campaign donors and judges.

For this reason, we next broaden our analysis to look at other types of interest groups beyond just business groups. The major parties organize interest groups into diverse coalitions of supporters from different industries and mobilize electoral support for their candidates. The parties, after all, are defined by their reputations for the policy positions. The Republicans broadly represent conservative positions that tend to be more sympathetic to business, more hostile to government regulation, and more punitive toward criminal defendants. The Democrats broadly represent more liberal positions that are more sympathetic to civil rights, less hostile toward government regulation, and more protective of criminal defendants. Of course, these are generalizations that pave over lots of nuance and exceptions, but the public understands these party brands, and party leadership cultivates them.

Major Party Money and Ideological Influence

To study the influence of money from the major party coalitions, we categorize certain interest groups as roughly belonging to one major party or the other.[91] The parties themselves raise, contribute, and spend money directly for their candidates across all levels of government, including state supreme court. However, we were interested in how successfully the parties coordinated interest groups as part of a campaign-finance coalition in support of their candidates.

The affiliated groups constituting the party coalition share certain preferences over public policy, including issues decided by state courts, and thus join in common interest to fund candidates likely to promote those preferences in office. These groups conclude that they "get more from government by funneling their resources through a party coalition to nominate and elect officeholders friendly to their interests than by buying policies one at a time from independent officeholders."[92] Republican-leaning groups in our data included not just business groups, but financial/real estate groups, insurance companies, medical groups, and conservative single-issue groups.[93] Democratic-leaning groups included labor unions, lawyers, and liberal single-issue groups.[94]

So categorized, campaign contributions to state supreme court justices, from the Democratic and Republican Party coalitions, are significantly predictive of the justices' voting on the bench.[95] More money from the Democratic Party coalition is associated with left-leaning votes across the gamut of state supreme court cases. In our dataset, left-leaning votes meant voting for the individual facing a business in general business disputes, for the employee in labor disputes, for the patient plaintiff in medical malpractice cases, or for the plaintiff in products liability and other torts cases. For instance, an increase of 10 percentage points in the proportion of an average justice's total fundraising that comes from the Democratic coalition increases the probability of a left-leaning vote in torts cases by 1 percent, controlling for other things.

The influence of campaign money from the Republican coalition seems even greater. As a simple matter, increases in the proportion of total contributions that comes from the Republican coalition likewise raises the likelihood of a right-leaning vote in cases across the board, controlling for other things. In our dataset, right-leaning vote meant voting for the business litigant in general business disputes, for the employer in labor disputes, for the doctor or hospital in medical malpractice cases, or for the business defendant in a products liability and other torts cases. But we find that the marginal effect of money from the Republican coalition is substantially larger than money from the Democratic side. For instance, an increase of 10 percentage points in the proportion of the average justice's fundraising that comes from the Republican coalition boosts the likelihood of a right-leaning vote for the defendant in torts cases by 7 percent, roughly seven times the influence of Democratic money. In the same way, an increase of 10 percentage points in the proportion of fundraising from the Republican coalition also increases the probability of right-leaning votes in products liability cases by 6 percent, in medical malpractice cases by 7 percent, in labor disputes by 7 percent, and in general business disputes by 6 percent.

The influence of campaign contributions was smaller for justices elected under nonpartisan elections than those elected under partisan elections, but the influence of money didn't go away entirely. The relationships between campaign money from the Republican and Democratic coalitions and judicial decisions were clearly stronger for justices elected in states that used partisan elections for state supreme court. Partisan elections attract

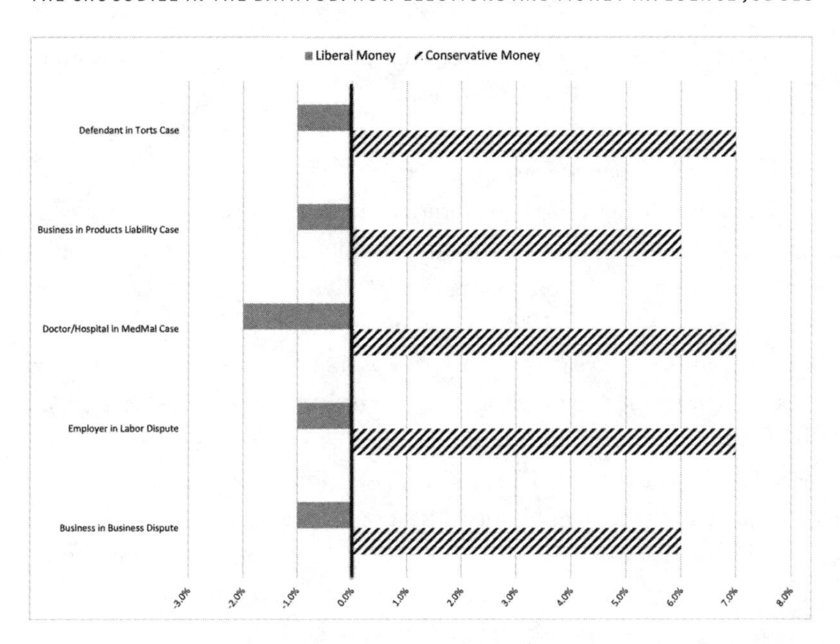

FIGURE 3.4 Relationship between Left- and Right-Leaning Contributions and Votes. Source: Re-created from analysis in Michael S. Kang and Joanna M. Shepherd, "The Partisan Foundations of Judicial Campaign Finance," *Southern California Law Review* 86 (2013): 1276.

more party involvement and commitment, as well as more partisan candidates in the first place. It therefore is no surprise that the connection between party money and decisions by partisan justices is stronger there than for justices in other states elected through nonpartisan systems.

However, in contrast to earlier analysis on business money and business cases, we still find a statistically significant relationship between contributions from the party coalitions and subsequent decisions by nonpartisan justices. Without question, the relationship was less robust. The effect of money was smaller in magnitude and statistically insignificant specifically for medical malpractice and torts cases. That said, we still found a statistically significant effect of party money on decisions by nonpartisan justices in business disputes, as well as labor cases, that were comparable in magnitude to the effects for partisan justices. The effect of money was less for justices elected under nonpartisan elections, but unlike the earlier analysis of business cases, the effect of party money was still significantly predictive of many judicial decisions. Money still matters in nonpartisan elections, though a bit less than in partisan elections.

Major Party Money and Election Cases

To follow up on our study of major party money, we decide to look at what the parties care about most—winning elections. The legal certification of an election winner has become more contested and litigated since *Bush v. Gore* in 2000.[96] Election litigation has gone up from an average of 94 cases per year in the five years before *Bush v. Gore* to an average of almost 250 cases per year since then.[97] *Bush v. Gore*, which effectively decided the 2000 presidential election, taught both parties that election litigation can win elections by deciding the rules that apply to who can run and which votes are counted. Sometimes election litigation happens before election day;[98] sometimes it happens after election day, as in *Bush v. Gore* itself. Either way, the parties know what rules they want and how the rules can help and hurt them. And judges—usually state judges—decide these questions.

One obvious way the parties can influence judges to decide in their favor in election cases is campaign finance. We look at how campaign contributions from the major party coalitions affect state supreme court decisions on election cases. Basically, we were interested in whether party money increases loyalty to the party in the cases where partisan loyalty matters the most—candidate-litigated election disputes. We look in our dataset for these types of election cases where a candidate sues or is sued proximate to an election, usually about an arcane question of election law such as the counting of ballots or the eligibility of a candidate in a particular race.[99] Common issues include whether a candidate was a legal resident of a particular jurisdiction as required to run for office there, whether certain ballots that weren't completely filled out could still be counted as valid votes, and whether a candidate was eligible for the ballot despite technical defects in their application for candidacy.

These cases do not encompass all of election law, broadly defined. For example, there are no campaign finance, voter identification, or voting rights cases in our dataset, nor any other issues that we thought were ideological or already identified as partisan valenced. We remove those cases to leave just those that are almost entirely characterized by highly technical, rare questions of law without much ideological content. One way of thinking about these cases is that they are very much like *Bush v. Gore*. That case was historically important and decided a presidential election, but the actual legal questions were how to understand rarely interpreted provisions of state election law that hardly anyone has thought about since. Similarly, these election cases are highly technical, obscure state or local law questions that are not consequential in terms of long-term law and precedent. However, how judges decided these cases was very consequential to the outcome of a *particular* election that the decision was trying to resolve.

Indeed, we purposely restrict our dataset for this study to these technical, nonideological cases. These cases, in other words, involved no consistent ideological position on the merits of these questions that could be identified as conservative or liberal, Republican or Democratic, as a matter of law.

Why did we do this? Well, we already know that Republican judges typically will decide ideological questions more conservatively than Democratic judges, and that Democratic judges will decide ideological questions more liberally than Republicans. We didn't want to simply look at those cases where judges' behavior was too predictably based on their ideological predisposition. Instead, these cases were ideological ciphers. There were no ideologically conservative or liberal positions, for example, on how to construe a state law question of who constitutes a resident for purposes of candidate eligibility, as far as we could tell. What's more, we thought these cases didn't involve identifiable long-term party interests one way or the other. A decision to include a disputed candidate as an eligible resident in this upcoming election, based on some obscure election law interpretation, could help the judge's party this time, but may just as easily hurt the judge's party the next time the question comes up—or the question might never come up again. In other words, deciding these cases one way or the other wouldn't predictably benefit the Democratic Party or the Republican Party over the long run.

And why did we want cases where the parties' long-term advantage was uncertain? Judges might care enough about their party's long-term interests that they could be willing to decide against their party's side in a particular case if it benefits their party even more over the longer term. In other words, we worried that judges might sacrifice the short-term gain as a tradeoff for a bigger long-term payoff. If judges were making such tradeoffs, this would make it hard to tell if a decision against their party in a particular case was really against their party's interests.

As a result, these election cases were unusual because their long-term stakes were unpredictable and not determined by ideology or partisanship. Admittedly, this is very different from most election cases. In voting rights cases, for instance, there is an ideological position of conservatives and liberals that all judges know ahead of time, and the Republicans and Democrats know how any particular legal resolution of the cases will help and hurt the parties over the long run. In most cases, judges know the long-term ideological and partisan stakes, and those stakes loom larger than the specific outcome in an individual case. But to the extent there are any conservative or liberal positions on these election cases in our study, they do not sufficiently align with the long-term political advantage for either party such that any pattern of partisan loyalty can be explained as ideological. This lays bare the partisanship of the judges for us to see.

As a consequence, we had a set of election cases where the long-term stakes are very unclear, but the short-term payoffs from the case are very clear—one party will gain an advantage in the current election depending on how the court decides. These cases are all about very salient *short-term partisan advantage*, which is what we want to measure. If Democratic judges consistently favor Democratic candidates in these cases, it is likely that they are doing so because they are influenced, consciously or not, by a desire to help their party rather than anything else. There isn't some alternate ideological story about what they're doing, nor is there any legal doctrinal story as far as we know. The same would hold true for Republican judges helping their party. These cases therefore give us a nice way to gauge judges' partisan loyalty, as opposed to something else that motivates judicial decisionmaking.

Looking at our data, we find that campaign money from the party coalition increases state supreme court justices' partisan loyalty in election cases—at least for Republicans. Republican justices are more likely to favor their own party in election cases by a statistically significant margin compared to Democratic justices, controlling for other factors. The partisan imbalance is large: Republican justices decided election cases in their party-favored direction at 38 percent higher rate than Democratic justices did. As reported in Figure 3.5, Republicans voted in favor of the Republican

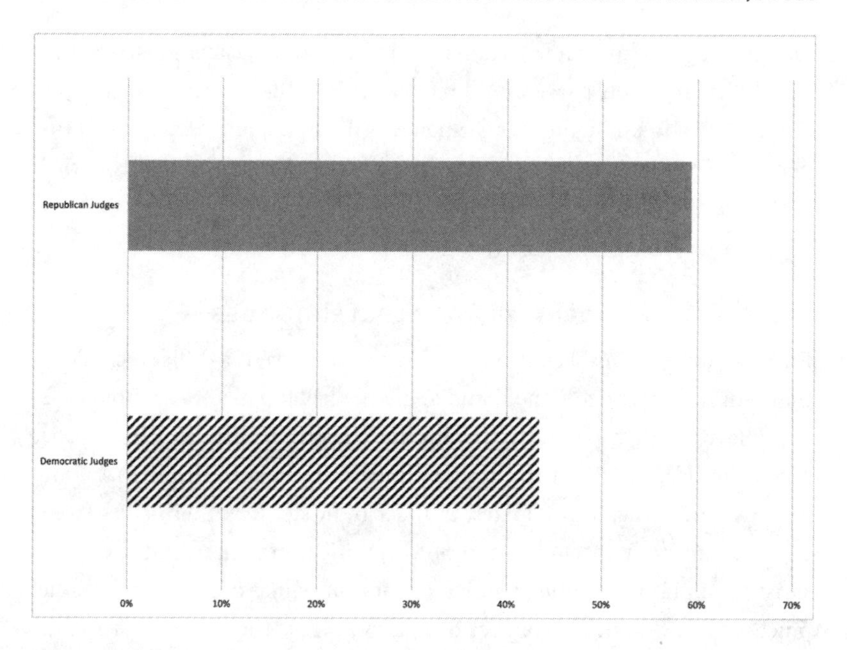

FIGURE 3.5 **Voting in Favor of Party or against Opposing Party in Election Cases. Source: Re-created from analysis in Michael S. Kang and Joanna M. Shepherd, "The Long Shadow of *Bush v. Gore*," *Stanford Law Review* 68 (2016): 1411.**

litigant, or against the Democratic litigant, almost 60 percent of the time, compared to just 43 percent for Democratic justices.

Moreover, partisan favoritism by elected Republican justices increases as a function of campaign contributions received from the Republican Party and from party-allied interest groups. We find that every additional $10,000 in contributions from the Republican side increased by 3 percent the likelihood that the average Republican justice would vote in favor of the Republican litigant or against the Democratic litigant. Conversely, every $10,000 in contributions from the Democratic side made the average Republican justice about 1 percent less likely to vote in favor of the Republican or against the Democrat.

In other words, we find that Republican justices generally display greater partisan loyalty than Democratic justices over our period of study. The result is partially a function of party campaign finance, with Republican Party loyalty increasing with party money received, while Democrats were neither loyal to their party in election cases nor affected by campaign money. Judges who decided against their party might have considered the possibility that their party would reduce or drop their support for them in the next election. Like Justice Clement in Michigan, judges who don't display the expected party loyalty in their decisions risk retribution from their party when it comes to re-election time.

THE ELECTION INCENTIVES OF ELECTED JUDGES

Running for judge, especially for state supreme court, is a difficult challenge that requires judges to uphold and apply the law but also raise money and curry favor with voters to win office and keep their job. As Chief Justice McCormack observed at the beginning of this chapter, running for judge is just weird. Judicial candidates, unlike candidates for other offices, aren't supposed to cater to public opinion or political pressures, but they must satisfy the public or other political actors—just like candidates for other offices—if they are to become and remain judges. These cross-cutting demands mean that elected judges confront a potential conflict of interest and must decide how best to balance their judicial duties and election incentives as part of their jobs.

In this chapter, we've described the state-of-the-art empirical literature on how judges negotiate this type of conflict of interest. We know judges are sensitive to factors that influence whether they will keep their job. As a general matter, our work shows that judges cater to whoever controls whether they retain their judgeship: the governor, legislature, or voters. This makes sense: These retention mechanisms are designed for the purpose of making state judges accountable to those political actors who decide whether they continue to have a job. They work just as planned. Specifically for elected judges, we know that they are affected by election worries and protect their re-election chances by deciding criminal cases differently, that is, more conservatively. And when judicial elections become more competitive with more TV advertising, especially attack ads, judges go further in a conservative direction to defend their flanks.

Armed with this understanding, we know also that campaign finance money is predictive of judicial decisions and suspect it has something to do with electoral incentives as well. Judges know they need campaign financing, and we find in our data that judges decide cases in ways that benefit their campaign contributors. We have focused a lot on business contributors and cases, but we've also studied and described our research on all kinds of donors and cases. Our quantitative work substantiates the anecdotal suspicions of judges and the public that, controlling for other things, elected judges are influenced by campaign money and favor their contributors' interests in a predictable fashion.

So, money matters a lot. Whether it comes from business groups, the major parties, or other interest groups as part of a party coalition, campaign money predicts how elected justices later vote. Money gets what it wants in judicial elections.

4 WHY MONEY MATTERS

AT THE BEGINNING OF THIS book, we introduced the U.S. Supreme Court case *Caperton v. Massey*, decided just over a decade ago in 2009. The facts of the *Caperton* case are notorious and inspired a John Grisham novel because they so graphically demonstrate the fears about big money in judicial elections. An ultra-wealthy coal-mining CEO spent millions on campaign ads to elect his favored state supreme court candidate, who then won office and saved the CEO's company from a $50 million verdict on appeal. Even a conservative U.S. Supreme Court thought that this decision violated constitutional due process and that the candidate should have sat out the appeal, given how indebted the candidate could have felt to the donor. The U.S. Supreme Court decided a judge who owes their job to an important donor shouldn't decide an appeal worth more than $50 million to that donor just a few years later.

Of course, none of this wild story in the *Caperton* case would have been imaginable to that state supreme court candidate, Brent D. Benjamin, back in 2004 when he first decided to run for the West Virginia Supreme Court. He moved to West Virginia shortly after graduating from law school in the 1980s and practiced law in the state for a couple decades before deciding to challenge incumbent state supreme court justice Warren McGraw as a Republican candidate in 2004. Benjamin was fortunate that his first-time election bid coincided with his donor Don Blankenship's newfound interest in the West Virginia Supreme Court. Blankenship's support would soon help power Benjamin's candidacy for statewide office.

Don Blankenship served as the longtime president, CEO, and chairman of the board of A.T. Massey Coal Company Inc., a giant coal-mining conglomerate operating across Appalachia. Blankenship ran Massey as his fiefdom and was virtually synonymous with Massey Coal Company. Many employees in the office had DAD's root beer mugs, which employees said stood as an acronym and constant reminder to "Do As Don Says."[1]

The company had been hit with a massive $50 million verdict in 2002 when a trial jury found the company, under Blankenship's iron-fisted leadership, liable for tortious interference and fraud against Harman Mining, the plaintiff Hugh Caperton's company. The jury in *Caperton v. Massey* found that Massey directed a subsidiary—Harman Mining's main customer—to breach its contract with Harman and stop buying coal from Harman, putting Harman Mining on the brink of failure. Don Blankenship and Massey then, according to the jury, fraudulently strung along Harman in purchase negotiations before cutting off those negotiations when Harman had no alternative other than going out of business. Massey's conduct was egregious, involving a fraudulent invocation of an "act of God" clause in the contract with Harman, and ultimately sent Harman into bankruptcy, but still, the eight-figure magnitude of the jury verdict was a surprise. Even for a company of Massey's size, a $50 million verdict would be a painful pill to swallow.

Everyone expected Massey to appeal the verdict up to the West Virginia Supreme Court. However, for bizarre reasons having partially to do with a missing trial transcript, the trial judgment wasn't finalized for almost three years. In the meantime, with Massey's appeal in *Caperton* soon to be decided by the West Virginia Supreme Court, Blankenship took a newfound interest in the 2004 supreme court election that would help determine the composition of the court for his company's upcoming appeal.

Nominally, the West Virginia Supreme Court at the time was uniformly Democratic, with five Democrats and no Republicans, elected through the state's then-partisan judicial elections for the court. In practice, though, the politics of the court were more complicated. One justice, Elliot "Spike" Maynard, was a Democrat in name only, a well-known conservative who later flipped his partisan identification to the Republican Party once the state's party leanings converted to the Republican side. Another justice, Robin Davis, was also an elected Democrat, but she regularly sided with Maynard in decisions and was distrusted by the liberal Democrats on the court, Warren McGraw, Larry Starcher, and Joseph Albright. As a result, McGraw's re-election bid in 2004 potentially could tip the balance of the court between the two factions in key cases like the *Caperton* appeal.

In this context, Blankenship took aim at McGraw's seat, with his *Caperton* appeal still pending. Although Blankenship's company lost at trial, Blankenship could reverse that defeat on appeal if he could change the composition of the state supreme court. As a wealthy man, Blankenship had the money to affect the race and boost a little-known candidate like Benjamin. In July 2004, Blankenship met with Benjamin through Republican operative Gregory Alan Thomas at the law offices of Steptoe & Johnson.[2] As Blankenship explained later to the *New York Times*, "I thought, if I want to beat this guy [McGraw] I ought to know who's running against him."[3] Benjamin, though, apparently didn't impress Blankenship, who said he told Benjamin during the meeting that "[he didn't] know who you are, but if you go around talking to business people about raising money, you need to do more listening than you do talking." Still, Blankenship "[did]n't like McGraw" and remained determined to change the composition of the West Virginia Supreme Court.

Blankenship invested roughly $3 million in the 2004 state supreme court election behind Benjamin. With Steptoe & Johnson's help, Blankenship set up a 527 organization, similar to what we today would call a Super PAC, to financially support Benjamin's campaign against McGraw. The 527 organization was named "And for the Sake of the Kids." Blankenship never established the promised charity, indicated by the name, to "provide needed clothing and other necessities to the most needy children of West Virginia."[4] The 527 organization was strictly a campaign-finance vehicle established for the 2004 election. At the time, there were no limits on individual financial contributions to 527 organizations for purposes of making independent campaign advertisements.

Blankenship, a well-paid executive, funded $2.46 million in negative campaign advertising against McGraw through "And for the Sake of the Kids," spent another $515,708 in advertising on his own, and then gave an additional $150,000 to other groups supporting Benjamin.[5] In a bruising, expensive campaign, Blankenship's $3 million of campaign spending in the race was greater than all other Benjamin supporters combined and three times what Benjamin's own campaign committee spent on the race.[6] No one can say for sure whether Blankenship's spending decided the race, but that magnitude certainly had a great chance to make a difference.

Boosted by Blankenship's generous election support, Brent Benjamin beat McGraw to become the first Republican elected to the West Virginia Supreme Court in more than eighty years. The most infamous of Blankenship's campaign ads belongs in the pantheon of inflammatory supreme court election ads, because it made a huge splash and stabbed the usual hot buttons of judicial politics. McGraw was part of a 3–2 court majority that granted probation to a convicted sex offender who briefly worked as an evening janitor at a Catholic school.[7] The ad blared that McGraw's vote let "a child rapist go free, to work in our schools." (You can see a screengrab from the ad in Chapter 2.) The true story was complicated, and McGraw protested that the ad was "absolutely untrue. I'm embarrassed to go out in public. They've absolutely destroyed me."[8] Blankenship would later brag that the child rapist ad "killed" McGraw.[9]

Blankenship had succeeded in changing the composition of the West Virginia Supreme Court in time for his company's appeal. When the *Caperton* appeal finally reached the West Virginia Supreme Court just over a year later in early 2006, the plaintiffs moved for Benjamin to recuse himself from the case. Hugh Caperton, the lead plaintiff, requested Benjamin's removal from decisionmaking in the case under Canon 3E(1) of the state Judicial Code of Conduct, which stipulated that a "judge shall disqualify himself or herself in a proceeding in which the judge's impartiality might be reasonably questioned."[10]

The plaintiffs argued that Blankenship "spent an unprecedented amount of money to see Justice Benjamin elected" and "Blankenship's inordinately immense campaign contributions would create reasonable doubts concerning Justice Benjamin's impartiality when confronted with a Massey case."[11] To the degree local sentiment serves as objective evidence of such reasonable doubts, the plaintiffs cited editorials in the *Pittsburgh Post-Gazette*, *Huntington Herald-Dispatch*, *Charleston Gazette*, and *Beckley Register-Herald*, a virtual sweep of the local news media, all calling for Benjamin to recuse himself for the reasons the plaintiffs offered.[12] The plaintiffs even commissioned a survey that claimed two-thirds of West Virginians likewise doubted Benjamin could be fair in the case, against just 15 percent who thought he could be.[13] It was hard for many to believe that Blankenship's very prominent and generous support for Benjamin might not affect Benjamin's objectivity in the case. It seemed at least to affect many people's perception of his impartiality, even if Benjamin himself felt he would be objective.

Still, Benjamin refused to recuse in the case and, perhaps predictably, cast the decisive 3–2 vote to overturn the $50 million jury verdict against the company of his former campaign champion, Don Blankenship. In a long concurrence, Benjamin argued narrowly that he could not be required to recuse based on the mere appearance of judicial bias or conflict of interest. He should not recuse, as he put it, merely because Blankenship's 527 organization "independently used its contributions to wage a campaign against my opponent four years ago."[14] Understandably, Benjamin seemed defensive regarding the plaintiffs' worries about his objectivity and raised a reasonable point that financial campaign support for a judge's election, without more, should not automatically require recusal in a future case.

That said, the plaintiffs had not argued that financial support from Blankenship by itself, *without more*, required recusal. Instead, the plaintiffs argued that the enormous amount of Blankenship's support of Benjamin's election was almost singular, in their words "impossible to overstate."[15] They emphasized that Blankenship spent more on Benjamin's election than the total amount spent by all other West Virginians combined.[16] What's more, they claimed that Benjamin had made no clarifying disclosures regarding the nature of his relationship, if any, with Blankenship or Blankenship's company.[17] The plaintiffs therefore argued that the overwhelming magnitude of Blankenship's support for Benjamin in his 2004 election, together with Benjamin's failures to disclose anything further about his relationship with the parties, raised reasonable doubts about his impartiality in the case sufficient to require recusal. The increasing politicization and intensity of West Virginia's judicial elections, as well as its judicial campaign finance, were being litigated in state supreme court.

Notably, two other state supreme court justices *did* recuse themselves in the *Caperton* case. In a twist fit for the John Grisham thriller the case eventually became, Justice Maynard had been photographed vacationing with Blankenship in France just months before the court was to hear the *Caperton* case.[18] Maynard and Blankenship had long been friends, but it was too much to see them sharing flutes of champagne on the French Riviera so close to Maynard presiding over Blankenship's case. Maynard earlier refused to recuse and actually voted to overturn the verdict against Blankenship at a previous stage of the appeal, but just nine days after the pictures went public, Maynard agreed to recuse himself and the court subsequently was forced to vote unanimously to at least rehear the appeal.[19]

Justice Starcher also ultimately agreed to recuse himself from the rehearing. Starcher had been publicly critical of Blankenship but refused to recuse from Massey cases on that basis, until he was quoted by the *New York Times* castigating Benjamin and Blankenship's relationship. Starcher told the *Times* that "it makes me want to puke to see massive amounts of out-of-state money come in and buy a seat on our court. . . . Now we have one justice who was bought by Don Blankenship."[20] Starcher recognized that his angry criticism of Blankenship made it plausible that his "impartiality might be reasonably questioned" under Canon 3E(1), even if he remained convinced of his own objectivity.

Benjamin, however, refused to recuse himself in the case, even then. In a long concurring opinion to the West Virginia Supreme Court decision reversing the jury verdict against Blankenship, Benjamin dismissed doubts about his potential impartiality regarding Blankenship as mere "drama . . . a diversion."[21] In fact, with Maynard and Starcher's recusals, Benjamin played an especially outsize role in the case. Maynard was the sitting chief justice, but his recusal elevated Benjamin to chief justice for the case. In West Virginia, the presiding chief justice actually appoints lower court judges to sit in place of any justices who are recused from a case. Maynard's and Starcher's recusals, along with Benjamin's refusal to recuse, meant that Benjamin not only participated in the case as chief justice, but he also appointed Maynard's and Starcher's replacements for the case. It was therefore no surprise at all that Benjamin had joined Maynard's replacement (whom he appointed) and Justice Davis as the 3–2 court majority to reverse the trial verdict.

The plaintiffs appealed this West Virginia Supreme Court decision against them and, against the odds, were granted a hearing by the United States Supreme Court. The U.S. Supreme Court grants hearings in only a few dozen cases per year, but the Court was compelled by the unusual facts of the *Caperton* case to decide this one. As we've already mentioned in Chapter 1, and as we'll discuss more thoroughly in the next chapter, the Supreme Court reversed the West Virginia Supreme Court in favor of Hugh Caperton and his fellow plaintiffs.

The Court held that Brent Benjamin had been constitutionally required by due process of law to recuse himself in the *Caperton* case and should not have participated in the decision. The Court explained that "there is a serious risk of actual bias—based on objective and reasonable perceptions—when a person with a personal stake in a particular case had a significant and disproportionate influence in placing the judge on the case by raising funds or directing the judge's election campaign when the case was pending or imminent."[22] It was, in short, constitutionally unfair for Benjamin to participate in the case when, under the circumstances, Blankenship had just spent so much money getting him into office.

The Court did not find, nor did the plaintiffs need to allege, that Blankenship bribed or agreed on an explicit quid pro quo with Benjamin. Instead, the Court ruled that "objective standards may also require recusal whether or not actual bias exists or can be proved."[23] Here, the objective circumstances of Blankenship's heavy involvement in the campaign for Benjamin's election, while the *Caperton* appeal was pending and foreseeable, offered "a possible temptation to the average . . . judge . . . to lead him not to hold the balance nice, clear, and true."[24]

As we mentioned earlier, we enthusiastically agree with the U.S. Supreme Court's decision in *Caperton* to hold that Benjamin's recusal was required in the case. The Court took seriously the objective risks raised by judicial campaign finance for judicial impartiality, certainly for the appearance of impartiality if nothing else. We have already presented empirical evidence of campaign finance's influence on judging in the last chapter. We think this is exactly the concern about judicial campaign finance—that it affects judges' decisionmaking in favor of their financial supporters.

This can be true even if the judges don't think they are affected by campaign finance. Remember that judges regularly report in surveys that they think campaign finance influences cases but generally don't think it affects *their own* decisionmaking. Brent Benjamin, we think, sincerely believed that Blankenship's financial support for him didn't affect his view of the

Caperton case. Although he and Maynard reportedly dined with Blankenship just days before the appeal was filed, Benjamin insisted that he wasn't personally close with Blankenship the way that Maynard was.[25] Even Blankenship concluded that "Brent Benjamin, rightfully or wrongfully, thinks I had nothing to do with his election."[26]

The *Caperton* story illustrates, at least for most readers, how big money judicial campaign finance matters, and this raises worries about impartial justice. We've explained earlier in the book the significant relationship between money spent in judicial elections and the way that judges decide cases, not unlike the way that Benjamin predictably decided in favor of his major supporter's appeal in *Caperton*. Worse, the more campaign money spent on their behalf, the more predictably judges decide cases in favor of their supporters' interests and preferences. The more money that political parties donate to judges, the more predictably those judges vote in favor of their side in election cases. The more money that interest groups donate to judges, the more predictably those judges decide cases in favor of those groups' interests and preferences. The more campaign ads and specifically attack ads that run in a state's supreme court elections, the more judges cover their flanks by voting more predictably against criminal defendants, regardless of their party affiliation or ideological predisposition.

What is less clear, at least so far, is exactly *why* the money matters. Do judges decide cases in favor of their supporters' interests because they are biased by their supporters' money? Or do they just decide cases as they see them, and it happens to align with their supporters' interests because they all share the same views of the law? Perhaps, in other words, Brent Benjamin and Blankenship are both conservatives with similar views about the law, so it's no surprise that Benjamin decided *Caperton* as Blankenship expected. Perhaps the predictable relationship between campaign money and judicial decisions is the result of this natural alignment between supporters and judicial candidates—a selection effect—rather than judges altering their decisions to favor their supporters.

This puzzle about causation—why campaign finance money seems to influence judicial decisions—is the focus of this chapter. We present the best empirical evidence to date, using social science methods, that judicial decisions are *not* just coincidence of agreement between supporters and judges. We show persuasively that judicial decisions follow the campaign money, at least in significant part because judges are biased toward their financial contributors. We cannot prove anything about Brent Benjamin, or any specific case, but over the run of cases, we think judges are biased by their need for campaign money and, specifically, by their need to run for re-election.

Both selection and biasing probably occur at the same time. When we talk about our research with other academics, they regularly press us on whether we think campaign finance influences judges through selection or biasing. Until now, we haven't focused on trying to prove one or the other. We show that campaign money gets its way in either case. That's enough to trouble most people who think seriously about the health of our justice system. Wealthy people shouldn't be able to dictate so directly how judges decide cases, especially cases that affect their interests.

In this chapter, though, we focus on identifying whether campaign finance biases judges and their decisions, rather than influencing decisions entirely through selection. For technical reasons that we explain later, it's difficult to prove that biasing happens at all. While it may be natural to suspect that judges are biased toward their contributors' interests, it is methodologically difficult to prove that biasing, as opposed to selection, is actually happening. We try here to distinguish between selection and biasing and to show that supreme court justices are affected by the need to raise campaign money for re-election.

The empirical results in this chapter represent the best social-science evidence to date that campaign finance significantly biases elected judges' judicial decisionmaking toward their contributors' interests. We show that selection effects cannot fully explain the power of campaign money. In other words, money matters not simply because it goes to the set of judges who already would decide cases a certain way, regardless of re-election concerns. Instead, campaign contributions predict later decisions by judges who receive them at least in part because judges eventually up for re-election need to curry favor with contributors who may help them keep their jobs. Re-election is a crucial incentive that produces money's biasing influence on judicial decisions.

This chapter sets out our deepest study on the biasing effect of campaign contributions. As a result, this chapter is the most technical in the book. We want to provide plenty of detail on our statistics and methods. There's even more detail, primarily for academic readers, in the Appendix. We use the latest data we could find to test our theory of judicial bias by looking at judicial decisions from 2010 through 2012. These decisions therefore were made during the *Citizens United* era, after that U.S. Supreme Court decision loosened campaign finance law in most states and promised higher spending in judicial elections to come.

WHY DOES IT MATTER HOW MONEY INFLUENCES JUDGES?

The question we ask at this point is why campaign money matters in all these ways. That is, why does campaign money so significantly predict judicial decisionmaking? As social scientists would put it, what is the causal mechanism here?

As we just explained, we can think of at least two important alternative pathways. The first is what social scientists would call a *selection* effect. Consider the perspective of a campaign donor with a clear set of policy views. To whom do you want to give your money? Someone who shares your views in the first place. As Senator Bill Bradley once put it, "Money not only determines who is elected, it determines who runs for office."[27] Candidates who already share your ideological views are likely to be attractive candidates for you to support. If you are pro-business, you'll seek out and support pro-business candidates. If you are pro-regulation, you'll seek out and support pro-regulation candidates, and so on.

In addition, candidates with more campaign finance support would, by virtue of those resources, be more likely to be elected. Once elected, those candidates would represent the views of their like-minded donors as they do their jobs as judges. In the end, then, campaign finance support from left-leaning donors would be correlated with left-leaning votes by the candidates they supported. And this happens, at least in part, because left-leaning donors directed money disproportionately to judges they anticipated would vote in their favor and made the right picks. The same would be true for right-leaning donors and right-leaning candidates as well. In the end, the money would line up with judges' decisions.

A second pathway by which campaign financing might correlate with judicial voting is more direct and perhaps even more worrisome—outright biasing. Let's assume that candidates may, or may not, be predisposed to the views of prospective campaign donors. However, candidates, and subsequently judges when they reach the bench, know the views of many wealthy campaign donors out there. They especially know the ideological views of their own campaign donors who have supported them in the past, and with whom they already have working relationships. As Bridget McCormack explained to us, "You go to these [fundraising] events, and people would say 'Well, what can you do for me?' which is a fair question to ask of most politicians running for office." What's more, judges know that they probably need continued campaign contributions from these donors to win re-election. They definitely know that they risk not receiving these needed contributions in the future if they don't vote as their donors expect them to vote.

As a consequence, even when judges don't think the contributors' views should win out in a particular case, they still may feel pressure to vote as their contributors want. Rather than worry about losing campaign contributions for the next election fight, justices may cover their bases and vote a little differently than they otherwise would, biasing themselves toward their contributors' views. A former chief justice of the Tennessee Supreme Court explained that "whether subtle or unintentional or not, there may be a tendency in the future for appellate judges to have one eye looking over their shoulder."[28] This *biasing* effect means justices would decide cases differently than they otherwise would, or differently than the applicable law directs, because they need to account for their re-election interests. If biasing occurs, then the judges' decisions will match up with their donors' preferences again.

In the past, we observed that either causal pathway means campaign donors ultimately get the policy results they wanted.[29] Money in this sense buys its preferred outcomes whether it does so by installing the right judges into office or whether it does so by biasing judges into doing what it wants. We assume both happen, but for now, we present the best, and perhaps only convincing, empirical evidence that at least *some* biasing seems to be occurring.

To understand our analysis, we have to first explain a little bit of social science methodology. The difficulty in figuring out whether any biasing is occurring is something social scientists call "endogeneity." As we explained, if biasing is happening, then justices' votes would align with their campaign donors' interests. The justices become biased toward the donors' interests, with an eye toward attracting donations for the next election, and thus decide cases in their favor. The donors then contribute to those justices. Campaign money and judicial decisionmaking match up.

However, the same statistical pattern could happen even if there is no biasing and only selection. Selection also would explain the close relationship between campaign money and judicial decisions if donors give their money to justices who were already going to decide in their favor. Donors thus give their money to these justices and keep doing so election after election, because they are confident that the justices will do what they prefer. Assuming the donors are right, the justices' decisions line up with the donors' interests, and again, there will be a close relationship between money and subsequent decisions. How can we tell, based on the same data, whether selection or biasing is happening?

One study by Morgan Hazelton, Jacob Montgomery, and Brendan Nyhan provides a clue. They looked at North Carolina Supreme Court candidates before and after the state adopted public financing for judicial races.[30] The advantage of this study is that they could see if removing the reliance on campaign finance contributors would affect candidates' decisions on the bench. What they found, in short, was that, after they were able to opt into public funding, justices became less favorable toward attorneys who had previously donated money to them. Two justices favored their donors less after they knew they would no longer need them for campaign finance support in their next election. A third justice seemed unaffected by the change to public funding. This study therefore suggested that the North Carolina justices were affected by re-election concerns before public funding—the biasing effect—but that this effect largely disappeared after justices knew they didn't need to curry favor with their donors anymore.[31]

While this study provided some very useful information, it was also limited. It studied only six justices, all in one state, whose tenure spanned the years before and after the state switch to public funding. As a result, it's hard to evaluate whether this tells us a lot about the influence of money, or just describes something peculiar about a handful of judges in North Carolina. Still, it's a good clue about what's going on and helps us introduce how we later try to tease apart the selection and biasing effects by looking at lame duck justices, who, like the North Carolina justices, were no longer reliant on their campaign finance donors for re-election.

A few other larger studies tried to control for judges' predispositions in order to isolate the direct influence of campaign funding from selection effects. For example, Damon Cann found evidence that, after controlling for judges' ideology, campaign contributions still have a biasing effect on judicial voting in the Georgia Supreme Court.[32] This suggests that campaign contributions seem to have some added influence beyond what each judge's natural ideological profile would predict. Other studies have examined whether campaign funding from a source *opposite* a judge's ideology can cause the judge to *deviate* from their usual tendency. For example, Damon Cann, Chris Bonneau, and Brent Boyea employ a matching research design to identify judges with the same ideological predispositions but differing campaign contributions to see if they have different voting patterns as a result of campaign financing. Their study found statistically significant differences in voting and therefore significant evidence of contributions' biasing influence on judicial voting, at least in the Michigan Supreme Court.[33] Similarly for the Texas Supreme Court, Madhavi McCall found that judges who were ideologically predisposed to vote in favor of defendants were significantly more likely to support the plaintiff if they had received contributions from the plaintiff's side.[34] So, these studies find that campaign money can blunt judges' natural ideological tendencies if it comes from the other side of the political spectrum.

Both biasing and selection effects are empirically plausible and likely explanations for the relationship between campaign contributions and judicial decisions. It is not only likely that both occur, but also that they reinforce each other. The fact that judicial candidates must fundraise and please voters to win elections and become judges attracts a certain type of candidate in the first place. Candidates who mind fundraising less and are more amenable to cultivating a network of contributors have advantages and are more likely to run for judge than candidates who abhor fundraising and playing to the crowd.

And these types of candidates, as other empirical work demonstrates, tend to be more ideologically extreme and predictable. As a result, a system of electing judges is likely to draw a set of judges and judicial candidates who are more ideologically extreme and predictable to suit contributors' tastes, and more conscious of fundraising and re-election concerns, than an appointive system. So, we do not think biasing and selection are mutually exclusive. One being true doesn't falsify the other. Indeed, both explanations are likely and make up parts of the big picture.

However, in this chapter, we try to prove that biasing, apart from selection, *is* a significant part of the story. There are important reasons we would want to know that campaign finance biasing of judges is occurring, apart from and perhaps in addition to selection effects. One simple reason is that most experts, lawyers, and judges think that biasing is more problematic than selection.

Remember that selection effects mean judges decide cases in line with their contributors' interests because contributors have done a good job of predicting in advance which candidates will do what they want. These candidates, once on the bench, simply decide cases as their contributors expected, and thus their decisions align with their contributors' preferences. This doesn't necessarily mean these judges are doing something wrong.

It is possible these judges believe in good faith and practice a judicial philosophy toward cases that their contributors know will lead to their preferred outcomes. Under this theory, the judges are deciding cases as they believe is correct under the law, and it just happens to match up with what their contributors want. The judges themselves, in this view, are not changing their views based on campaign finance or re-election considerations. This is simply favorable selection of judges from the perspective of their contributors.

Now, this theory of selection is somewhat naïve. You might think that selection is the reason campaign money lines up with judicial decisions but have a dimmer view about how it works. You might assume that judicial candidates, before they even decide to run, know what views they need to espouse to attract campaign financing. Some candidates know their views won't attract enough fundraising and therefore never run for office. Candidates with views hostile to contributors' interests might therefore get weeded out before the field of candidates is even set. Remember that Marsha Ternus, with whom we began the book, said she wouldn't want to be a judge if it meant she had to fundraise and campaign. In contrast, other candidates want to be judges under these conditions and know they need to bend toward their contributors' preferences, regardless whether these reflect their own true views.

Campaign finance therefore skews the *selection* of candidates who run at all, let alone who wins once the field of candidates is set. We know, for instance, that campaign fundraising tends to favor more ideologically extreme candidates over moderate centrist ones. Under this view, campaign contributors get their way through selection of a preferred set of judges who favor their preferences. Money skews the set of possibilities from the outset and gets what it wants.

That said, *biasing* effects might be even worse than this dim view of judicial selection. Remember that biasing effects would result if judges, once already in office, change how they decide cases with campaign finance and re-election considerations in mind. Judges know how they think their cases should be decided but nonetheless change or otherwise adjust their decisions to ingratiate themselves with campaign donors. This is a big problem for the rule of law. Judges should decide cases correctly rather than bending the law to curry favor with contributors. Under a theory of selection effects, at least the judges are deciding cases the way that they think is correct under the law. Under a theory of biasing, though, judges are deciding cases differently, *incorrectly* in some sense, rather than what they would otherwise think the law indicates. Judges do their jobs differently in favor of their contributors so they have a better chance of winning re-election and keeping their jobs.

Of course, we cannot say for sure whether judges consciously decide cases in favor of contributors with this re-election calculus front of mind. Certainly, the anecdotal evidence about and from judges suggests strongly that they are aware of the relationship between their decisions, campaign contributions, and their chances of re-election (the proverbial crocodile in their bathtub, as we have discussed). But we cannot peer into judges' heads and know whether they actively bias their decisions in favor of contributors, or if they only subconsciously change their decisions toward contributors' interests, without acknowledging it to themselves.

Regardless, if biasing is an important part of why campaign money matters so much, it indicates a different set of fixes to remedy the problem. If selection is the root of the problem, then it suggests that the basic idea of electing judges doesn't work well. Money buys the candidates it wants from the start, and that's why the money lines up with later judicial decisions by those candidates once in office. The problem, then, is the election process for which campaign money is so important to filtering out candidates and ensuring that certain candidates win in the first place, from the very start.

However, if the problem is less about selection and more about biasing, then the problem is not simply judicial elections as a general matter. If campaign money matters because judges are too concerned about re-election, then we might not need to do away with judicial elections altogether. It might turn out that judges need money to get elected in the first place, but they do a fair and professional job as judges once in office. The problem instead could be biasing. Judicial decisions line up with campaign money because judges care prospectively about the money they need for the next election and curry favor with future contributors for that reason. Then, if the possibility of re-election is removed, incumbent judges would no longer have these biasing incentives, leaving them free and able to judge properly. The fact of their initial election would not necessarily bias them. Re-election, not election, would be the problem. So, taking re-election off the table, by limiting judges to a single term in office, would free judges from this biasing effect that is responsible for the link between campaign money and decisions.

LAME DUCK JUDGES AND WHAT THEY TELL US ABOUT JUDICIAL BIAS

"Lame duck" justices are legally restricted from winning another term because they will hit mandatory retirement age under state law before their current term ends. They therefore know at the very start of this final term that they will not be able to run again for re-election. For these justices, there is no point currying favor with campaign donors for the next election since there is no next election for them. Re-election is off the table. Lame duck justices therefore are free to decide as they want without worrying about campaign donors or attracting campaign contributions the way that other justices must.

Biasing, as we have explained above, doesn't make any sense when it comes to lame duck justices. If lame ducks decide cases as their campaign donors want, even with re-election off the table, then it must be because their donors picked the right horses, not anything to do with re-election or biasing. If so, then these lame ducks must be so ideologically committed to deciding cases the way that their donors prefer, despite the fact that they no longer need to. Selection thus would explain why their last term decisions still line up with their donors' preferences—the donors picked justices who will decide cases as they wanted, and this didn't change when the justices were no longer eligible for re-election.

As a consequence, we look at these lame duck justices in their final term to see if there remains a statistically significant relationship between campaign fundraising and their decisionmaking.[35] If lame ducks vote the same way during their final term as other justices awaiting their next re-election, then it suggests that donors are effectively picking the right justices, whose ideological preferences dictate decisions all the way through the lame duck term until retirement. Justices would be voting true to their ideological commitments and wouldn't vote any differently during their final term.

But if biasing is at least part of the story, then we would expect a different statistical pattern in decisions during their final term. We would expect to see the lame ducks behaving differently in their last term, because they no longer have re-election to worry about. Lame ducks aren't subject to the temptation of biasing themselves for re-election or campaign finance purposes. They might finally be free to judge cases as they see them, without concerns about how it affects their re-election chances. If biasing helps explain the relationship between money and judicial decisions, then the lame ducks will vote differently in their final term than other justices and appear less affected by money.

When we've looked at the data in the past, we found that lame duck justices *do* vote differently than other justices when it comes to campaign money and judicial decisions. Lame ducks basically did not seem affected much by campaign money.[36] Their campaign contributions weren't as correlated or predictive of their voting during their final term. We found this to be true for business group contributions and lame duck voting on business cases. Unlike other justices, at least partisan elected ones, the lame duck justices in their final term display much less or no influence of money on judicial voting in favor of business. Likewise, unlike other justices, lame duck justices in their final terms don't seem as affected by campaign money from the major party coalitions. Democratic Party coalition money doesn't pull their judicial decisionmaking to the left, nor does Republican Party coalition money pull them to the right.

The same is true again for election cases. Lame duck justices no longer displayed greater partisan loyalty in election cases as a function of campaign money once they reached their final term. In fact, if anything, campaign contributions from the Republican coalition actually seemed to *decrease* partisan loyalty by Republican justices in their final term, while Democratic money had no effect at all. The connection between campaign money and judicial decisionmaking virtually disappeared when we looked at lame duck justices in their final term. Re-election, or more precisely the absence of any chance of re-election, matters a lot.

These striking results for lame duck justices inspired this book, and we will expand quite a bit on these results in the next section of this chapter. For now, though, there are a couple lessons we want to underscore before continuing.

First, the lame duck evidence tells us that biasing is *at least part* of the story of campaign money's influence on supreme court justices. We wouldn't argue that selection doesn't matter at all. In fact, we think selection does matter. Probably campaign donors are smart about where their money goes and focus their giving on candidates already predisposed in their direction. But the lame duck evidence indicates that biasing occurs too, and in a significant and robust way. Perhaps candidates bend toward monied preferences in the first place to attract money and only feel freer to judge as they see the law once the pressure to fundraise is gone. The need to fundraise may bias the whole field of potential candidates from the outset. This would be hard to detect unless you look at our lame duck justices.

Just as important, it seems that sitting justices may be, consciously or unconsciously, voting differently to attract campaign money and improve their re-election chances, at least until they reach their final term. This possibility of outright biasing, of justices not voting as they see the law but to boost their re-election prospects, is more worrisome than selection. Selection effects are inherent in judicial elections where we know wealthy donors will push the system toward their preferences by throwing campaign money behind preferred candidates. That comes with the territory. However, even fans of judicial elections could be worried by justices who vote according to their campaign contributors' preferences out of fear about the next election. As bad as selection may seem, electing justices who are biased by campaign money is even worse.

Second, the lame duck evidence suggests that re-election worries exert a lot of pressure on justices and deeply affects their performance. Reformers who are concerned about money in judicial elections often excoriate competitive elections for judges and want to replace judicial elections with appointments. Competitive judicial elections can be undignified free-for-alls and draw judicial candidates into posturing, fundraising, and mudslinging as we see with candidates for other offices. However, at least when it comes to the influence of campaign money, our lame duck findings suggest that it may be *re-election*, not election, that is the greater problem. When elected justices are freed from re-election pressure, campaign money doesn't seem to affect them nearly as much, regardless of how undignified and pressure-packed the initial election process was that put them there. Re-election, and the pressures it puts on justices, needs a lot more attention.

Why is re-election so influential on judges and how they do their job? The next re-election weighs heavily on supreme court justices because they worry about losing their jobs. Remember that re-election to the state supreme court is no certainty. Supreme court elections have become more professionalized, partisan, expensive, and heated over the years. Political professionals and campaign finance contributors eventually realized that state supreme courts have a big impact on state policy and have been increasing their investment in supreme court elections. As one union official put it, "We figured out a long time ago that it's easier to elect seven judges than to elect 132 legislators."[37]

Campaign money matters for re-election. More money is a necessary and valuable resource for candidates, especially when re-election looks like it will be competitive and uncertain. So it's no surprise, once you think about it, that justices would be affected by campaign finance considerations. We hate to suggest that justices would care so much about re-election and campaign finance that it would change how they decide matters of justice, but it shouldn't be shocking if it turns out to be true as an empirical matter.

It's important to remember that justices care about campaign fundraising because it helps win re-election, not because they get to keep the money for their own personal use. Campaign fundraising is useful only because it helps justices fight off challengers and get their message to the public. Justices aren't affected by campaign finance contributions because they are greedy people. They can't use campaign money to buy a new house or car for themselves but instead value it only because they need it to keep their jobs. As political scientist Bruce Cain once reminded, "51 percent of the vote dominates an infinite amount of campaign money."[38] In other words, re-election is the goal, and campaign money is only a means (albeit a very useful means) to that goal, not an end in itself.

For this reason, the need to raise campaign money disappears once judges are no longer running for re-election. They should care about campaign fundraising only because they are worried about re-election. When the possibility of re-election is removed, campaign money is no longer a motivation.

A DEEP DIVE INTO LAME DUCK JUDGES AND JUDICIAL BIASING

We empirically examine whether lame duck justices on state supreme courts vote differently from justices still eligible for re-election. Judges who face mandatory retirement under state law—our lame ducks—know from the start of their final term that they are not eligible for re-election. When re-election is taken off the table for them, so are the re-election incentives to bias their decisionmaking. They simply have no re-election to worry about, nor any campaign contributors to satisfy.

We focus on these lame duck judges here and think our results are the best, most comprehensive empirical evidence to date establishing that elected judges are biased by re-election fundraising concerns rather than by selection effects alone. Judges in their last term are significantly less inclined to vote in favor of their campaign donors' interests, when controlling for other factors. This sudden shift in a judge's final term suggests that it's re-election and the need to raise campaign funds that biases judges to vote in favor of their contributors' interests earlier in their careers.[39]

Figure 4.1 shows the thirty-two states that have mandatory retirement laws compelling judges to retire sometime between ages seventy and ninety.

By examining the voting of judges in their last term before mandatory retirement, we can test whether judges continue to favor their contributors' interests when they no longer need to attract campaign funds. If lame duck judges continue to favor their contributors' interests in the same way, it would suggest that selection is largely responsible for their voting. In other

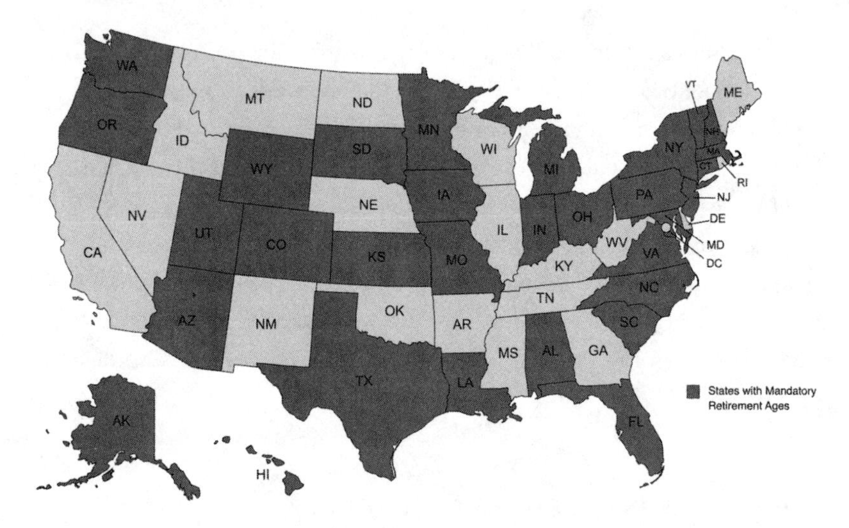

FIGURE 4.1 States with Mandatory Retirement. Source: Data collected from websites of individual state judicial systems and National Center for State Courts, "Mandatory Retirement Ages," https://cdm16501.contentdm.oclc.org/digital/collection/judicial/id/308.

words, it would indicate that elections produce judges that are predisposed to favor their contributors' interests, and those judges continue to vote in that way even when they are retiring. In contrast, if judges' support for their contributors' interests is significantly weaker during their lame duck period, it would support a biasing theory that the need to raise future campaign funds drives judges' voting in favor of contributors' interests.

To explore the degree to which judges are influenced by the prospective need for campaign financing in future elections, we compiled a new dataset of judicial decisions and judge characteristics. Our dataset of judicial decisions consists of the decisions of over 650 state supreme court justices in over 3,000 business-related cases decided between 2010 and 2012 across all fifty states.[40] We supplemented these data with both institutional variables that describe aspects of the judicial system of each state and with detailed information about each judge's background and career.

The sample of cases that we analyze includes cases between a business litigant and a non-business litigant. Our analyses focus on business cases for several reasons. First, data availability: Business cases make up almost one-third of the cases before the state supreme courts, making them a big part of what state supreme courts do and a major reason why contributors care about supreme court elections.

Second, an analysis of judges' votes in business cases and contributions from business groups to those judges is likely one of the best ways to study the relationship between campaign finance and judicial decisions. Compared to other interest groups, business groups typically have more substantial resources to devote to judicial campaigns. Indeed, over the past two decades, business groups have been among the largest direct contributors to judicial campaigns and have dominated interest group spending on television campaign advertising.

Third, business groups typically have a focused agenda and clearer preferences than other interest groups. Business groups generally favor pro-business, pro-tort reform judges and decisions that tend to limit plaintiffs' recoveries in lawsuit damages. By contrast, the plaintiffs' bar in many states is typically more diverse in their economic interests because they represent a larger range of clients. The magnitude of contributions from business groups and clarity of business groups' preferences provides an ideal case study to empirically isolate the influence of money on votes.

Although we focus on business cases and business contributions, we nonetheless believe that our results have important implications for all wealthy campaign donors. Any contributor that is able to marshal sufficiently large campaign contributions likely exerts similar influence over the judiciary. We therefore think our results generalize beyond business cases and contributions, as we've already found in some of our other studies that we discussed in the previous chapter.

The ideal way to determine whether judges vote differently when they no longer have to worry about raising campaign funds for future elections would be to collect years of data on specific judges' votes over their careers. For example, if we had multiple years of voting data both from periods when judges were facing re-election and from their mandatory last term, we could track exactly how a judge's votes change when retention is off the table. This is what social scientists would call a longitudinal design, or a panel study. Unfortunately, this presents a difficult task because each judge has a unique career path, including different election dates and mandatory retirement terms, which would demand an immense amount of data gathering to collect enough non–lame duck and lame duck votes. Data on state supreme courts is collected by the year, and even a single year of data requires extensive case analysis and coding to quantify votes. Thus, the most ideal longitudinal analysis is not currently feasible.

However, our data does include some judges who entered their lame duck period during the 2010 to 2012 period we studied. For these judges, we have data both on the votes cast during a term when they were eligible for re-election and on the votes cast during their subsequent final term as a lame duck. Now, we don't have data for that many votes—only 318 votes from six judges—so we shouldn't read too much into our results, but they are consistent with our suspicions. During the periods in which these judges were facing re-election and raising campaign funds, they voted for the business litigant 55 percent of the time. But when they entered their lame duck period and no longer had to worry about raising funds from businesses, they voted for the business litigant only 52 percent of the time. Again, these results are from only a few judges and are not statistically significant, but this mini longitudinal analysis does show a decrease in judges' favoring business litigants.

For the primary empirical tests, though, we employ a rigorous statistical analysis using multiple regressions to measure the relationship between campaign contributions from business groups and judicial decisions in business cases. A regression analysis isolates the relationship between the dependent variable (in our case, judges' pro-business votes) and each of the explanatory variables that we describe below. In this way, our analyses can separate the influence of money on judges' voting from, say, the judges' ideology or the underlying state law. For our technically inclined readers, we describe our regression methodology further in the Appendix.

The dependent variable in our analyses is whether a judge voted for or against the business litigant in a given case. A judge is coded as voting for a litigant if the judge voted to make the litigant any better off, regardless of whether the judge voted to reverse a lower court or to change the damage award. Our large sample of cases allows us to measure the relationship between contributions from business groups and judges' voting for business litigants over a wide range of cases. We know that the outcomes of most individual cases in our analysis have little, if any, impact on most companies as a general matter. And not every vote for a business litigant is necessarily an instance of pro-business bias. This statistical noise makes our job in analyzing the data harder because even a meaningful correlation might be drowned out. However, if we still find an empirical relationship in our data despite this noise, our study will be even more convincing because we will have found a strong enough statistical relationship that we can detect it through all the noise.

The main explanatory variables that we focus on in our analysis involve the dollar value of campaign contributions from business groups in each judge's most recent election.[41] Our measure of business group contributions aggregates the contributions from several different sectors that are generally supporters of pro-tort reform and pro-business judges: agriculture, communications, construction, defense, energy, finance, real estate and insurance, health care, transportation, and a general business category. To test the role of mandatory retirement on the relationship between campaign money and judicial decisions, we add an interaction term between this measure of business contributions and an indicator variable for whether a judge is in their lame duck term. An interaction term reveals how the relationship between business contributions and voting differs for lame duck judges versus judges facing re-election.

In our analysis we also include a number of control variables that help us rule out other explanations for our results. Before we can say that campaign finance money influences judges' decisions, our control variables measure the effect of and thereby account for other influences on judicial decisionmaking. The control variables we include fall into three categories: judge-level variables, state-level variables, and case-level variables. All these variables may influence how a judge votes in a given case. That is, a judge's vote may be partly determined by their own characteristics, such as ideology; partly determined by state characteristics, such as the conservatism of the state's laws; and partly determined by case characteristics, such as which litigant appealed to the state supreme court. The control variables are again described in more detail in the Appendix.

Table 4.1 provides descriptive statistics for each of the variables we include in our analysis.

TABLE 4.1: Descriptive Statistics of Variables in Regression Analysis

Variable	*Mean*	*Standard Deviation*
Pro-Business Vote	0.49	0.49
Business Contributions	$84,790	$234,855
Non-Business Contributions	$196,443	$397,244
Retention Election Indicator	0.31	0.46
Nonpartisan Re-election Indicator	0.32	0.47
Partisan Re-election Indicator	0.14	0.35
Democratic Judge Indicator	0.41	0.49
Republican Judge Indicator	0.43	0.50
State Tort Climate	-0.043	0.46
Citizen Ideology	60.9	17.1
Government Ideology	51.9	14.1
Business Petitioner Indicator	0.48	0.50
Case Strength	-0.02	44.0

HOW MUCH DOES MONEY MATTER ONCE RE-ELECTION IS OFF THE TABLE?

We perform several different analyses to determine how the prospective need for campaign funds influences judges. First, we explore the baseline relationship between contributions from business groups and judges' voting in business-related cases. Figure 4.2 reports the marginal effect of business contributions on the likelihood of a judge casting a pro-business vote, holding all other control variables equal.[42] The figure shows that increasing business contributions are associated with an increase in the likelihood of judges casting pro-business votes. The more money contributed by business, the more likely the average judge will vote in favor of the business litigant in a case.

However, the relationship in Figure 4.2 can be explained by either selection effects or biasing effects of campaign funding. As we discussed, it's possible that greater contributions are related to pro-business votes because business groups happen to fund judges who are more likely to vote in favor of business interests in the first place. Alternatively, the relationship could be explained by judges who are biased in favor of business interests in hopes of attracting future business contributions.

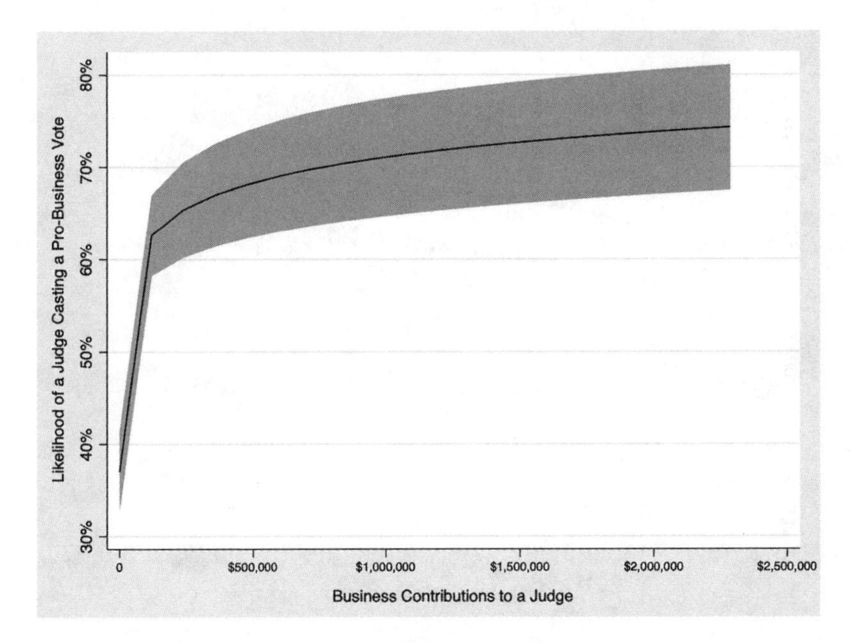

FIGURE 4.2 Relationship between Business Contributions and Pro-Business Votes.

To tease apart selection from biasing, we can check whether judges become more likely to vote for business litigants as their next election draws nearer. Prior studies have found that the behavior of elected judges does in fact change in response to an impending retention event; judges deviate from earlier voting patterns, impose longer criminal sentences, and side with the majority in death penalty cases as re-election approaches.[43] That said, it is not clear that judges should increase their voting in favor of business interests only as their next election approaches, because business groups seem likely to consider a judge's full voting record whether or not their voting became more pro-business toward the end. Perhaps re-election becomes more significant to judges it approaches because they are thinking about it more frequently or actively fundraising at the time. Whatever the reason, re-election appears to become more salient to justices as re-election time draws nearer and poses a bigger influence on them as it does.

We find that campaign finance money carries more weight with judges as the next election approaches. Figure 4.3 reports the difference in the marginal effects of business contributions on the likelihood of a judge casting

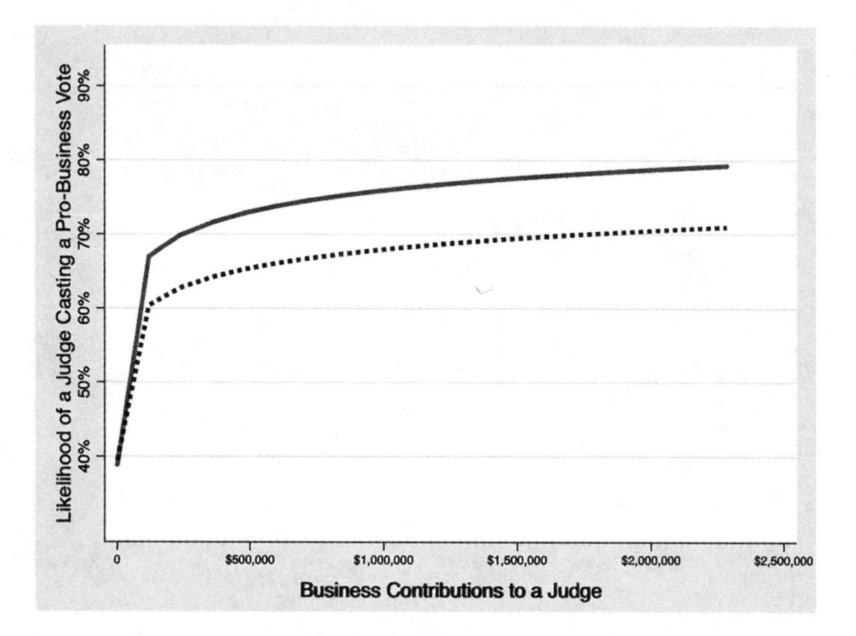

FIGURE 4.3: Business Contributions and Pro-Business Votes as Retention Election Approaches.

a pro-business vote for judges with fewer than two years until their next election versus judges with two or more years until their next election.[44] The figure shows that, although there is a relationship between business contributions and pro-business votes throughout a judge's term, contributions are associated with a greater increase in the likelihood of pro-business votes in the two years prior to a judge's re-election.

Figure 4.3 shows that money is associated with an increased likelihood of pro-business votes prior to a judge's next election. However, to further explore the degree to which judges are influenced by the prospective need for campaign financing in future elections, we next examine whether judges who cannot run for re-election are, as a result, freed from campaign finance concerns.

Table 4.2 presents the results of an estimation measuring the role of mandatory retirement on the relationship between business campaign contributions and pro-business votes.[45] We report only the results of the campaign contribution variables and interaction terms for brevity; the full results, again, are reported in the Appendix. Because of our empirical

TABLE 4.2 Business Contributions and Votes: Impact of Mandatory Retirement

	Percentage increase (or decrease) in the likelihood of a judge casting a pro-business vote
Doubling of Business Contributions for *Non–lame Duck Judge*	33.8%*
Doubling of Business Contributions for *Lame Duck Judge*	17.3%*
Doubling of Non-Business Contributions for *Non–lame Duck Judge*	-21.2%*
Doubling of Non-Business Contributions for *Lame Duck Judge*	-7.6%*
# of observations	9,920

methodology, the results should be interpreted as the percentage increase (or decrease) in the likelihood of a judge casting a pro-business vote if the business campaign contributions to that judge doubled.[46]

The results in Table 4.2 indicate that a doubling of business contributions is associated with a 33.8 percent increase in the likelihood of a judge who is not in their mandatory last term casting a pro-business vote. However, for lame duck judges, this increase is cut approximately in half; a doubling of business contributions is associated with only a 17.3 percent increase in the likelihood of a lame duck judge voting for the business litigant. Similarly, while a doubling of contributions from *non*-business sources is associated with a 21.2 percent decrease in the likelihood of a non–lame duck judge casting a pro-business vote, the doubling is associated with only a 7.6 percent decrease in a lame duck judge's likelihood of voting for the business litigant. The differences in the likelihood of voting for business litigants between lame duck judges and non–lame duck judges are statistically significant.[47]

These results support the biasing theory: The need to obtain future campaign support influences how judges vote. Without the pressure to be reelected and raise money, campaign contributions are less likely to influence the judicial decisions of lame duck judges. In other words, when mandatory retirement liberates judges from future campaign fundraising concerns, the money they raised has a much weaker influence on how they vote. Money still matters, but judges have much more freedom to judge when the possibility of re-election is removed.

ARE THERE OTHER EXPLANATIONS FOR WHY CAMPAIGN MONEY HAS LESS INFLUENCE ON LAME DUCK JUDGES?

Before we can confidently conclude that judges are biased by campaign finance and re-election pressures, we need to rule out some plausible counter-explanations for why lame ducks defy the usual relationship between votes and money. Although our previous analysis used lots of control variables to isolate the role of campaign contributions from other influences, we still want to make sure that there's not something special about lame duck judges that explains our results. It might be that lame duck judges differ importantly in other ways that complicate our conclusions. We use the following robustness checks to rule out the possibility that other differences are the reason for our results.

To illustrate what we're talking about, we know lame duck judges nearing retirement are older, on average, than non–lame ducks. Given that fact, perhaps older judges are affected less by campaign finance money for any number of reasons. They have shorter careers ahead of them and may care less about job security when retirement is approaching. Or, perhaps older judges are more set in their ways and care less about campaign funders' preferences. If older judges are different than younger ones in ways that affect judicial decisionmaking, and lame ducks are older than non–lame ducks, perhaps then our finding of a significant difference between lame ducks and non–lame ducks above is really more about age than the absence of re-election prospects. This is what social scientists and statisticians would call a confounding variable. In this hypothetical, it's the confounding variable of old age that actually explains why lame ducks don't seem biased by campaign finance money.

To test this and other possible confounding variables, we perform a series of what are called "robustness checks" to make sure that differences other than re-election pressures aren't accounting for our lame duck results. These robustness checks rule out other possible explanations, like old age, for the contrast between lame duck judges and non-retiring judges. By eliminating counter-explanations, we are left with only one logical explanation for the difference between lame duck and non-retiring judges: When judges no longer need to raise campaign funds or run for re-election, campaign finance has less influence on how they vote.

DOES MONEY MATTER LESS TO OLDER JUDGES?

Our first robustness check focuses on the influence of the judges' age on the relationship between business contributions and pro-business votes, basically testing the hypothetical we mentioned above. Because lame duck judges are generally older than other judges, it is possible that age accounts for the differences between these groups. Perhaps, as judges age, either their ideological preferences shift away from business interests, or they become less concerned with attracting or maintaining future campaign funds.

We control for the age of each judge in two ways. First, we include each judge's age as a control variable to isolate the influence of age from the influence of mandatory retirement. Second, we take advantage of the fact that eighteen states do not have mandatory retirement ages. That is, in eighteen states, there are older judges not facing mandatory retirement who are approximately the same age as older judges facing mandatory retirement in thirty-two other states. Controlling for our usual explanatory variables, the only factor that differs between these two sets of older judges is whether they will need to attract future campaign funds. Thus, to restrict our analysis to judges of a similar age, we include in our second robustness check only judges over age sixty.[48]

Table 4.3 reports the results of the campaign contribution variables from both robustness checks that control for the influence of age. The first column shows that, even when age is included as a control variable to isolate its influence, lame duck judges respond differently to campaign contributions than non–lame duck judges do. A doubling of business contributions is associated with a 32 percent increase in the likelihood of a judge who is not in their mandatory last term casting a pro-business vote, but the doubling is associated with only a 15.6 percent increase in the likelihood of a lame duck judge voting for the business litigant. This difference is statistically significant. When controlling for age, the influence of contributions from non-business sources is also weaker for lame duck judges compared to non–lame duck judges. In fact, the relationship between non-business

TABLE 4.3 Business Contributions and Votes: Robustness Check for Age

	Percentage increase (or decrease) in the likelihood of a judge casting a pro-business vote	
	Age included as an explanatory variable	*Estimation sample restricted to judges over age 60*
Doubling of Business Contributions for *Non–lame Duck Judge*	32.0%*	30.7%+
Doubling of Business Contributions for *Lame Duck Judge*	15.6%*	17.6%*
Doubling of Non-Business Contributions for *Non–lame Duck Judge*	-20.4%*	-19.3%*
Doubling of Non-Business Contributions for *Lame Duck Judge*	-6.3%	-6.2%
# of observations	9,651	6,707

contributions and pro-business votes is statistically insignificant for lame-duck judges, suggesting that the money doesn't have a statistically reliable influence on lame-duck judges' voting.

The second column in Table 4.3 shows that, even when we restrict our analysis to judges over age sixty, older lame duck judges are different from older judges not facing mandatory retirement. For older judges who do not face mandatory retirement, a doubling of business contributions is associated with a 30.7 percent increase in the likelihood of a judge casting a pro-business vote. In contrast, for older judges in their mandatory last term, a doubling of business contributions is associated with only a 17.6 percent increase in the likelihood of voting for the business litigant. Again, the difference in the influence of money on lame duck and non–lame duck judges is statistically significant. Non-business contributions follow a similar pattern: A doubling of non-business contributions reduces the likelihood that an older non–lame duck judge will cast a pro-business vote by 19.3 percent. In contrast, the doubling of non-business contributions does not have a statistically significant relationship with the pro-business voting of lame duck judges, suggesting that the money doesn't have any systemic influence on these judges' voting.[49]

This robustness check shows that the weaker influence of money on votes for lame duck judges cannot be explained by the age of these judges. Even when we control for older age, campaign contributions have a different effect on lame duck judges than on judges not facing mandatory retirement. The need to obtain future campaign support influences how even older judges vote.

IS THERE SOMETHING SPECIAL ABOUT STATES WITH MANDATORY RETIREMENT?

Next, we perform a robustness check to see whether there is something special about states with mandatory retirement that explains the relationship between campaign money and judicial decisions. Perhaps states with mandatory retirement for judges also happen to have particularly business-friendly law or other things that increase the likelihood of judges there voting in favor of business litigants, relative to other states without mandatory retirement.

We would be very surprised if we found states with mandatory retirement to be very different from other states. As we showed earlier in Figure 4.1, states with mandatory retirement ages are quite representative of the country. They are not concentrated in a particular region and do not seem to be distinctive in any obvious way. However, Table 4.4 does show that states utilizing mandatory retirement are more likely to use merit selection to select judges and retention elections to retain judges. Similarly, states without a mandatory retirement age are more likely to use nonpartisan elections. But our robustness check will see whether the big differences between lame duck judges and other judges remains the same when we limit our analysis to only the mandatory retirement states.

Table 4.5 reports our results for just the thirty-two states with mandatory retirement ages. Compared to the nationwide results, the differences between lame duck judges and non–lame duck judges in mandatory retirement states are even more pronounced. A doubling of business contributions is associated with only a 16.9 percent increase in a lame duck judge's likelihood of voting for the business litigant, but a 37.8 percent increase in the likelihood of a judge not in their mandatory last term casting a pro-business vote. Similarly, a doubling of campaign contributions from

TABLE 4.4 Number of States with Different Selection and Retention Methods

	States with Mandatory Retirement Age	*States without Mandatory Retirement Age*
	Method of Selection	
Gubernatorial/Legislative	5	2
Appointment Merit Selection	16	5
Nonpartisan Election	5	8
Partisan Election	6	3
	Method of Retention	
Gubernatorial/Legislative Reappointment	6	2
Retention Election	14	5
Nonpartisan Re-election	5	8
Partisan Re-election	5	2
Permanent Tenure	2	1

TABLE 4.5 Business Contributions and Votes: Unique State Features Robustness Check

	Percentage increase (or decrease) in the likelihood of a judge casting a pro-business vote
Doubling of Business Contributions for *Non–lame Duck Judge*	37.8%*
Doubling of Business Contributions for *Lame Duck Judge*	16.9%*
Doubling of Non-Business Contributions for *Non–lame Duck Judge*	-26.5%*
Doubling of Non-Business Contributions for *Lame Duck Judge*	-9.8%*
# of observations	6,249

non-business sources is associated with only a 9.8 percent reduction in the likelihood of a lame duck judge voting for the business litigant, but a 26.5 percent reduction in the same likelihood for a non–lame duck judge. The differences between the voting of lame duck judges and non–lame duck judges are statistically significant.

These results confirm that the relationship between campaign contributions and votes cannot be explained by differences among states with mandatory last terms and those without. In fact, when we restrict our sample to states with mandatory retirement, there appears to be an even greater difference in how lame duck judges vote compared to their counterparts not facing mandatory retirement.

DO ALL JUDGES IN THEIR LAST TERM VOTE THE SAME WAY?

Finally, we test whether lame ducks behave differently from other judges who are also in their final term, but for reasons other than mandatory retirement. Judges may leave their position because they are appointed to another job, because of an illness or death, because of a voluntary retirement, or because they are not reappointed or lose a re-election. While all of these events result in a judge serving their last term, they are different from mandatory retirement. When judges face mandatory retirement under state law, they know for certain they will no longer need to attract campaign funds. By contrast, most other events that cause a judge not to serve another term, such as death, incapacity, or losing a re-election bid, are at least a bit more uncertain at the start of a judge's final term in office. As a result, we would usually expect business contributions to continue influencing pro-business votes for judges who are in their last term for any reason other than mandatory retirement.

Table 4.6 reports the results of estimations that separately compare the voting of judges not in their last term to two different sets of judges: (1) judges who are in their last term because they are voluntarily retiring and (2) judges who are in their last term for any reason other than mandatory retirement, including voluntary retirement, illness or death, appointment to another job, and a failed retention. For judges who are not in their last term, a doubling of business contributions is associated with about a 25 percent increase in the likelihood of a pro-business vote. However, for judges in their last term for a reason other than mandatory retirement, the likelihood of pro-business voting increases to about 45 percent. Thus, compared to non–last term judges, the relationship between campaign contributions and votes actually becomes *stronger* for judges in their last term for any reason other than mandatory retirement. In contrast, the results for lame duck judges reported back in Table 4.2 showed that the relationship between business contributions and pro-business votes became weaker for lame duck judges compared to non–lame duck judges.

Similarly, while a doubling of contributions from non-business sources is associated with about a 15 percent decrease in the likelihood of a non–last term judge casting a pro-business vote, the doubling is associated with a 27 percent decrease in pro-business voting for judges in their last term for a reason other than mandatory retirement. By contrast, Table 4.2 reported that the relationship between non-business contributions and voting against the business litigant was weaker for lame duck judges compared to non–lame duck judges.

Our earlier results show that, when lame duck judges know they will not seek retention or need to attract campaign funds because they face mandatory retirement, campaign contributions have a far weaker influence on their voting. This last robustness check actually shows that when judges are in their last term for any other reason, contributions actually have a stronger influence on those judges. Unlike lame duck judges, many of these

TABLE 4.6 Business Contributions and Votes: Robustness Check for Other Last Term Judges

	Percentage increase (or decrease) in the likelihood of a judge casting a pro-business vote	
	Last term because of voluntary retirement	*Last term for any reason other than mandatory retirement*
Doubling of Business Contributions for *Non–Last Term Judges*	24.7%*	24.5%*
Doubling of Business Contributions for *Last Term Judges*	45.8%*	45.3%*
Doubling of Non-Business Contributions for *Non–Last Term Judges*	-15.5%*	-15.2%*
Doubling of Non-Business Contributions for *Last Term Judges*	-27.0%*	-26.9%*
# of observations	9,920	9,920

judges don't know they are serving their last term. They are likely to assume the possibility of re-election remains on the table and still have incentives to vote in favor of contributors' interests to serve their fundraising needs.

Why does the influence of campaign money increase for certain retiring judges? Perhaps campaign donors help out certain retiring judges after they leave the bench, and, if true, this might explain the stronger influence money has on them. It is hard to know what's really going on here without a lot more investigation. Regardless, the important takeaway from this robustness check is that mandatory retirement, and not simply serving in one's last term, reduces the relationship between campaign money and votes. For our purposes, we can safely conclude here that lame duck judges in their final term again behave differently than all other judges.

WHAT HAVE WE SHOWN?

Our solution to the methodological challenges of establishing campaign finance's biasing influence on judges is to focus on lame duck judges in their final term. We look at elected state supreme court justices in the final term they are allowed by law and compare them with other justices who still are eligible for another re-election. Generally speaking, we find that campaign contributions are significantly correlated with judicial decisions in favor of the contributors' interests. However, for lame duck justices in their final term, campaign money has a much weaker influence. We then go on to consider and rule out empirically a bunch of the likeliest counter-explanations for why lame ducks defy the usual influence of money. Elected justices who are no longer eligible for re-election, and know so in advance, are liberated from much of the influence of campaign finance considerations and have more freedom to judge.

Our results provide powerful evidence that biasing is at least a very important part of the story of campaign money's influence on supreme court justices. Once seated, judges bend toward monied preferences as they worry about campaign fundraising for their re-election. They become freer to judge once the pressure to fundraise is gone, and much of the effect of campaign money, anywhere from one-third to half of the predictive relationship in our data, withers away. Our results suggest that the biasing effect is significant. The need to obtain future campaign support influences how judges vote. And when judges no longer have to worry about getting re-elected or raising campaign funds, the money they have raised in past elections has a smaller impact on how they vote.

To be clear, we find that the effect of campaign money doesn't completely disappear for lame duck judges. This doesn't surprise us, because as we've explained, campaign donors likely channel their money to candidates who are inclined to agree with their views and decide cases as the donors hoped and anticipated. In other words, selection effects play a role in campaign money's influence. But our results also show that selection effects play a lesser role than most critics of judicial elections might think and certainly don't explain the whole story.

Moreover, as we discuss in the next, final chapter, the evidence that re-election concerns exert critical pressure on judges has important implications for reforms. Reformers concerned about the effect of money in judicial elections often condemn competitive elections in favor of appointments. To be sure, competitive elections can be undignified and pressure-packed. However, our lame duck findings suggest that it's judicial re-elections, in contrast to the original election, that are the bigger problem. When elected judges no longer have to worry about re-election and currying favor with potential donors, the campaign money they've raised in the past has a much weaker influence on how they vote. Re-election, and the pressures it puts on judges, needs more attention in the conversations about reform.

5 HOW TO FIX JUDICIAL ELECTIONS AND CAMPAIGN FINANCE

THE PROBLEM OF CAMPAIGN MONEY in judicial elections is a pervasive and growing threat to equal justice. We've shown here that campaign money as an influence on judges' decisionmaking is not just overblown hype. Of course, there's a lot of attention to the rising spending on judicial campaigning, the increasing politicization of the judicial election process, and how hyperpartisanship in American politics is creeping into how we select our state judges. However, we've documented empirically, both in our own work and that of other scholars, that campaign money does bias judges and how they decide their cases. Campaign money sways judges to decide cases in the favor of their financial donors, and the problem is growing as donors spend more and more money on judicial elections. Judges and the public are right to suspect, as they do, that money buys favorable outcomes in our current system of judicial elections.

We've shown that the connection between campaign money and judicial decisions is not just coincidence. As we acknowledged at the outset of this book, donors channel their contributions and spending to judicial candidates who are ideologically predisposed to decide cases as the donor prefers. So, it's not a surprise that elected judges decide cases as their donors might want. But importantly, we establish empirically here, using massive amounts of data from state supreme courts and elections, that judges are actually biased by campaign money in how they decide cases. It appears that judges decide cases differently than they otherwise would because they need to curry favor with donors and raise campaign money from them to get re-elected.

We focus on lame duck judges to help tell our story. Lame duck judges, who are ineligible for re-election and therefore are freed from fundraising concerns, decide cases as if campaign money has little influence on them. We want to underscore this lesson from the book—when we take away the need to fundraise for re-election, campaign money seems to have a much smaller influence on how judges decide cases. The effect of money doesn't go away entirely, but if we're looking for a way to fix the problem of campaign money in judicial elections, this is as close to a magic bullet as we're likely to find. We need to get rid of re-election incentives on judges if we want them not to be as influenced by money.

Each previous chapter in this book began with a vignette about a state supreme court justice who ran and won a statewide election and experienced the campaign finance pressures that come with that achievement. The judges in this book braved those pressures to do their job with integrity. And we think most judges try very hard to serve justice and decide cases in an unbiased manner. The judges are not the bad guys in this story by any means. Instead, the system places pressures on judges that make it harder for them to do the jobs they intend to do. We can honestly say that every judge with whom we've spoken, for this book and otherwise in our work, acknowledged these pressures inherent in the system.

Re-election pressures ultimately affect how cases are decided whether judges are consciously aware of those influences or not. The judges didn't ask for big-money elections and all these pressures. Indeed, almost every judge we know would prefer a different system where campaign money and re-election pressures played a minimal role. We advocate for a reformed system that might free judges from these pressures and allow them to judge without re-election incentives playing such an influential force.

In this final chapter, we focus on this next step, on normative payoffs—judicial election reform. People who share our concerns about the influence of money on judicial elections often advocate for abolition of judicial elections and replacing them with appointment systems. We're not opposed to getting rid of judicial elections and turning to judicial appointment. After all, getting rid of judicial elections would get rid of campaign finance because there would be no election campaigns to run. But as we'll explain, we think judicial elections are not the real problem—judicial re-election is. And judicial elections, after all, are very popular with the public and unlikely to go away soon.

So, we focus on reform possibilities that largely retain judicial elections as the method of judicial selection but remove the incentives for judges to position themselves for re-election. We want to get rid of judicial re-election, not necessarily elections altogether. There are a number of ways to get there. We review many of them here. Ultimately, though, we recommend as the most promising path forward judicial elections, at least for state supreme court, with a long single term limitation and without the possibility of re-election or reappointment.

CAPERTON V. MASSEY AND THE RE-ELECTION PROBLEM

Caperton v. Massey is the most important judicial campaign finance case of the last fifty years. It presents such illustrative facts that have made it the poster child case for anyone worried generally about campaign finance, much less campaign finance specifically for judicial elections. We've discussed the case already, but we return to it once more because of its centrality to our concerns. We think it's important to highlight what the Supreme Court got right about campaign finance, but even more important to highlight what it got wrong. It tells a lot about what we should do next to fix the problem.

Remember that Don Blankenship spent $3 million on campaign support to elect Brent Benjamin to the West Virginia Supreme Court while an appeal of a $50 million jury verdict against his company Massey Coal Co. was pending. Benjamin won election and then cast the decisive vote in a 3–2 decision overturning that verdict on appeal. Blankenship later bragged to his girlfriend, in a taped conversation uncovered in a criminal prosecution that sent Blankenship to prison for mining safety violations, that "[he] won . . . [and] saved Massey $70 million."[1] (Indeed, the jury verdict had ballooned to $70 million with accrued interest by the time the appeal was decided.) The plaintiffs in the case appealed the West Virginia court's decision all the way to the United States Supreme Court, which unexpectedly heard the case. Hugh Caperton and the other plaintiffs argued that Benjamin should have recused himself from the case because Blankenship's extraordinary financial support for Benjamin's election raised "the probability of actual bias on the part of the judge . . . too high to be constitutionally tolerable."[2]

In analyzing the constitutional merits, the U.S. Supreme Court analogized the due process problem to the facts in *Tumey v. Ohio*, the classic statement of the law for judicial recusal. The Supreme Court cited the maxim that "no man is allowed to be a judge in his own cause; because his interest would certainly bias his judgment, and, not improbably corrupt his integrity."[3] The problem in *Tumey* was that a village mayor was serving as the judge in cases where he received a salary supplement only if he convicted the defendants. He was essentially paid out of fines imposed upon his convicted defendants, but he would not be paid his supplement if the defendants were acquitted and, as a consequence, no fines were assessed. The Court sensibly found that the arrangement violated due process because, among other things, the judge had a "direct pecuniary interest in the outcome."[4] The Court explained that the "temptation to the average man as a judge . . . which might lead him not to hold the balance nice, clear and true between the State and the accused, denies the latter due process of law."[5]

The analogy to *Caperton* was obvious. In both *Tumey* and *Caperton*, the judge had a financial interest in deciding the case a certain way, whether or not the law supported that result. In *Tumey*, the judge had financial incentive to convict defendants so he would be paid personally for his work. He faced a conflict of interest that compromised the defendants' right to a fair hearing under the law, what we call due process in constitutional law. In *Caperton*, the judge benefitted personally from Blankenship's financial generosity to his campaign effort and had a personal incentive to reciprocate that generosity. As the Court explained it, someone in the judge's position would feel "a debt of gratitude to Blankenship for his extraordinary efforts to get him elected."[6]

The Court acknowledged that there had been no proof, indeed not even an allegation in the case, that Benjamin had engaged in any formal quid pro quo with Blankenship. That is, no one accused or tried to show Benjamin and Blankenship had explicitly agreed that Benjamin would reciprocate Blankenship's earlier generosity by deciding the case in Blankenship's favor. The Court nonetheless reasoned that Blankenship's "significant and disproportionate influence" in getting Benjamin elected, coupled with the timing of the election and Blankenship's case, presented a realistic concern that Benjamin's impartiality would be compromised in a case involving Blankenship.[7] The Court reasoned "there is a serious risk of actual bias—based on objective and reasonable perceptions—when a person with a personal stake in a particular case had a significant and disproportionate influence in placing the judge on the case."[8]

After Blankenship had spent $3 million to get the judge, Benjamin, elected to the West Virginia Supreme Court, it was only natural, the Court concluded, that Benjamin would feel the tug of reciprocity and indebtedness in deciding his case. Benjamin violated due process of law by failing to remove himself from taking part in Blankenship's case, given their history and relationship, which threatened to compromise his objectivity. The U.S. Supreme Court reversed the West Virginia Supreme Court's decision and sent the case back for new proceedings without Benjamin taking part.

We think the U.S. Supreme Court correctly decided the *Caperton* case. Our research, which we've described in this book, supports exactly what the Court suspected: Campaign contributions influence judges' subsequent decisionmaking by biasing them measurably in the contributors' favor. Even if Benjamin never agreed to reciprocate Blankenship's support by deciding in his favor, many judges in Benjamin's position do end up deciding in favor of their contributors' interests, whether they do so consciously or not. This is true despite the fact that most judges don't think their own objectivity is compromised by election and campaign finance considerations.

What's more, the namesake plaintiff in the case, Hugh Caperton, quite reasonably wondered, when seeing Benjamin deciding his case, "How in the world is this fair?"[9] Even if Benjamin's objectivity hadn't been affected by his relationship with Blankenship, it was reasonable for Caperton to worry that it was and feel he was treated unfairly in the case. We can't say that Benjamin himself was biased in his decision for his former campaign supporter in Caperton's case, but we can say that judges as a general matter in this type of scenario behave as if they are biased, deciding disproportionately in favor of the supporters' interests.

However, our empirical research also identifies a complication with the Court's reasoning in the *Caperton* case. Of course, we agree that campaign finance support biases judges and think that the Court was right to find Caperton's due process rights were violated when Justice Benjamin participated in the case. That said, the Court's reasoning for its decision highlights an important distinction that we try to make in our research and underscore here in the book: We think judges are affected more by their *future* campaign finance needs than by gratitude for *past* campaign finance support.

The Supreme Court's justification for finding a due process violation in the case seemed to be grounded in a theory that Justice Benjamin's objectivity might be biased by indebtedness to Benjamin and a desire to reciprocate Benjamin's past support. As the Court put it, the plaintiff's theory was that "Justice Benjamin would nevertheless feel a debt of gratitude to Blankenship for his extraordinary efforts to get him elected."[10] Such an instinct on Benjamin's part, the Court explained, might be "strong and inherent in human nature."[11]

Indeed, social science research establishes that the human impulse for reciprocity is extremely powerful.[12] As another West Virginia justice told the *New York Times* at the time, "It's very hard not to dance with the one who brung you."[13] This understanding explains why so many observers suspect that the influence of campaign finance on officeholders operates through this instinct to repay past favors, especially important ones that helped put officeholders into the prestigious jobs they hold. The Court seemed to base its decision, in important part, on this theory of "retrospective gratitude" in *Caperton*.[14]

We find, though, that the Court is wrong to focus so much on retrospective gratitude rather than forward-looking, *prospective* bias in judicial campaign finance. The human impulse for reciprocation may be strong, but we found that it matters less than one might suspect in judicial decisionmaking. Retrospective gratitude should be the same for all elected judges, lame duck or not, if it ever is. Indeed, gratitude perhaps should be even stronger for lame ducks, many of whom have been elected more than once with the repeated help of their supporters. But we find that lame ducks don't exhibit the same bias toward their contributors' interests. When judges are legally prohibited from running for another term and have no re-election pressures to consider anymore, our results show that these lame duck judges do not display bias in their contributors' favor. Retrospective gratitude doesn't bias them, and the usual effect of campaign money on their decisions seems largely to fall away. Gratitude therefore doesn't offer a great explanation for why judges usually are so biased toward their contributors when it has little impact on lame ducks who ought to be just as grateful for past support and feel the same pull of reciprocity. Even Don Blankenship observed, before *Caperton* was decided, that "politicians don't stay bought, particularly ones that are going to be in office for 12 years."[15]

Our research on lame ducks highlights instead the importance of *prospective* re-election considerations. The Court puts too much emphasis on retrospective gratitude in *Caperton* and not enough on how the need to run for re-election in the future, and raise campaign money to do so, might bias judges. Justice Benjamin might be tempted toward bias in favor of Blankenship in the *Caperton* case, not because of backward-looking gratitude, but a forward-looking need to raise money for the next election. Like almost all elected judges, Justice Benjamin would've known he needed to win re-election to keep his job for another term. And as Justice Scalia wrote, judges can't mount "judicial campaigns without funds for campaigning, and funds for campaigning without asking for them."[16] Given that Blankenship had been Benjamin's biggest supporter by far in the last election, it would have been natural to anticipate Blankenship as a potentially enthusiastic and generous supporter of Benjamin's re-election.

Under these circumstances, might Benjamin have been careful not to alienate Blankenship if he could avoid it? Even if re-election considerations didn't drive Benjamin's decision in favor of Blankenship, it would have been reasonable for Hugh Caperton to wonder if they biased Benjamin at all against him. Indeed, we find that judges in Benjamin's position often do seem to decide cases in ways that favor their contributors' interests. And they do so mainly when re-election is a possibility; the lame ducks don't seem similarly affected. Re-election seems to be the crucial consideration in these calculations, whether conscious or not. It was reasonable for the Court to worry, in setting constitutional expectations, that judges generally might be so affected by re-election and their future campaign finance needs, regardless of whether Benjamin himself was.

Our colleague, the constitutional law scholar Marty Redish goes even further than we do along these lines. He argues that *any* requirement that judges be re-elected or reappointed violates the Constitution. Redish contends that "as long as a judge knows that the voting public, legislature, or executive holds the power to remove her as a result of her decisions on the bench, the very real possibility exists that she will—if only subconsciously—shape those decisions in a manner designed to win their favor."[17] This risk that judges will bend their decisions to the preferences of whoever decides whether they keep their jobs "presents a threat to due process 'too high to be constitutionally tolerable.'"[18]

Redish therefore considers unconstitutional any mechanism, whether competitive re-election, retention election, or executive or legislative reappointment, where judges might contemplate how their decisions could affect their prospects for continuing as a judge. He would declare unconstitutional, as a result, the current retention processes for forty-seven of fifty state supreme courts and virtually all state lower courts. Similarly, an amicus brief in *Caperton* predicted that the Court's ultimate ruling in the case would make "extraordinarily difficult for states" to hold judicial elections, not just re-elections, and throw judicial elections as a general matter into constitutional trouble.[19]

We don't need to go so far here as Marty Redish does, but we agree that a fix for money in judicial elections starts with identifying retention incentives as the root of the problem. The question is, if we don't go quite so far as throwing out judicial elections altogether, how do we fix the problem?

WHAT'S HAPPENED SINCE *CAPERTON*?

Unfortunately, the Supreme Court's decision in *Caperton v. Massey* didn't fix the problem of campaign finance's biasing effect on judges. Chief Justice Roberts worried in dissent that the decision would swamp the courts with recusal motions, all based on similar claims of bias that "inevitably lead to an increase in allegations that judges are biased, however groundless those charges may be."[20] Roberts observed that the facts of *Caperton* weren't so extreme, compared to other judicial campaigns, in terms of spending or spending's impact on the election outcome. As a consequence, Chief Justice Roberts complained that the *Caperton* decision would produce an overreaction to judicial campaign finance. As he put it, "I believe we will come to regret this decision as well, when courts are forced to deal with a wide variety of *Caperton* motions, each claiming the title of 'most extreme' or 'most disproportionate.'"[21] Judges would be forced to constantly consider recusal based on campaign spending and perhaps even be forced actually to recuse under the authority of the Court's decision in *Caperton*.

We agree with Roberts on his former point that the facts of *Caperton* weren't so extreme. As we described earlier, there are plenty of state supreme court races where campaign spending rivals what we saw in Brent Benjamin's 2004 election. It was not such an extreme example of modern judicial campaign finance that we can dismiss or marginalize it as a one-time event. As we see it, though, that's actually the bigger problem. The Court's decision in *Caperton* simply acknowledges the reality that our research substantiates: Campaign spending is extremely high and politicizing, which has resulted in measurable judicial bias, conscious or subconscious, in favor of campaign contributors' interests.

However, it turns out that Chief Justice Roberts's latter worry that *Caperton* would lead to an overreaction to judicial campaign finance hasn't panned out at all. A recent decade-long study of the decision's impact concluded that "those prognosticators who predicted that *Caperton* would have little impact on the judiciary were correct."[22] Litigants weren't able to use the decision to overturn judicial judgments. Indeed, there were only twenty-one reported cases in the decade following the decision where litigants even made *Caperton*-based recusal claims. In only one of those twenty-one cases did the court find that a judge should've recused himself for campaign finance reasons like those in *Caperton*.

And only a handful of states meaningfully revised their recusal rules for judges after *Caperton* to account for campaign finance considerations. New York announced a rule that no case should be assigned to judge who received $2,500 or more in the preceding two years from the lawyers or parties.[23] New York, though, was the exception. According to the Brennan Center for Justice, even five years after *Caperton*, twenty-two of thirty-nine states that held judicial elections still lacked any guidelines for judicial recusal based on campaign spending.[24] Most states that actually revised their recusal standards did so only by adding campaign finance spending as a consideration, among many, within their flexible guidelines for recusal. Several of those states made clear that recusal would be required only in "extraordinary circumstances."[25]

What's more, we haven't seen a big shift to new campaign finance rules for judicial elections either. In fact, since *Caperton* was decided in 2009, two states that had public financing for judicial elections, Wisconsin and North Carolina, have actually since *repealed* public financing systems, after Republican majorities captured the state legislatures in those states. Only one state has adopted a system of public funding for judicial elections since *Caperton*: West Virginia. Despite some litigation over certain provisions of the system, Allen Loughry became the first supreme court justice in the state to opt into public funding and win election in 2012.

West Virginia, however, is the lone recent example of a state reforming campaign finance rules for judicial races after *Caperton*, and currently, there are no additional states where public financing is under serious consideration for new adoption. *Caperton*, in other words, has changed judicial campaign finance law hardly at all.

We support campaign finance reform and think it might help mitigate the problems of money in judicial elections. If new rules properly regulate the amounts of money spent in judicial elections and promote transparency, we agree that they could help reduce the overall influence of campaign money on judges.[26] One of us has written extensively about campaign finance law along these lines.[27] A problem for campaign finance reform, though, is that the U.S. Supreme Court under Chief Justice Roberts is increasingly hostile to campaign finance regulation under the First Amendment and has struck down a wide range of such regulations since *Citizens United*.[28] Indeed, a Wisconsin Judicial Task Force explained in its report that it chose not to address campaign finance regulation in its discussion of judicial independence because of the Supreme Court's hostility to regulation and "declined to tilt at campaign reform windmills."[29] Campaign finance reform is a good idea, for judges and other politicians, but it's tough sledding as a matter of constitutional law, and it's probably not enough by itself.

As a consequence, the problems that the Supreme Court identified in *Caperton* and that we substantiate here—that elected judges are affected by campaign finance considerations and may bias their decisions in favor of their contributors—really haven't been addressed since *Caperton*. The story remains the same despite that decision. Elected judges who face reelection in the offing still have a crocodile in their bathtub looming over their campaign finance needs, and thus their decisions on the bench. Litigants still are right to worry that these judges will be influenced by campaign finance considerations and be biased toward those who have or may make contributions (and biased against those who haven't or likely won't).

Indeed, Brent Benjamin's subsequent career after *Caperton* illustrates the risks for elected judges who don't cater to their supporters well enough. The aftermath of the case, involving the Benjamin's later re-election bid, opposed by his former supporters, tells us even more about judicial campaign finance and elections than most people realize. The facts of *Caperton* are reasonably well known, but its aftermath is hardly known at all, even by scholars of campaign finance law. Originally the beneficiary of big-money judicial campaign finance, Brent Benjamin eventually saw the politics of judicial elections turn decisively against him when it was time twelve years later for him to run for re-election.

After initially helping his campaign patron Don Blankenship escape a $50 million verdict in *Caperton*, Benjamin actually disappointed his election backers with his subsequent decisions. Remember that Benjamin seemed genuinely convinced that Blankenship's support wasn't critical to his 2004 election. Blankenship himself sensed little gratitude after the election from Benjamin, who didn't thank Blankenship in his victory speech and claimed afterward that he never asked Blankenship for money.[30] Chastened later by the U.S. Supreme Court's decision in *Caperton*, Benjamin recused himself in all cases involving Massey.[31] So, Brent Benjamin wasn't going to help Massey Corporation anymore, at least not directly in its own litigation.

Worse, from his former supporters' perspective, Benjamin disappointed conservatives in several key cases deeper into his judicial term as a supreme court justice. In one case, Benjamin cast a decisive 3–2 vote to grant standing to drug addicts to sue pharmacies and doctors allegedly involved in exacerbating their addiction. As one lawyer put it, "Conservative business people, who are mostly Republicans, expected that after [Benjamin] got elected that he would rule their way all the time, and he hasn't done that. In a couple of high-profile cases, he voted, I think the business community would say, the wrong way."[32] A conservative group formerly run by Gregory Thomas, the Republican operative who introduced Benjamin to Blankenship and ran Blankenship's 527 organization, pivoted to mobilize *against* Benjamin's re-election in 2016. This new group, West Virginia Citizens Against Lawsuit Abuse, campaigned against him and claimed that "[n]early every organization that supported his election in 2004 now supports other candidates."[33]

Benjamin could no longer draw upon these past supporters to finance his re-election campaign in 2016. Benjamin acknowledged at a conference at University of Virginia Law School, shortly before the 2016 election, that he "underestimated" the campaign finance complications of running for judicial office. He admitted that he had been "tone deaf" in refusing to recuse himself in the *Caperton* case itself.[34] These were remarkable admissions from the former poster child for big-money judicial campaign finance. But Brent Benjamin's supreme court career demonstrated the dangers of the crocodile in the bathtub when elected judges don't decide cases as their supporters expect. Benjamin was proud of his record, establishing a new business court, as well as drug and veterans' courts in West Virginia, and deciding cases on the merits in ways that might upset his former supporters. Arguably, he ended up having an admirable supreme court career as justice, despite the rocky start. But the people and politics who put you into office can be the same ones that punt you out of office unless you serve their interests on the bench. The crocodile might eat you if you don't continue to feed it raw meat.

Benjamin, ironically, turned in 2016 to the new public financing system in West Virginia for judicial candidates. Benjamin explained that "from a personal standpoint, I made the decision I could not judge cases and then know that my campaign committee was going to those very same people appearing in front of me . . . asking for money."[35] The system had been established in the wake of the *Caperton* case, as a potential remedy for the problems of big-money judicial elections that Benjamin's earlier election in 2004 had surfaced.

Now, alienated from his former support, Benjamin applied for public funding, and his former allies-turned-enemies fought to knock him out of office. They recruited Republican lawyer Beth Walker to challenge him, and the Republican State Leadership Committee donated more than $2 million to her campaign effort.[36] They spent more than $3 million on campaigning to push Walker to election victory in a multi-candidate 2016 race where almost $5 million total was spent.[37] Benjamin, with his half million in public funds, received just 12.47 percent of the vote in fourth place. As he told us later, "I do not regret my decision to use public financing... but sadly I don't think one can win that way unless all candidates in a race do it."

Brent Benjamin had once been a cautionary tale for anyone concerned about big-money judicial campaign finance and how wealthy campaign donors could influence legal outcomes by throwing around their enormous wealth in judicial elections. Twelve years later, Benjamin served as a different sort of cautionary tale, though an equally powerful one. Judges who alienate their boosters, even for the best of reasons, risk losing their support and then ultimately their jobs in their next re-election bid.

SO, WHAT CAN WE DO ABOUT THE BIASING EFFECT OF JUDICIAL CAMPAIGN MONEY?

One major reform that would transform everything is to abolish judicial elections. Getting rid of judicial elections would get rid of judicial campaign finance. To paraphrase Justice Scalia once again, if we didn't have judicial elections and instead chose state judges a different way, then we wouldn't have judicial campaigns. If we didn't have judicial campaigns, judges wouldn't have fundraising or campaign contributors to worry about. As a result, abolition of judicial elections is a popular reform proposal that many critics of judicial campaign finance advocate. Get rid of judicial elections altogether, and we solve the problem of judicial campaign finance in the process.

Former U.S. Supreme Court Justice Sandra Day O'Connor famously made it her cause after her retirement from the Court to replace competitive judicial elections and address the problem of judicial campaign finance. As she put it, judicial elections have fed the "serious problem that so many people in our country think that judges are just politicians in robes."[38] And the even bigger worry was that, in her view, "in some states, perhaps that's what they are."[39] Although O'Connor's criticisms of judicial elections went beyond campaign finance, she nonetheless blamed campaign finance for politicizing the state judiciary. She explained that "elections have become big business in many parts of our country. Every judicial race brings a flood of money from partisan groups."[40] For that reason, O'Connor wanted "to see the states move in the direction of the federal judicial system" where judges are appointed, not elected, and don't have to campaign or raise money for an election bid. She put it bluntly about judicial elections: "They're awful. I hate them."[41]

Justice O'Connor was hardly alone in her arguments against judicial elections. The American Bar Association (ABA) formally opposes the use of judicial elections as well. The ABA explained that "increasingly expensive state judicial campaigns focus on narrow issues of intense political interest, contributing to the public's perception that judges are influenced by their contributors."[42] The Conference of Chief Justices criticized state judicial elections as "high-dollar free-for-alls marked by dueling campaign salvos by organized interest groups, often located outside the state of election."[43] The American College of Trial Lawyers, Michigan Bar Association, New York State Bar Association for American Progress, U.S. Chamber Institute for Legal Reform, and Brennan Center for Justice, among others, have criticized and advocated for the abandonment of judicial elections at the state level.

If we got rid of judicial elections, how would we instead choose our judges? Some form of appointment system would be the obvious replacement. As we explained earlier, states used to rely on political appointment, by the governor or legislature (or both), to select state judges. A handful of states still select judges by initial appointment for either lifetime terms or periodic reappointment. More importantly, the federal system offers a ready model for comparison between state methods of judicial election and the federal appointment of judges that critics like Justice O'Connor often cite.

At first glance, the federal system appears to address all our concerns about re-election and campaign finance influences. Federal judges are nominated by the president and confirmed by the Senate to lifetime terms under Article III of the U.S. Constitution. Judges don't have to run for office, campaign, or raise money for campaigning. And once appointed to the federal bench, they sit for a lifetime, unless they choose to resign their seat or are impeached. So, federal judges should be totally free to judge.

The problem with abolishing state judicial elections, most basically, is that it's not going to happen. Judicial elections, in one form or another, have been the dominant method for selecting state judges in the United States since the nineteenth century, and no state has dropped judicial elections in more than forty years. To our knowledge, currently no state is even seriously considering getting rid of judicial elections wholesale, or specifically for their state supreme court. States that have modified their judicial election system have generally moved at most to a hybrid of merit selection. In fact, some of the aforementioned groups critical of elections actually advocate a shift to merit selection, where judges are initially appointed but run for reappointment in yes-or-no retention elections without challengers.

Why have states not abolished judicial elections and moved back to appointment? Simply put, judicial elections are very popular with the public. A supermajority of Americans approves of electing judges notwithstanding concerns about campaign finance. National surveys find roughly two-thirds of Americans prefer judicial elections over gubernatorial appointment of state judges.[44] State-level surveys find similar public opinion in states weighing judicial election reform.[45] For instance, roughly three-quarters of North Carolinians support direct election of judges by voters and disagree with the idea that "appointing judges is better than electing them."[46] Similarly, 70 percent of Missouri voters support judicial retention elections, with 80 percent of Missourians believing that these elections are an effective way to hold judges accountable.[47]

Voters enjoy wielding the power to select and reject their state judges. Even if voters generally re-elect incumbents and vote along partisan lines in judicial elections, regular voters seem to think judges require electoral discipline and are not so different from other elected politicians in this respect. As the ABA recognized almost twenty years ago and has proved correct since then, "support for judicial elections remains entrenched in many states" such that reform suggestions are better served in looking for ways to improve judicial elections rather than do away with them altogether.[48] Indeed, since then, no state has abandoned judicial elections for state supreme court. What's more, in South Dakota and Nevada, voters actually rejected ballot measures that would've replaced judicial elections with merit selection consistent with the ABA's recommendations, and they did so by overwhelming margins. Legislative bills proposing merit selection to replace judicial elections likewise failed in Texas, Louisiana, Washington, and Minnesota.

More fundamentally, abolition of judicial elections is unpopular with voters without necessarily making the selection process less political or prone to political influence. Any form of judicial selection brings its own form of politics and sources of bias, whether it's partisan judicial elections, merit selection, gubernatorial appointment, or other plausible alternatives. As Marty Redish explains, for every form of judicial selection, "judges owe their appointment to someone or some group."[49] No form of judicial selection, in other words, is perfect. Judges initially appointed by the governor owe their jobs to the governor and their shared political party relationships. Judges appointed through merit selection owe a debt not only to those players, but also the group constituting the state selection commission, usually tied to the state bar association.

The point here isn't that these different forms of judicial selection are illegitimate, or that there aren't better or worse systems for selecting judges. However, we should be conscious of the fact that, when it comes to judicial selection, there must be some method of selection, and every method of selection brings with it a nontrivial degree of political patronage and indebtedness.

Take, for example, the presidential appointment of federal judges. Federal judges under Article III of the U.S. Constitution are appointed by the president, with the advice and consent of the Senate, and serve lifetime tenure during good behavior. Lifetime appointment provides a secure measure of political insulation from pressures for judges once on the bench, because they aren't accountable to anyone after appointment and keep their jobs for life. However, when it comes to the initial selection and appointment of candidates for the federal bench, the process is still intensely political and competitive. Many attorneys would like to serve as federal judges, and only those with political capital with the major parties, especially the president's party, will merit serious consideration for selection.[50] What's more, even nominees favored by the president will survive the Senate confirmation process and receive a positive vote only if they have sufficient political support and avoid disqualifying opposition, with the help of political allies and fellow partisans.

The federal appointment and confirmation process is, in its own way, just as politicized as state judicial elections. *CQ Roll Call* investigated the campaign finance contributions of judicial nominees over the last decade and found that both Democratic nominees under President Obama and Republican nominees under President Trump made significant contributions to their respective parties' lawmakers.[51] More pointedly, three of every five federal judges appointed over the period had made political contributions specifically to senators sitting on the Senate Judiciary Committee, which oversees the confirmation process.[52] Senior federal judge John Walker, Jr., declared in an article published by the *Atlantic* that "the nomination and confirmation process for federal judges is broken."[53] Both parties now try to block the opposition's judicial nominees on ideological grounds, in what has become open warfare on judicial appointments.[54] Although partisans have different perspectives on the partisan fray, the confirmation process reached a modern low in terms of partisanship when Republican Senators refused even to grant a hearing, much less a confirmation vote, to Democrat Merrick Garland, who was nominated by President Obama for the Supreme Court in March of the 2016 election year.[55] The open seat, as a result, was not filled by President Obama and remained vacant until Obama's successor, Republican President Donald Trump, began his term by nominating Neil Gorsuch and thereby maintained a Republican majority on the Supreme Court. Trump extended that majority by naming Amy Coney Barrett to replace Justice Ruth Bader Ginsburg only months before the end of his presidential term.

Given the magnitude of each U.S. Supreme Court appointment, it is no surprise that big money politics and campaigning now invades the federal confirmation process. Of course, Senate confirmation differs from state judicial elections. There is no traditional public campaigning by the candidate, and ultimately the U.S. Senate confirms presidential nominees, rather than a state's voters choosing a judge through an election. As such, the nominees themselves do not fundraise or produce their own ads like state supreme court candidates.

However, the political parties, their politicians, and allied interest groups actively campaign to influence public opinion and affect the confirmation process in the Senate.[56] After spending $27 million on ads to block Merrick Garland's nomination,[57] Judicial Crisis Network led conservative groups in support of Neil Gorsuch's confirmation to fill the vacant seat and itself committed more than $10 million to the nomination.[58] A year later, Brett Kavanaugh's confirmation effort drew even more money, including $12.3 million in media ad spending from Judicial Crisis Network alone.[59] By Amy Coney Barrett's rushed confirmation in 2020, big spending by affiliated groups was not only unsurprising but expected and commonplace. Judicial Crisis Network reportedly spent $6.3 million over five weeks on national television ads,[60] in addition to millions from other similarly minded groups.[61] Nor does the trend of big money campaigning to affect the federal nomination process stop with Supreme Court appointments; it now covers lower-court appointments as well.[62]

In short, getting rid of judicial elections is probably not politically feasible in the short term, and the most obvious substitute of executive appointment doesn't offer a perfect solution, even when it comes to money's influence. Luckily, our research suggests quite a bit of hope for reform by other more modest means. Our research tells us that judicial elections aren't inherently bad when it comes to the influence of campaign money. Our research also provides answers about how we can fix the problem of campaign money and judicial bias without necessarily getting rid of judicial elections altogether. If we listen to the data, we have some possible solutions.

HOW DO WE MAKE JUDICIAL ELECTIONS BETTER?

If there's anything you take away from this book, it should be that campaign money appears to influence elected judges, but mainly when they have to run for re-election. Judges aren't irredeemably corrupted by campaign fundraising and judicial elections to win their seat. Instead, elected judges appear to be biased in their decisionmaking on the bench mostly by their need to raise money for their re-election. The influence of money is prospective, looking forward to re-election, rather than retrospectively looking backward to their debts and gratitude for money contributed to their last election. This insight, based on the data we've collected and presented here, tells us a lot of what we need to know for effective reform of judicial campaign finance and elections.

When judges don't have re-election to worry about, the biasing influence of money largely goes away. So, how do we reform judicial elections with respect to these biases? We should get rid of judicial *re-election*. When judges are no longer eligible for re-election, and therefore don't need to worry about raising money for their re-election campaigns, they make different decisions that no longer seem biased in favor of their contributors. Removing the prospect of re-election changes judicial decisions and seems to debias judges from the influence of money.

We can remove the prospect of re-election in different ways, which we'll discuss. But we emphasize that the particular way we remove re-election is less important than that we do so in some way. As we'll recommend, one way to get rid of re-election is to limit judges to a single term. Judges might have to run a campaign and win a judicial election to gain office, but once in office as an incumbent, they could be prohibited from running for a second term. Like our lame duck judges facing mandatory retirement, all judges would be legally ineligible for re-election and therefore freed from campaign finance pressures as judges. Another way of getting rid of re-election would be to give state judges lifetime tenure, like federal judges. Once elected to office, they wouldn't need to be re-elected to retain their jobs. They would serve for life, subject to removal only for misconduct. Once again, this would mean no re-election worry and therefore no campaign finance–related bias.

Obviously, another way to get rid of judicial re-elections is to get rid of judicial elections altogether as means of selecting judges in the first place. If we switch to, for instance, gubernatorial appointments for judicial selection and do away with judicial elections, we obviously wouldn't have judicial *re*-elections either. The important thing to underscore is that we don't need to go that far. We've already conceded that getting rid of judicial elections wholesale would be politically unlikely. Voters prefer judicial elections, and no state in a long while has come close to entirely getting rid of them.

Fortunately, our research tells us that getting rid of judicial elections altogether is probably not necessary. If we're focused on the biasing effect of campaign money on judges, our findings show that judges who win office through judicial elections aren't irretrievably corrupted by the election process, as ugly as elections may seem to many. From that finding, we conclude that judicial elections are not inherently corrupting. Elected judges who aren't facing re-election, like our lame ducks, aren't terribly influenced by their past fundraising and campaign finance activity. When they don't have to worry about re-election, they don't seem affected by gratitude toward past donors or by a perceived need to reciprocate past favors. So again, judicial *elections* themselves are not the main source of the problem. It's judicial *re-elections* that we should focus on and eliminate. We don't need to get rid of judicial elections altogether, at least when it comes to reducing bias from campaign money.

We view this realization as critical to realistic reform. To the degree we're hung up on the evils of judicial elections in toto, we lose focus on what gives political money its main influence over judges and run headlong into public resistance to abolishing elections altogether. Judicial elections, at least when it comes to the influence of money, *aren't* all bad. Elections and campaign fundraising don't necessarily compromise judicial integrity, as we show. Not only is it unlikely that we could get rid of judicial elections wholesale, we also don't think we need to.

Instead, we need to get rid of judicial re-elections. In this book, for the first time in the commentary and literature on judicial elections, we provide the empirical substantiation for this nuanced insight. While newly supported here, we think the insight itself is intuitive and probably one that others share. For all the focus on getting rid of judicial elections, even the ABA observed that "the worst selection-related judicial independence problems arise in the context of judicial reselection."[63] When judges need to win another election to keep their jobs, "it is then that judges may feel the greatest pressure to do what is politically popular rather than what the law requires."[64]

As we noted earlier, our colleague Marty Redish goes even further to argue that requiring judges to run for re-election should be outlawed. As he puts it, "The very argument used to justify judicial elections—as an opportunity to hold judges accountable—renders such elections unconstitutional."[65] Other important reform groups, like the Brennan Center, endorse getting rid of judicial re-elections for similar reasons.

How should we get rid of judicial re-elections? We suggest that state judges be legally limited to a single long term in office without the possibility of re-election to multiple terms. Every elected judge would start their initial term with the certainty that it will be their first and last term in that judicial position. Like our lame duck judges, then, they would have the security from the start of their term that they need not worry about running for re-election or raising money for the next campaign. They would be outright barred from running again and would be free to judge according to their conscience without regard for the campaign finance considerations that seem to bias elected judges as we've described.

In other words, let's make all judges lame ducks from the jump. Lame duck judges behave differently than judges who need to run for re-election to keep their jobs and must decide cases with a crocodile in their bathtub, poised to bite them if they decide in ways that alienate potential supporters and donors. Freeing judges from this worry should be a primary goal of judicial selection reform, and informed by our research, we think a so-called "one-and-done" model, where judges can run for and serve only a single long term, does a lot of good without requiring us to abandon judicial elections altogether.

THE CASE FOR A SINGLE TERM LIMIT WITH A LONG SINGLE TERM

We urge that the single term limit for state elected judges, particularly for state supreme court, be a lengthy one for multiple reasons. First, a single term must be long enough to make judgeships attractive to quality candidates even when they aren't permitted to run for additional terms. We want good candidates to run for judge and don't want our proposed term limit to negatively affect the quality of the candidates who decide to run. However, limiting judges to a single term means even winning candidates may need to look for another job after their single term rather than remaining in office. That is, good candidates who hope to win office and then stay in that position for multiple terms may decide a single term isn't attractive enough to be worth leaving their current job or even running a campaign in the first place. Many state judges leave their legal practice to run for judge and, if successful, stay in a judicial position for the rest of their career through retirement. A single term makes this unlikely for many candidates, particularly younger ones.

We can mitigate this potential effect on candidate quality by lengthening the single term of office. Right now, for instance, state supreme court terms currently vary from six years on the low end to fourteen years on the high end, with most states somewhere in between. If we limit our sample to *elected* state supreme courts, terms vary from six years (Alabama, Georgia, Idaho, Minnesota, Nevada, Ohio, Oregon, Texas, Washington) on the low end to twelve years (Virginia, West Virginia) on the high end. Of course, almost all these term lengths are predicated on the fact that judges are eligible for multiple terms after the expiration of their first. Based on data from 1947 to 1994, we know state supreme court justices served an average of 12.69

years in office, with an average term length of 8.29 years.[66] In our 2010s data, judges served an average of roughly 15 years in office. So, we know that on average, state supreme court justices successfully won retention, whether through reappointment or re-election, and served more than one term.

Setting a single term under our proposal at fourteen years is likely not to significantly shorten average state supreme court career length. A fourteen-year term is on the highest end of the current range of state supreme court terms, matched only by the New York Court of Appeals (which serves as the state's highest court). This very long term by current standards therefore goes as long as possible without going beyond what any state currently provides—and we have no reason to believe that New York's experience with a fourteen-year term has caused problems as a result of its length.

What's more, by extending the single term to this length, we can help ensure that our single term limit doesn't significantly shorten state supreme court careers. Although justices wouldn't be able to extend their tenure by winning additional terms, their single term would be longer than it would be currently in all but one state, thereby mitigating any shortening effect of our term limit. Justices would be limited to no more than fourteen years on the state supreme court, but they would be guaranteed no less than fourteen years provided they do not die, resign, or get impeached during their term. As a result, under a single fourteen-year term limit, even without any possibility of additional terms, the average state supreme court tenure should not differ significantly from the average (from 1947 to 1994) of twelve and a half years.

So, we would expect that judicial candidates wouldn't necessarily think the single term limit makes a state supreme court seat less attractive. They could run for office with a similar expectation about how long they would serve in that role and, indeed, with a guarantee about a longer minimum tenure. State supreme court justices, from 1947 to 1994, won their seats for the first time at the average age of 53.26 years old.[67] In our data from the 2010s, the average age for first-time judges was only a bit younger at 52.2 years old. And with a single term limit, we doubt the average age of candidates would decrease significantly. We expect that the average supreme court tenure wouldn't change much, but we know the single term limit would eliminate any tenure beyond fourteen years, so we can't imagine that this makes the job more attractive to candidates younger than the current average. Younger candidates are precisely the ones who would be most interested in and most likely to earn the longest tenures without a term limit by winning additional terms. As a consequence, the average age of candidates probably wouldn't decrease significantly.

If we are right, the average candidate, in their fifties, could expect that a single fourteen-year term has a good chance to take them through retirement age, as is the case for most justices now.[68] In other words, we hope and expect that a single term limit, with a long fourteen-year term, wouldn't dramatically change the incentives for candidates and therefore not affect candidate quality very much. Indeed, studies of term limits for legislative office find that the average age of candidates under term limits doesn't change significantly from candidates who run for office where there aren't term limits.[69]

Second, we would recommend a single long term because it would help improve judicial quality in other ways. One cost of a term limit is that every judge is in their first and only term, without any judges accruing greater judicial experience. By extending judges' single term to a lengthy fourteen years, we can ensure that judges accumulate meaningful experience, and their work has a chance to improve with that experience over time. Indeed, there is evidence that judges write better opinions by multiple measures when they have longer terms.[70] One study shows that not only do judges write opinions that are cited by other judges at a higher rate (a sign of quality), but they also write more dissenting opinions to articulate objections to their colleagues' decisions.[71]

Judges likewise appear to become more predictable in their decisions with longer terms. It seems that litigants become more familiar with judges and their philosophies over time, and perhaps the judges themselves develop clearer philosophies as well, such that longer terms improve predictability and consistency.[72] For all these reasons, the ABA recommends that states opting for a single-term limit should make that term at least fifteen or more years,[73] even longer than our proposal.

One reason that judges appear to perform better with longer terms, even without a term limit, is that judges act more independently when there are many years before they are required to stand for re-election or retention. That is, judges who are at the beginning of a longer term are less likely to think ahead to what they must do to keep their jobs. There's therefore some evidence that they tend to decide cases with less worry about satisfying voters or campaign supporters.

Legal historian Jed Shugerman, for example, shows that state judges elected to longer terms during the nineteenth century, when states shifted to judicial elections, were more likely to defy their political party and special interests.[74] Judges with greater seniority also are more likely to reverse death penalty sentences despite the potential reaction of public opinion.[75] And judges elected to a long term would be doubly removed from political and campaign finance considerations if they are ineligible for re-election under a single-term limit. Judges who have more time and worry less about job security seem to perform their jobs better.

Third, many of the potential worries about term limits are not as salient when applied to judges. Empirical research on legislative term limits finds that these limits don't tend to affect candidate or legislator characteristics too much, or at least not as much as one might expect.[76] The type of person who runs for and wins office doesn't appear to be too different. But legislative term limits increase turnover and reduce the average length of legislative careers for the obvious reason that legislators are eligible to serve only a limited number of terms. As a result, legislators in the aggregate have less experience and less motivation on average to become adept at a job that they'll be forced by law to give up.[77]

The argument that term limits can thus reduce the collective capacity of a legislature is an important one for *legislative* term limits. However, we think this argument doesn't apply very well to courts and judges, especially not for a state supreme court. Judicial candidates, on average, are older and more experienced in their legal careers than legislative candidates. Compared to state legislators, judicial candidates who win a state supreme court seat tend to be highly qualified, competitive candidates who are fairly senior in their professional careers. As a result, judicial candidates already tend to be experienced lawyers who have most of the relevant expertise for the job before they first join the bench. Of course, these candidates don't have firsthand experience as state supreme court justices, but their practice experience as lawyers is highly relevant to the job. And justices will learn and accumulate experience as judges much as they would've without a term limit.

As we explained above, we don't expect judicial tenure on state supreme courts to change much under a single-term limit, so the average experience for sitting justices also shouldn't change much. Overall, we don't expect term limits to reduce experience on the state supreme court because justices would serve roughly as long as they do now, provided that their single term is lengthy, as we propose. One consequence of inexperience for term-limited legislators is that they tend to rely more heavily of professional staff and lobbyists, who have more experience with the legislative process than elected legislators who are restricted in how long they can serve. One study of legislative term limits, for instance, reported that lobbyists felt overwhelmingly that term-limited legislators were less knowledgeable about issues and how the legislature operates, while relying more on staff.[78]

However, judges aren't subject to the same sort of open-access lobbying as state legislators and executives. The professional rules of the legal process and the judiciary strictly limit the parties' ex parte access to judges in their cases and block off the sort of lobbying so prevalent in the legislative process. Those who seek to influence judges would lose even more influence when judges aren't eligible for re-election. They wouldn't be able to dangle the possibility of campaign finance support, or opposition, over the heads of judges in the same way that they do today when judges have to consider their re-election prospects. Indeed, there's some evidence that campaign finance investment by contributors goes down when legislative term limits are introduced because influence over legislators who can serve only a limited time is worth less.[79] From our perspective, less money in judicial elections as a result of term limits would be a good thing.

If professional staff increase in influence with term limits, we think this is less of a worry for judges than legislators. Simply put, professional staff matters a lot less for judges than they do in the legislature. Judges tend to do their jobs largely by themselves, with minimal support staff, at least relative to the state legislature or executive.[80] Judges are helped in their substantive work mainly by a handful of judicial clerks who generally serve short terms, often right out of law school. There simply isn't much staff to advise judges on their substantive decisionmaking that is anywhere comparable to the bureaucracy surrounding the legislative process.

Indeed, we hope that term-limited judges, once liberated from re-election concerns, might feel freer to judge by their conscience rather than political considerations. Studies generally find that judges with greater political insulation and greater job security tend to be less influenced by public opinion. And at least one important study finds that term limits for legislators produces just such a "Burkean shift" where term-limited officials seem "oriented more toward conscience than district."[81] For legislators, this effect of term limits might be worrisome at some point. Elected legislators might feel too free to disregard their constituents' wishes and fail in their representational duties. Legislators are supposed to represent their constituents in government and be responsive to their wishes. But judges are different. Judges are elected, but they aren't mere delegates put on the bench to do what their voters want. Judges are beholden to law, not just their constituents. We need judges to be freer from public opinion and serve justice even when it defies public opinion in a particular case. Term limits might encourage this Burkean shift that well suits the specialized judicial role.

Admittedly, getting states to enact a single-term limit is no political slam dunk either. More than a decade ago, Colorado and Montana seriously considered imposition of term limits for their supreme courts but ultimately rejected them.[82] More recently, though, the Arkansas and Wisconsin Bar Associations recommended similar proposals for a single long term. A Wisconsin State Bar Judicial Task Force rejected judicial appointments, with the recognition that "Wisconsin has always elected its judges" as a political reality, but instead recommended a single sixteen-year term for state supreme court, which would be "long enough to attract highly qualified candidates, but not so long as to create nearly life tenure."[83] An Arkansas Bar Task Force similarly suggested a single fourteen-year term (with a shift to appointment) because "extending the length of the Justice's term and thereby eliminating the need for a retention election frees the Justice to vote according to conscience and the rule of law and not according to political necessity."[84] And as we discuss next, there's been growing political support at the U.S. Supreme Court level for a single-term limit as well. Our findings hopefully provide academic substantiation for a term limit that can help support these nascent political efforts.

LIFE TENURE?

If judicial insulation from political pressures is a good thing, why not have judges serve lifetime terms, like federal judges? Judges elected to a lifetime term are certainly protected from political influence and never need to worry about losing their job because they decided a case differently than the voters wanted. They keep their jobs, subject only to the minimal threat of impeachment, almost regardless of how they decide their cases. In fact, federal judges are constitutionally entitled to lifetime appointment precisely for this reason.

The Framers thought, as Alexander Hamilton wrote in the *Federalist Papers*, that "complete independence of the courts of justice is peculiarly essential in a limited Constitution."[85] The Framers prioritized judicial independence in response to what they saw as the corruption of judges under English rule. During the time, judicial commissions were issued "during the pleasure of the Crown," leading to tensions between colonial legislatures and governors appointed by the King.[86] Indeed, the Framers lamented the English judiciary's subservience to the Crown in the Declaration of Independence, exclaiming as a grievance that "[The King] made Judges dependent on his Will alone, for the tenure of their offices."[87] Given this history, the Framers advocated for lifetime judicial appointment because they feared the "danger of an improper complaisance" to the other branches of government since "periodical appointments, however regulated, or by whomsoever made, would, in some way or other, be fatal to their necessary independence."[88] The Framers pretty accurately foresaw our modern problems with judicial elections and reappointment at the state level today.

All that said, lifetime judicial appointment is still quite rare in the modern world. Only three states allow their state supreme court justices to hold their seats for life, or at least until a mandatory retirement age. The federal judiciary in the United States receives lifetime tenure, but it is the outlier among national supreme courts worldwide. According to law professors Steve Calabresi and Jim Lindgren, the United States is the only major democratic country with life tenure for its highest constitutional court. As Calabresi and Lindgren explain, "Judicial independence is not an unqualified good."[89] True, with lifetime tenure, judges are well insulated from political pressure, but at the great offsetting cost of a judiciary that rarely changes membership and installs judges for long stretches of time without democratic renewal. "A regime that allows high government officials to exercise great power, totally unchecked, for periods of thirty to forty years, is essentially a relic of pre-democratic times."[90] Lifetime tenure, in sum, is just too long a time for judges to serve in the same position without replacement.

Again, the example of the federal judiciary is instructive. Calabresi and Lindgren point out that the terms of U.S. Supreme Court justices grew longer in length over time, with the average term jumping from 14.9 years from 1789 to 1970, to 26.1 years from 1970 to 2006.[91] With justices serving an average of a quarter century in place, the time between vacancies on the Court also increased. From 1789 to 1970, a Supreme Court seat opened up every 1.9 years on average.[92] This figure increased by roughly 50 percent since 1970 to 3.1 years. What's more, there have been three of the five longest stretches between vacancies in relatively recent years, including a decade-long stretch of unchanged Court membership between August 3, 1994, and September 4, 2005.[93]

The problem with lifetime tenure is that it allows too little opportunity for fresh blood on a court and therefore too little opportunity for the democratic process to periodically update supreme court membership. We want judicial independence from a long, secure term free from re-election worries, but lifetime tenure probably goes too far. A quarter-century strikes us as excessively long, with justices serving deep into their seniority, when fourteen-year single terms probably provide all the judicial independence that we need. The federal system on this score is not necessarily a model for states to follow, and only a handful have done so.

For all these reasons, many experts, including Calabresi and Lindgren,[94] advocate term limits even for the U.S. Supreme Court justices, in light of the data Calabresi and Lindgren present. In fact, Democrats in Congress introduced the Supreme Court Term Limits and Regular Appointments Act in late 2020 with exactly the same idea in mind.[95]

The Presidential Commission on the Supreme Court, convened by President Joe Biden in 2021 to consider possible reforms, came close to the same conclusion in analyzing proposed eighteen-year terms for U.S. Supreme Court Justices to replace Article III life tenure.[96] As Tom Ginsberg testified before the Commission, "Were we writing the United States Constitution anew, there is no way we would adopt the particular institutional structure that we have for judicial tenure."[97] In other words, reform momentum seems to be pushing the federal judiciary, with its lifetime tenure, toward the very same solution of a single long term that we advocate here for state judges.

Mind you, we don't necessarily oppose lifetime terms for elected state supreme court justices, if the alternative is short terms where justices run frequently for re-election. We do think that state judges need more political insulation than they do at the moment. Life terms are one way to accomplish that goal, even if we think they are an imperfect solution. However, we think that single elected fourteen-year terms are a better way to provide judicial independence and limit the influence of campaign finance on judges without running into the problems of the federal system.

Again, a major advantage of a single-term limit, as opposed to virtually all other prominent reform ideas, is that this is a relatively modest, politically feasible fix. Limiting state supreme court justices to a single elected term doesn't require states to eliminate judicial elections, which probably isn't realistic in most states. It also doesn't require states to extend judicial terms to a lifetime, which isn't popular among the states and would follow a federal model that is increasingly drawing criticism. Although no state has adopted a term limit for its supreme court yet, this idea enjoys broad support among experts in the area and likely requires the least modification to how state select their justices while still removing the problem of re-election that we've identified here. At least one state, Florida, has recently considered term limits,[98] and as we've noted, there's growing consideration of the limitation even for the U.S. Supreme Court in light of the problems with the federal appointment process.

To be clear, we're focused on getting rid of judicial re-election, however the means. We're not quite so particular about how we get there, whether it's elimination of judicial elections altogether, lifetime terms, or, as we propose, a single-term limit. But we also think a single-term limit is probably the most politically feasible, simplest reform that accomplishes our hope of freeing judges from re-election concerns and the potential bias that comes with campaign finance.

LAST WORDS

In the end, we hope two lessons stand out from our research and this book. First, judicial elections do not inevitably lead to campaign finance influences on judges and judicial decisionmaking. Elected judges who are term limited and cannot run for another term do not seem as influenced by their past donors and biased toward the interests that funded their judicial careers. Elections aren't inherently corrupting for judges.

Second, the source of campaign finance biases on elected state judges seems instead to be the pressure to raise money for re-election. We find that judges who are eligible for re-election behave differently than judges who aren't and therefore are not worried about where the money for their next race will come from. In other words, as we say one last time, it's judicial re-election that brings the influence of money into play, not judicial elections in general. So, we advocate for reforms that will remove the temptations and pressures associated with re-election.

There is more than one way to remove re-election from the minds of judges, and we advocate specifically for a long single term for the reasons we've just described. The most important thing is to get rid of re-election one way or another, because this is the source of the biasing pressure from campaign finance money that threatens judicial integrity.

Re-election is the crocodile in the judge's bathtub that they must worry about to keep their job. Until we get rid of this constant worry, judges won't be free to judge impartially as justice demands.

Appendix

METHODOLOGY

We estimate a multilevel logit model in most analyses. Our multilevel model controls for dependence across both decisions in individual cases and specific state supreme courts' decisions. That is, judges' decisions in a particular case are unlikely to be independent of each other; there is likely a relationship between how one judge votes in a case and how another judge votes in the same case because of the underlying facts, law, and other relevant factors to the case. Similarly, the decisions in different cases made by judges on the same court are likely not independent because the judges share not only the court in common, but also the state, its laws, and other environmental influences. Our model accommodates this dependence so we can precisely isolate the influence of business contributions on judicial votes.

The control variables we include fall into three categories: judge-level variables, state-level variables, and case-level variables. Our judge-level control variables include non-business campaign contributions, party affiliation, and the type of retention election. First, we include the dollar value of campaign contributions from non-business groups in each judge's most recent election.[1] This variable provides a measure of the potential influence from interests and sectors opposed to (or unrelated to) business interests.

It also controls for the total amount of money raised by different judges—$200,000 in business contributions should have a different impact when the total amount raised is $300,000 versus when $2 million is raised in total.

Next, we include each judge's party affiliation.[2] We know from the empirical literature that Republican judges are generally more conservative and more likely than Democratic judges to vote for business litigants regardless of campaign finance considerations. We control for party affiliation to separately account for the relationships between, on the one hand, ideology and voting, and on the other, campaign finance and voting.

We also include the type of election that the judges in each state face for retention—partisan, nonpartisan, or an unopposed retention election. Different types of elections have different degrees of competitiveness and require the candidates to raise different magnitudes of money. Including the type of retention election as an explanatory variable will control for different judges' need to attract future campaign funds.

Our state-level control variables include the state tort climate, the ideology of the state's citizens, and the ideology of the state government. We include a variable capturing the tort liability climate to isolate the influence of business contributions on pro-business votes from the underlying state law.[3] In states with existing law that favors business interests, we would expect judges to vote in favor of business interests regardless of contributions. We also include variables that measure the liberalism of citizens in the state and the liberalism of the state government.[4] Judges' voting may be influenced by the attitudes of the public and of other governmental officials in the state if they fear that displeasing these groups could negatively impact them.

Finally, we include two case-specific control variables that capture the likelihood of the business litigant winning the case without regard to a judge's pro-business bias. First, we include a variable indicating whether the business litigant is the petitioner filing the appeal in each case. Because petitioners are more likely to win on appeal, this variable captures the judge's natural propensity to vote for the petitioner.[5]

Second, we include a variable that measures the strength of the business litigant's legal case. This control variable is important because some cases are so strong (or weak) that judges will vote for (or against) business interests regardless of their ideological predisposition or the influence of campaign contributions. To create a measure of case strength, the study first estimates the model without the case strength variable. The results of this estimation allow us to predict how many of the other judges will vote for the business litigant in each case. The difference between this predicted number and the actual number of the other judges voting for the business litigant provides our measure of case strength. That is, suppose that the model predicts that, based on the judges' ideological predisposition, retention election, campaign contributions, the state tort climate, the citizen and government ideology, and the litigant petitioning the court, four of the six other judges would support the business position. In reality, if five of the other judges supported the business position, the case strength variable would indicate a stronger than average case. In contrast, if only one other justice voted in favor of business instead of the predicted four, the case strength variable would indicate that the case was very weak.

RESULTS

The following tables present the full results of the multilevel logit estimations. We present the results in odds ratios for ease of interpretation. The odds ratios can be used to interpret the magnitude of the relationship between each explanatory variable and the dependent variable. An odds ratio greater than one indicates a positive relationship between the explanatory and dependent variable and an odds ratio less than one indicates a negative relationship. Given the log transformation of our contribution variables, the precise interpretation of each odds ratio for the contribution variables is the percentage increase (or decrease) in the odds of a pro-business vote for a doubling of the business contributions, with all other variables held constant. For example, in Table A.1, the odds ratio of 1.289 for Business Contributions indicates that a doubling of business contributions is associated with, on average, a 28.9 percent increase in the likelihood of casting a pro-business vote. In contrast, the odds ratio of 0.822 for Non-Business Contributions indicates that a doubling of non-business contributions is associated with a 17.8 percent decrease (1 – 0.822) in the odds of casting a pro-business vote.

The interpretation of odds ratios becomes more complicated with the interaction between our contribution variables (continuous variables) and the indicator for non–lame duck judges (nominal variable). In this situation, the odds ratio on the simple contribution variable is interpreted as the percentage increase (or decrease) in the odds of a pro-business vote for a doubling of the business contributions for lame duck judges (i.e., the non–lame duck indicator = 0). The interpretation of the odds ratio on the interaction term is the *additional* change in odds for non–lame duck judges (i.e., the non–lame duck indicator = 1). To determine the percentage increase (or decrease) in the odds of a pro-business vote for a doubling of the business contributions for non–lame duck judges, we have to multiply the odds ratio of the simple contribution variable by the odds ratio for the interaction term. For example, in Table A.2, the odds ratio on Business Contributions of 1.173 indicates that, for lame duck judges, a doubling of business contributions is associated with a 17.3 percent increase in the likelihood of a judge voting for the business litigant. The odds ratio on the interaction between Business Contributions and an Indicator for Non–Lame Duck Judges of 1.141 indicates that, for non–lame duck judges, a doubling of business contributions is associated with a 33.8 percent (1.173*1.141=1.338) increase in the likelihood of a judge voting for the business litigant.

We also report the p-value associated with each logit coefficient. The p-value for each variable indicates whether there is sufficient evidence in the data to conclude that the variable has a relationship with judges' voting. A smaller p-value indicates that there is strong evidence that the variable does have a relationship. Researchers generally use a p-value cutoff of 0.05 (or, to a lesser extent, 0.10) as the demarcation between a statistically significant and statically insignificant result. For simplicity we include a "*" to indicate statistical significance at the 0.05 level and a "+" to indicate statistical significance at the 0.10 level. A p-value of less than 0.05 indicates that there is strong evidence of a meaningful relationship between the variable and judges' voting; a p-value greater than 0.05 indicates that the evidence is not strong enough to conclude that a meaningful relationship exists between the variable and judges' voting.

TABLE A.1 Full Set of Results for Figure 4.2: Relationship between Business Contributions and Pro-Business Votes

Variable	*Odds Ratio (p-value)*
Business Contributions	1.289* (0.000)
Non-Business Contributions	0.822* (0.000)
Partisan Re-election Indicator	2.17* (0.001)
Nonpartisan Re-election Indicator	1.13 (0.531)
Retention Election Indicator	1.24 (0.424)
Democratic Judge	0.645* (0.002)
Republican Judge	1.46* (0.005)
State Tort Climate	0.579* (0.001)
State Citizens Ideology	1.01 (0.101)
State Government Ideology	0.988+ (0.071)
Business Petitioner Indicator	0.587* (0.000)
Case Strength	1.072* (0.000)
# of observations Chi-squared statistic	10,104 3217

TABLE A.2 Full Set of Results for Figure 4.3: Business Contributions and Pro-Business Votes as Retention Election Approaches

Variable	*Odds Ratio (p-value)*
Business Contributions	1.21* (0.000)
Indicator for Fewer than 2 Years until Retention	1.15 (0.319)
Business Contributions* Fewer than 2 Years Until Retention	1.05+ (0.079)
Non-Business Contributions	0.84* (0.000)
Partisan Re-election Indicator	2.88* (0.001)
Nonpartisan Re-election Indicator	1.25 (0.381)
Retention Election Indicator	1.17 (0.620)
Democratic Judge	0.617* (0.039)
Republican Judge	1.58* (0.041)
State Tort Climate	0.526* (0.001)
State Citizens Ideology	1.01 (0.183)
State Government Ideology	0.989 (0.193)
Business Petitioner Indicator	0.571 * (0.000)
Case Strength	1.079* (0.000)
# of observations	10,104
Chi-squared statistic	2659.3

TABLE A.3 Full Set of Results for Table 4.2: Business Contributions and Votes: Impact of Mandatory Retirement

Variable	*Odds Ratio (p-value)*
Indicator for Non–lame Duck Judge	1.39* (0.041)
Business Contributions	1.173* (0.001)
Non- Business Contributions	0.924* (0.047)
Business Contributions* Indicator for Non–lame Duck Judge	1.141* (0.017)
Non-Business Contributions *Indicator for Non–lame Duck Judge	0.853* (0.000)
Partisan Re-election Indicator	1.970* (0.005)
Nonpartisan Re-election Indicator	1.044 (0.833)
Retention Election Indicator	1.178 (0.561)
Democratic Judge	0.637* (0.001)
Republican Judge	1.423* (0.010)
State Tort Climate	0.566* (0.002)
State Citizens Ideology	1.009 (0.175)
State Government Ideology	0.991 (0.203)
Business Petitioner Indicator	0.579* (0.000)
Case Strength	1.071* (0.000)
# of observations	9,920
Chi-squared statistic	3144.9

TABLE A.4 Full Set of Results for Table 4.3: Business Contributions and Votes: Robustness Check for Age

	Odds Ratio (p-value)	
Variable	*Age included as an explanatory variable*	*Estimation sample restricted to judges over age 60*
Indicator for Non–lame Duck Judge	1.10	1.14
	(0.582)	(0.463)
Business Contributions	1.156*	1.176*
	(0.003)	(0.001)
!Non-Business Contributions	0.937	0.937
	(0.106)	(0.109)
Business Contributions* Indicator	1.142*	1.112+
for Non–lame Duck Judge	(0.018)	(0.079)
Non-Business Contributions	0.850*	0.862*
*Indicator for Non–lame Duck Judge	(0.000)	(0.003)
Partisan Re-election Indicator	2.02*	1.717+
	(0.006)	(0.052)
Nonpartisan Re-election Indicator	1.056	0.893
	(0.797)	(0.635)
Retention Election Indicator	1.318	0.948
	(0.350)	(0.868)
Democratic Judge	0.618*	0.804
	(0.001)	(0.217)
Republican Judge	1.393*	1.475*
	(0.017)	(0.027)
State Tort Climate	0.627*	0.526*
	(0.015)	(0.003)
State Citizens Ideology	1.007	1.005
	(0.278)	(0.496)
State Government Ideology	0.990	0.995
	(0.162)	(0.519)
Business Petitioner Indicator	0.573*	0.546*
	(0.000)	(0.000)
Case Strength	1.072*	1.071*
	(0.000)	(0.000)
# of observations	9,651	6707
Chi-squared statistic	3040.78	2137.85

TABLE A.5 Full Set of Results for Table 4.5: Business Contributions and Votes: Unique State Features Robustness Check

Variable	*Odds Ratio (p-value)*
Indicator for Non–lame Duck Judge	1.532* (0.012)
Business Contributions	1.169* (0.001)
Non-Business Contributions	0.902* (0.010)
Business Contributions* Indicator for Non–lame Duck Judge	1.179* (0.007)
Non-Business Contributions *Indicator for Non–lame Duck Judge	0.815* (0.000)
Partisan Re-election Indicator	2.568* (0.001)
Nonpartisan Re-election Indicator	1.557+ (0.058)
Retention Election Indicator	1.159 (0.733)
Democratic Judge	0.706 (0.106)
Republican Judge	1.801* (0.007)
State Tort Climate	0.528* (0.003)
State Citizens Ideology	1.002 (0.809)
State Government Ideology	0.997 (0.689)
Business Petitioner Indicator	0.598* (0.000)
Case Strength	1.071* (0.000)
# of observations	6,249
Chi-squared statistic	1950.2

TABLE A.6 Full Set of Results for Table 4.6: Business Contributions and Votes: Robustness Check for Other Last Term Judges

	Odds Ratio (p-value)	
Variable	*Last term because of voluntary retirement*	*Last term for any reason other than mandatory retirement*
Indicator for Non–Last Term Judge	0.836	0.798+
	(0.105)	(0.057)
Business Contributions	1.458*	1.453*
	(0.000)	(0.000)
Non-Business Contributions	0.730*	0.731 *
	(0.000)	(0.000)
Business Contributions* Indicator for Non–Last Term Judge	0.855*	0.857*
	(0.003)	(0.003)
Non-Business Contributions *Indicator for Non–Last Term Judge	1.158*	1.160*
	(0.002)	(0.002)
Partisan Re-election Indicator	2.240*	2.262*
	(0.001)	(0.001)
Nonpartisan Re-election Indicator	1.204	1.199
	(0.354)	(0.364)
Retention Election Indicator	1.246	1.231
	(0.430)	(0.452)
Democratic Judge	0.587*	0.597*
	(0.000)	(0.000)
Republican Judge	1.353*	1.360*
	(0.031)	(0.028)
State Tort Climate	0.589*	0.600*
	(0.003)	(0.004)
State Citizens Ideology	1.011+	1.011+
	(0.082)	(0.090)
State Government Ideology	0.987+	0.987+
	(0.060)	(0.055)
Business Petitioner Indicator	0.575*	0.577*
	(0.000)	(0.000)
Case Strength	1.071*	1.071*
	(0.000)	(0.000)
# of observations	9,920	9920
Chi-squared statistic	3158.4	3158.6

Notes

Chapter 1

1. Allan W. Vestal, "Vindication: Varnum v. Brien at Ten Years," *Drake Law Review* 67 (2019): 463, 470.

2. See A.G. Sulzberger, "Ouster of Iowa Judges Sens Signal to Bench," *The New York Times*, November 3, 2010.

3. 570 U.S. 744 (2013).

4. 576 U.S. 644 (2015).

5. See Mike Glover, "Gay Marriage Foes Back Push to Oust Iowa Justices," *Associated Press*, October 25, 2010.

6. "Iowa Gay Marriages Foes Emboldened by Judges' Removal," *The Gazette*, November 3, 2010, 8:57 a.m., https://www.thegazette.com/campaigns-elections/iowa-gay-marriage-foes-emboldened-by-judges-removal/ (quoting Dan Moore, co-chairman of Fair Courts for Us).

7. Grant Schulte, "Iowans Dismiss Three Justices," *The Des Moines Register*, November 3, 2010 (quoting Bob Vander Plaats).

8. Sulzberger, "Ouster of Iowa Judges" (quoting Chemerinsky, then-dean of UC Irvine Law School).

9. Williams-Yulee v. Fla. Bar, 575 U.S. 433, 472 (2015) (Scalia, J., dissenting).

10. Gerald F. Uelmen, "Crocodile in the Bathtub: Maintaining the Independence of State Supreme Courts in an Era of Judicial Politicization," *Notre Dame Law Review* 72 (1997): 1133.

11. American Bar Association (ABA), "Justice in Jeopardy: Report of the American Bar Association Commission on the 21st Century Judiciary" (2003): 1–2.

12. Total campaign spending in 2015–16 was the highest spending unadjusted for inflation, though second highest when adjusted for inflation to 2003–2004.

13. Brady Dennis, "Super PACs, Donors Turn Sights on Judicial Branch," *The Washington Post*, March 29, 2012 (quoting Roy Schotland).

14. Annemarie Mannion, "Retired Justice Warns Against 'Politicians in Robes,'" *Chicago Tribune*, May 30, 2013 (quoting Justice Sandra Day O'Connor).

15. Debra Cassens Weiss, "Most Countries Don't Hold Judicial Elections," *ABA Journal*, May 27, 2008, 1:31 p.m. CT, https://www.abajournal.com/news/article/most_countries_dont_hold_judicial_elections.

16. Institute for the Advancement of the American Legal System, "Quality Judges Initiative FAQs: Judges in the United States," https://iaals.du.edu/sites/default/files/documents/publications/judge_faq.pdf.

17. Tracey E. George and Albert H. Yoon, "The Gavel Gap: Who Sits in Judgment on State Courts?" (2017): 3, https://www.acslaw.org/wp-content/uploads/2018/02/gavel-gap-report.pdf.

18. *Id.*

19. Michael Lewis, *Moneyball: The Art of Winning an Unfair Game* (New York: W. W. Norton & Co., 2003).

20. See, e.g., Harry Glorikian and Malorye Allison Branca, *MoneyBall Medicine: Thriving in the New Data-Driven Healthcare Market* (New York: Routledge, 2017).

21. See, e.g., Paul Caron and Rafael Gely, "What Law Schools Can Learn from Billy Beane and the Oakland Athletics," *Texas Law Review* 82 (2004): 1483; Jeremy Potter, "Legal Education and Moneyball: The Art of Winning the Assessment Game," *Connecticut Public Interest Law Journal* 11 (2012): 327.

22. See, e.g., Jim Nussle and Peter Orszag, *Moneyball for Government*, 2nd ed. (New York: Disruption Books, 2015).

23. Joan Biskupic, "Supreme Court Case with the Feel of a Best Seller," *USA Today*, February 17, 2009.

24. Caperton v. A.T. Massey Coal Co., 556 U.S. 868 (2009).

25. *Caperton*, 556 U.S. at 882.

26. *Id.* at 884.

27. *Id.* at 886.

28. *Id.* at 879 (internal quotation marks omitted).

29. See generally Frank B. Cross and Emerson H. Tiller, "What Is Legal Doctrine?," *Northwestern University Law Review* 100 (2006): 517.

30. See, e.g., Francisco J. Benzoni and Christopher S. Dodrill, "Does Judicial Philosophy Matter: A Case Study," *West Virginia Law Review* 113 (2011): 287; Jeremy Buchman, "The Effects of Ideology on Federal Trial Judges' Decisions to Admit Scientific Expert Testimony," *American Politics Research* 35 (2007): 671.

31. See generally Jeffrey Segal and Harold J. Spaeth, *The Supreme Court and the Attitudinal Model* (New York: Cambridge University Press, 2002) (advancing an "attitudinal model" of judicial decisionmaking).

32. See, e.g., Maya Sen, "Diversity, Qualifications, and Ideology: How Female and Minority Judges Have Changed, or Not Changed, Over Time," *Wisconsin Law*

Review (2017): 367; Adam B. Cox and Thomas J. Miles, "Judging the Voting Rights Act," *Columbia Law Review* 108 (2008): 1; Jason L. Morin, "The Voting Behavior of Minority Judges in the U.S. Courts of Appeals: Does the Race of the Claimant Matter?" *American Politics Research* 42 (2014): 34.

33. *Id.*

34. See Sue Davis, Susan Haire, and Donald R. Songer, "Voting Behavior and Gender on the U.S. Courts of Appeal," *Judicature* 77 (1993): 129; Christina L. Boyd, Lee Epstein, and Andrew D. Martin, "Untangling the Causal Effects of Sex on Judging," *American Journal of Political Science* (2010): 389.

35. Marsha Ternus, Arizona lecture, January 19, 2012. https://www.c-span.org/video/?303787-2/judicial-independence#!

36. See, e.g., "Americans Overwhelmingly Favor Election of Judges but Disapprove of Judicial Campaign Fund-Raising, Fearing It Affects Fairness," *Annenberg Public Policy Center,* May 23, 2007.

37. New York eliminated judicial elections for initial selection and retention in 1977 and switched to a system of judicial nominating commissions.

38. *Caperton*, 556 U.S. at 894, 898 (Roberts, C.J., dissenting).

Chapter 2

1. Stuart Taylor and New York Times News Service, "Blackmun Holds Court with Humor," *Chicago Tribune*, July 25, 1988.

2. Stephen B. Bright, "Political Attacks on the Judiciary: Can Justice Be Done Amid Efforts to Intimidate and Remove Judges from Office for Unpopular Decisions?," *NYU Law Review* 72, no. 2 (May 1997): 308, 336.

3. Melissa S. May, "Judicial Retention Elections After 2010," *Indiana Law Review* 46, no. 59 (2013): 60.

4. Maya Srikrishnan, "Conservatives Nationwide Target Tennessee Supreme Court Justices," *Los Angeles Times*, August 6, 2014 (quoting White).

5. *Id.*, 314, 336.

6. Bright, "Political Attacks on the Judiciary," 332.

7. 928 S.W.2d 18 (Tenn. 1996).

8. Odom v. Tennessee, 2017 WL 4764908 (Tenn. Ct. Crim App. 2017).

9. Bright, "Political Attacks on the Judiciary," 332.

10. *Id.*, 313, 331.

11. *Id.*, 332.

12. *Id.*, 336.

13. *Id.*

14. Margaret L. Behm and Candi Henry, "Judicial Selection in Tennessee: Deciding 'The Decider,'" *Belmont Law Review* 1, no. 143 (2014): 19, https://www.belmont.edu/law/academics/review/pdfs/Behm.pdf.

15. Justice White told us that while she "loved [Justice Birch]," she thought "some of the language in the opinion could've been crafted in a more sensitive way. And particularly the use of the phrase 'the worst of the worst,' that's what really set

people off." One regret she expressed was that "I wish I had written so that what all people found with me could've been based on what my true expression of what I thought the law required, rather than just my signature on [Birch's] opinion."

16. Colman McCarthy, "Injustice Claims a Tennessee Judge," *The Washington Post*, November 26, 1996.

17. Srikrishnan, "Conservatives Nationwide Target Tennessee" (quoting White).

18. Bright, "Political Attacks on the Judiciary," 333.

19. *Id.*

20. *Id.*

21. John Paul Stevens, "Opening Assembly Address, American Bar Association Annual Meeting, Orlando, Florida, August 3, 1996," *St. John's Journal of Legal Commentary* 12, no. 21 (1996): 30–31.

22. Paula Wade, "White First Casualty of Yes-No Option on judges Soft-on-Crime Charge Costs Seat," *Memphis Commercial Appeal*, August 2, 1996, Al.

23. *Id.*

24. See Adam Liptak, "U.S. Voting for Judges Perplexes Other Nations," *The New York Times*, May 25, 2008, https://www.nytimes.com/2008/05/25/world/americas/25iht-judge.4.13194819.html.

25. *Id.*

26. See generally Mitchel Lasser, *Judicial Deliberations: A Comparative Analysis of Transparency and Legitimacy*, 1st ed. (Oxford University Press, 2009).

27. See Adam Liptak, "Rendering Justice, With One Eye on Re-Election," *The New York Times*, May 25, 2008, A1.

28. Herbert M. Kritzer, "Constituencies in Judicial Retention Processes," *Journal of Institutional and Theoretical Economics* 166, no. 1 (2010): 115–16.

29. John O. Haley, "The Japanese Judiciary: Maintaining Integrity, Autonomy and the Public Trust" in *Law in Japan: A Turning Point*, ed. Daniel Foote (University of Washington Press, 2007).

30. *Id.*

31. Amanda Driscoll and Michael J. Nelson, "Judicial Selection and the Democratization of Justice: Lessons from the Bolivian Judicial Elections," *Journal of Law and Courts* 3, no. 1 (2015): 116.

32. *Id.*,122. After the 2017 judicial elections, however, then-President Evo Morales dismissed almost one hundred judges through the country's Magistrates Council in an attempt to undermine judicial independence. See "Bolivia: Dozens of Judges Arbitrarily Dismissed," *Human Rights Watch*, April 29, 2019, 9:00 a.m. EDT, https://www.hrw.org/news/2019/04/29/bolivia-dozens-judges-arbitrarily-dismissed.

33. Liptak, "U.S. Voting for Judges" (quoting Lasser).

34. U.S. Const. art. II, § 2, cl. 2.

35. U.S. Const. art. III, § 1.

36. See Burt Neuborne, "The Myth of Parity," *Harvard Law Review* 90, no. 6 (April 1977): 1105, 1121–22 (arguing that a competence gap exists between state and

federal judges partly because federal judgeships are better compensated, more prestigious, and more difficult to obtain relative to state judgeships).

37. See Caleb Nelson, "A Re-evaluation of Scholarly Explanations for the Rise of the Elective Judiciary in Antebellum America," *The American Journal of Legal History* 37, no. 2 (April 1993): 190.

38. Jed Handelsman Shugerman, *The People's Courts: Pursuing Judicial Independence in America* (Cambridge, Mass.: Harvard University Press, 2012), 49–52.

39. *Id.*, 57–60; John N. Shaeffer, "A Comparison of the First Constitutions of Vermont and Pennsylvania," *Vermont History* 43, no. 1 (Winter 1975): 37.

40. Evan Haynes, *The Selection and Tenure of Judges* (The National Conference of Judicial Councils, 1944), 99.

41. Shugerman, *The People's Courts*, 60–62.

42. Shugerman, *The People's* Courts, 66–77; Winbourne Magruder Drake, "The Mississippi Convention of 1832," *Journal of Southern History* 23 (August 1957): 359–64.

43. 31 U.S. 515 (1832).

44. William G. Bishop and William H. Attree, *Report of the Debates and Proceedings of the Convention for the Revision of the Constitution of the State of New York* (Albay: Evening Atlas, 1846): 883.

45. *Id.*, 671–72.

46. Nelson, "A Re-evaluation of Scholarly Explanations," 193.

47. Shugerman, *The People's Courts*, 105.

48. H. Fowler, *Report of the Debates and Proceedings of the Convention for the Revision of the Constitution of the State of Indiana*, vol. 2 (Indianapolis, W.B. Burford Print Col, 1850) (remarks of delegate Judge Borden).

49. Arthur Charles Cole, ed., *The Constitutional Debates of 1847* (Springfield, Ill.: Trustees of the Illinois State Historical Library, 1919): 462.

50. "Debate in the House of Representatives on the Proposed Amendment of the Constitution, Remarks of Mr. Biddle of Philadelphia, February 8, 1850," *Pennsylvania Telegraph*, February 20, 1850.

51. Kentucky Constitutional Convention, *Report of the Debates and Proceedings of the Convention for the Revision of the Constitution of the State of Kentucky* (Frankfort, Ky.: A.G. Hodges & Co., 1849), 273 (statement of Francis M. Bristow).

52. Nelson, "A Re-evaluation of Scholarly Explanations," 195 (quoting constitutional debates of 1847); Cole, *Constitutional Debates*, 462 (statement of David Davis).

53. For a discussion of the role of political parties in partisan elections, see Michael Kang and Joanna Shepherd, "The Partisan Price of Justice: An Empirical Analysis of Campaign Contributions and Judicial Decisions," *NYU Law Review* 86, no. 69 (April 2011): 107–11.

54. Gilbert E. Roe, *Our Judicial Oligarchy* (New York: B.W. Huebsch, 1912), 14 (citing Governor Chester Aldrich).

55. Shugerman, *The People's Courts*, 167–73.

56. *Id.*, 168; F. Andrew Hanssen, "Learning about Judicial Independence: Institutional Change in the State Courts," *Journal of Legal Studies* 33 (June 2004): 449–51.

57. Shugerman, *The People's Courts*, 170.

58. Kermit L. Hall, "Progressive Reform and the Decline of Democratic Accountability: The Popular Election of State Supreme Court Judges, 1850–1920," *American Bar Foundation Research Journal* 9 (1984): 361–62.

59. Shugerman, *The People's Courts*, 177–81.

60. Shugerman, *The People's Courts*, 177–94.

61. 18 Cal. State Bar J. 222 (1943).

62. Shugerman, *The People's Courts*, 197–207; Charles B. Blackmar, "Missouri's Nonpartisan Court Plan from 1942 to 2005," *Missouri Law Review* 72 (2007): 200–204.

63. Shugerman, *The People's Courts*, 212–18.

64. Shugerman, *The People's Courts*, 218–23.

65. Indiana, New Jersey, Ohio, and Pennsylvania. However, Pennsylvania switched from a seven-year term to a life term in 1790. National Center for State Courts, "History of Reform Efforts: Formal Changes since Inception" (2019), http://www.judicialselection.us/judicial_selection/reform_efforts/formal_changes_since_inception.cfm?state=.

66. Massachusetts Constitutional Convention, *Official Report of the Debates and Proceedings in the State Convention, Assembled May 4th, 1853, to Revise and Amend the Constitution of the Commonwealth of Massachusetts* (Boston: White & Potter, 1853), 776 (remarks of Benjamin F. Hallett).

67. *Id.*, 700 (remarks of Foster Hooper).

68. *The Natchez*, July 14, 1832.

69. Sherman Croswell and Richard Sutton, *Debates and Proceedings in the New York State Convention for the Revision of the Constitution* (Albany: Albany Argus, 1846), 456.

70. James Sample, Charles Hall, and Linda Casey, "The New Politics of Judicial Elections 2000–2009: Decade of Change," *Judicature* 94, no. 2 (2010).

71. Brian J. Ostrom, Neal B. Kauder, and Robert C. LaFountain, eds., *Examining the Work of the State Courts, 1999–2000: A National Perspective from the Court Statistics Project* (Williamsburg, Va.: National Center for State Courts, 2001), 76.

72. American Bar Association (ABA), "Justice in Jeopardy: Report of the American Bar Association Commission on the 21st Century Judiciary" (2003): 15.

73. Explanations involve the role of the underwriting cycle, conspiracy among insurance companies, increased liability actions, and uncertainty. For an assessment of alternate explanations of the crisis, see, for example, Kenneth S. Abraham, "Making Sense of the Liability Insurance Crisis," *Ohio State Law Journal* 48 (1987): 399; George Priest, "The Current Insurance Crisis and Modern Tort Law," *Yale Law Journal* 96 (1987): 1521; Michael J. Trebilcock, "The Social Insurance-Deterrence Dilemma of Modern North American Tort Law: A Canadian Perspective on the

Liability Insurance Crisis," *San Diego Law Review* 24 (1987): 929; Ralph A. Winter, "The Liability Crisis and the Dynamics of Competitive Insurance Markets," *Yale Journal on Regulation* 5 (1988): 455.

74. See G. Calvin MacKenzie, "The Revolution Nobody Wanted," *Times Literary Supplement*, October 13, 2000.

75. J. Christopher Heagarty, "The Changing Face of Judicial Elections," *North Carolina State Bar Journal* 7, no. 4 (Winter 2002): 20.

76. See generally Anthony Champagne, "Campaign Contributions in Texas Supreme Court Races," *Crime, Law and Social Change* 17 (1992): 91.

77. Phil Hardberger, "Juries Under Siege," *St. Mary's Law Journal* 30 (1998): 4–5.

78. American Judicature Society, "Alabama, Judicial Selection in the States" (2019) https://www.judicialselection.us/judicial_selection/index.cfm?state=AL.

79. Jonathan Groner, "Mississippi: Battleground for Tort Reform," *Legal Times*, January 26, 2004.

80. Model Code of Judicial Conduct, Canon 7(B)(1)(c) (1989).

81. Republican Party of Minn. v. White, 536 U.S. 765, 788 (2002).

82. Rachel P. Caufield, "The Changing Tone of Judicial Election Campaigns as a Result of White," in *Running for Judge: The Rising Political, Financial, and Legal Stakes of Judicial Elections*, ed. Matthew J. Streb (New York University Press, 2007), 36.

83. Citizens United v. Federal Election Comm'n, 558 U.S. 310 (2010).

84. Alicia Bannon, Cathleen Lisk, and Peter Hardin, *The Politics of Judicial Elections 2015–2016: Who Pays for Judicial Races?* (New York: Brennan Center for Justice, 2017), 8.

85. OpenSecrets.org, "Outside Spending, by Super PAC," (2010–2020) https://www.opensecrets.org/outside-spending/super_pacs.

86. Bob Biersack, "8 Years Later: How Citizens United Changed Campaign Finance," *OpenSecrets*, February 7, 2018, https://www.opensecrets.org/news/2018/02/how-citizens-united-changed-campaign-finance/.

87. Bannon, Lisk, and Hardin, *The Politics of Judicial Elections*, 8.

88. Outside spending by interest groups is campaign spending by non-party groups such as nonconnected PACs, Super PACs, and other 501(c) and 527 organizations that do not formally coordinate with parties or candidates.

89. Douglas Keith and Eric Velasco, "The Politics of Judicial Elections 2019–2020: Special Interests Are Spending More than Ever on State High Court Races. Here's Why," *Brennan Center for Justice*, January 25, 2022: 2.

90. *Id.*, 4.

91. *Id.*, 2, 7.

92. Deborah Goldberg, Craig Holman, and Samantha Sanchez, *The New Politics of Judicial Elections, 2000: How 2000 was a Watershed Year for Big Money, Special Interest Pressure, and TV Advertising in State Supreme Court Campaigns* (Washington, D.C.: Justice at Stake Campaign, 2002), 14.

93. Bannon, Lisk, and Hardin, *The Politics of Judicial Elections*, 32–34.

94. Deborah Goldberg, Sarah Samis, Edwin Bender, and Rachel Weiss, *The New Politics of Judicial Elections, 2004: How Special Interest Pressure on Our Courts has Reached a "Tipping Point"—and How to Keep our Courts Fair and Impartial* (Washington, D.C.: Justice at Stake Campaign, 2004), vii.

95. Bannon, Lisk, and Hardin, *The Politics of Judicial Elections*, 32.

96. U.S. Chamber, Institute for Legal Reform, "U.S. Chamber Enters Political Debate for Next White House," August 23, 2004.

97. Goldberg et al., *New Politics of Judicial Elections, 2004*, 9.

98. Bannon, Lisk, and Hardin, *The Politics of Judicial Elections*, 35–39.

99. Scott Greytak, Alicia Bannon, Allyse Falce, and Linda Casey, *Bankrolling the Bench: The New Politics of Judicial Elections, 2013–14* (Washington, D.C.: Justice at Stake Campaign, 2015), 54.

100. FairCourtsPage, "Don Blankenship Ad against Warren McGraw," March 13, 2009, YouTube video, 0:33, https://www.youtube.com/watch?v=cmatVomyFjA.

101. The Clean Courts Committee, "Vote No on Overstreet," October 20, 2020, YouTube video, 0:30, https://www.youtube.com/watch?v=XOYWQoFo77U.

102. Joe Kelly, "Wisconsin Judge Files Defamation Case Over Political TV Ads," *Courthouse News Service*, April 3, 2020; Brennan Center for Justice, "Buying Time 2020—Wisconsin," February 6, 2020.

103. Bannon, Lisk, and Hardin, *The Politics of Judicial Elections*, 36.

104. Douglas Keith, Patrick Berry, and Eric Velasco, "The Politics of Judicial Elections 2017–18: How Dark Money, Interest Groups, and Big Donors Shape State High Courts," *Brennan Center for Justice*, December 11, 2019: 5.

105. Holly Kathleen Hall, "Justice for Sale? The Shadow of Dark Money in State Judicial Elections," *Communication Law Review* 19, no. 1 (2020): 26.

106. Steve Rathje, Jay J. Van Bavel, and Sander van der Linden, "Out-group Animosity Drives Engagement on Social Media," *PNAS* 118, no. 26 (June 23, 2021): 1.

107. Facebook.com, "Ad Library," https://www.facebook.com/ads/library/?active_status=all&ad_type=political_and_issue_ads&country=US.

108. James Sample, Lauren Jones, and Rachel Weiss, *The New Politics of Judicial Elections 2006: How 2006 Was the Most Threatening Year Yet to the Fairness and Impartiality of Our Courts—and How Americans are Fighting Back*, (Washington, D.C.: Justice at Stake Campaign, 2007), 7.

109. The Brennan Center estimates sources of outside spending by identifying sources of TV ad buys. Bannon, Lisk, and Hardin, *The Politics of Judicial Elections*, 25.

110. Bannon, Lisk, and Hardin, *The Politics of Judicial Elections*, 2.

111. *Id.*

112. J.T. Stepleton, "Monetary Competitiveness in State Legislative Races, 2015 and 2016" *FollowtheMoney.org*, November 1, 2017, https://www.followthemoney.org/research/institute-reports/monetary-competitiveness-in-2015-and-2016-state-legislative-races.

113. Greytak et al., *Bankrolling the Bench*, v.

114. Gerald F. Uelmen, "Crocodiles in the Bathtub: Maintaining the Independence of State Supreme Courts in an Era of Judicial Politicization," *Notre Dame Law Review* 72, no. 4 (1997): 1133.

115. Justice at Stake/Brennan Center, "National Poll, 10/22–10/24, 2013," https://www.brennancenter.org/sites/default/files/press-releases/JAS%20Brennan%20NPJE%20Poll%20Topline.pdf.

116. *Id.*

117. Greenberg Quinlan Rosner Research Inc., "Justice At Stake—State Judges Frequency Questionnaire, November 5, 2001–January 2, 2002" *BrennanCenter.org*, 2002: 3–4.

118. *Id.*, 9.

119. *Id.*, 5.

120. Christie Thompson, "Trial by Cash," *The Atlantic*, December 11, 2014 (quoting Gary R. Wade).

121. Annemarie Mannion, "Retired Justice Warns Against 'Politicians in Robes,'" *Chicago Tribune*, May 30, 2013 (quoting Justice Sandra Day O'Connor).

122. Sample, Hall, and Casey, "The New Politics of Judicial Elections 2000–2009," Foreword.

123. See American Bar Association Coalition For Justice, *Roadmaps - Judicial Selection: The Process of Choosing Judges* (2008), 2, 8; American Bar Association (ABA), "Justice in Jeopardy: Report of the American Bar Association Commission on the 21st Century Judiciary" (2003): 1–2, https://www.americanbar.org/content/dam/aba/migrated/judind/jeopardy/pdf/report.authcheckdam.pdf.

124. N.Y. State Bd. of Elections v. López Torres, 128 S. Ct. 791, 801 (2008).

125. *Id.* at 803 (Kennedy and Breyer, JJ., concurring).

126. *Id.*

127. *Id.* at 801 (Stevens and Souter, JJ., concurring).

128. *Id.* (quoting Justice Thurgood Marshall).

129. National Center for State Courts, "History of Reform Efforts: Formal Changes Since Inception" (2019), http://www.judicialselection.us/judicial_selection/reform_efforts/formal_changes_since_inception.cfm?state=. The other state to reform judicial selection, Rhode Island (1994), replaced a system under which the state legislature selected judges with a merit selection system, but maintained permanent tenure for state supreme court justices.

Chapter 3

1. Chisom v. Roemer, 501 U.S. 380, 400 (1991).

2. Williams-Yulee v. Fla. Bar, 575 U.S. 433, 437 (2015).

3. See generally John Hart Ely, *Democracy and Distrust: A Theory of Judicial Review*, (Cambridge, Mass.: Harvard University Press, 1980): 153.

4. See Paul Egan, "Michigan Supreme Court Election Is a Low-Key Affair," *Detroit Free Press*, October 28, 2016, 11:00 p.m. EST, https://www.freep.com/story/news/politics/2016/10/28/michigan-supreme-court-election/92668800/.

5. See Michigan Campaign Finance Network, "America's Most Expensive, Most Secretive Judicial Election," October 29, 2012, https://mcfn.org/node/168/americas-most-expensive-most-secretive-judicial-election.

6. See David Eggert, "TV Ad Criticizes Bridget McCormack for Volunteering to Represent Suspected Terrorists," *MLive*, October 30, 2012, 8:50 p.m., https://www.mlive.com/politics/2012/10/conservative_judicial_group_ru.html.

7. See Barbara S. Gillers et al., "A View from the Bench," *Legislation and Public Policy* 18 (2015): 552.

8. See Roger Weber, "Michigan Supreme Court Candidate Bridget McCormack Responds to Attack Ad," *ClickonDetroit*, November 1, 2012, 7:35 p.m. EDT, https://www.clickondetroit.com/news/2012/11/01/michigan-supreme-court-candidate-bridget-mccormack-responds-to-attack-ad/.

9. See The Reliable Source, "How Michigan Judicial Candidate Bridget Mary McCormack Got 'The West Wing' Cast for her Campaign Video," *The Washington Post*, September 20, 2012, https://www.washingtonpost.com/blogs/reliable-source/post/how-michigan-judicial-candidate-bridget-mary-mccormack-got-the-west-wing-cast-for-her-campaign-video/2012/09/20/a2d53326-0347-11e2-91e7-2962c74e7738_blog.html.

10. See Cotton Delo, "Michigan Supreme Court Campaign Credits Facebook Ads with Margin of Victory," *Ad Age*, December 4, 2012, https://adage.com/article/campaign-trail/michigan-supreme-court-campaign-credits-facebook-ads/238604.

11. See Paul Egan, "Michigan GOP Could Drop Support for Judge Over Gerrymandering Vote," *Detroit Free Press*, August 1, 2018, https://www.freep.com/story/news/local/michigan/2018/08/01/gop-judge-gerrymandering-michigan/877968002/; Ellen Shanna Knoppow, "Justice Elizabeth Clement: On Politicizing the Courts, Child Welfare, the LGBTQ Community and RBG," *PrideSource*, April 16, 2019, https://pridesource.com/article/justice-elizabeth-clement-on-politicizing-the-courts-child-welfare-the-lgbtq-community-and-rbg/.

12. See Beth LeBlanc, "Michigan Justice Faced 'Bullying' Over Redistricting Plan," *Detroit News*, September 24, 2018, https://www.detroitnews.com/story/news/local/michigan/2018/09/24/justice-clement-bullying-redistricting-proposal/1412350002/.

13. Greenberg Quinlan Rosner Research and American Viewpoint, "Justice At Stake State Judges Frequency Questionnaire (2002)," January 31, 2002, https://www.brennancenter.org/sites/default/files/2001%20National%20Bipartisan%20Survey%20of%20Almost%202%2C500%20Judges.pdf; "Justice At Stake Frequency Public Poll Questionnaire (2001)," https://www.brennancenter.org/sites/default/files/2001%20National%20Bipartisan%20Survey.pdf (showing that 36 percent of the public thinks campaign contributions have "a great deal of influence" while 40 percent think campaign contributions have "some influence").

14. *Id.* (finding 26 percent of judges think campaign contributions have great or some influence on judicial decisionmaking).

15. A penny is too small and flat to gain enough momentum to kill someone. Natalie Wolchover, "Could a Penny Dropped Off a Skyscraper Actually Kill You?," *Scientific American*, March 5, 2012, https://www.scientificamerican.com/article/could-a-penny-dropped-off/.

16. It is actually a 51–49 percent chance, where you are more likely to land on the face that it started on. Persi Diaconis, Susan Holmes, and Richard Montgomery, "Dynamical Bias in the Coin Toss," *SIAM Review* 49, no. 2 (June 2007), https://statweb.stanford.edu/~susan/papers/headswithJ.pdf.

17. Sugar does not affect the behavior of children. Mark L. Wolraich, David B. Wilson, and J. Wade White, "The Effect of Sugar on Behavior or Cognition in Children: A Meta-Analysis," *JAMA* 274, no. 20 (November 1995): 1617.

18. Kyle D. Cheek and Anthony Champagne, "Partisan Judicial Elections: Lessons from a Bellwether State," *Willamette Law Review* 39 (2003): 1358–59.

19. *Id.*

20. Chris W. Bonneau and Melinda Gann Hall, *In Defense of Judicial Elections* (New York: Routledge, 2009), 2.

21. Gerald F. Uelmen, "Crocodiles in the Bathtub: Maintaining the Independence of State Supreme Courts in an Era of Judicial Politicization," *Notre Dame Law Review* 72, no. 4 (1997): 1133.

22. National Center for State Courts, "Methods of Judicial Selection," http://www.judicialselection.us/judicial_selection/methods/selection_of_judges.cfm?state= (last visited August 26, 2021).

23. *Id.*

24. *Id.*

25. Michael S. Kang and Joanna M. Shepherd, "The Partisan Price of Justice: An Empirical Analysis of Campaign Contributions and Judicial Decisions," *NYU Law Review* 86, no. 1 (April 2011): 79 (summarizing principal systems of judicial selection).

26. *Id.*

27. American Bar Association (ABA), "Justice in Jeopardy: Report of the American Bar Association Commission on the 21st Century Judiciary" (2003): 96.

28. See, e.g., Kang and Shepherd, "The Partisan Price of Justice," 94 (noting that judges facing retention events deviate from earlier voting patterns, impose longer criminal sentences, and are more likely to side with the majority in death penalty cases).

29. David R. Mayhew, *Congress: The Electoral Connection*, 2nd ed. (New Haven and London: Yale University Press, 2004), 6.

30. James Madison, "The Federalist No. 57," in *The Federalist*, ed. Jacob E. Cooke (Middletown, Conn.: Wesleyan University Press, 1961), 384–85.

31. *Id.*

32. Lawrence Lessig, *Republic, Lost: How Money Corrupts Congress—and a Plan to Stop It* (New York: Twelve Books, 2012).

33. Andrea Seabrook and Alex Blumberg, "Take the Money and Run for Office," March 30, 2012, in *This American Life*, podcast, https://www.thisamerican life.org/461/take-the-money-and-run-for-office (quoting then–U.S. Rep. Barney Frank).

34. For state supreme court elections between 2016 and 2020, incumbents ran for re-election 82.09 percent of the time. See Ballotpedia, "State Judicial Elections, 2021," https://ballotpedia.org/State_judicial_elections,_2021.

35. See generally Stephen J. Choi, Mitu Gulati, and Eric A. Posner, "The Law and Policy of Judicial Retirement: An Empirical Study," *Journal of Legal Studies* 42, no. 1 (January 2013): 111.

36. Richard Posner, *Overcoming Law* (Cambridge: Harvard University Press, 1995), 117.

37. For example, in Maryland between 1987 and 2000, the state legislature did not deny reappointment to any incumbent judge that sought reappointment. Connecticut General Assembly, "Judicial Selection" (December 2000), https://www.cga .ct.gov/pri/archives/js/20001201FINAL_Full.pdf.

38. Between 1964 and 2006, out of 6,306 judicial retention elections only 56 judges were not retained. Larry Aspin, "Trends in Judicial Retention Elections, 1964–2006," *Judicature* 90 (2007): 210.

39. Douglas Keith, Patrick Berry, and Eric Velasco, "The Politics of Judicial Elections, 2017–18: How Dark Money, Interest Groups, and Big Donors Shape State High Courts," *Brennan Center for Justice*, (December 11, 2019): 1.

40. See Ballotpedia, "State Supreme Court Elections, 2020," https://ballotpedia .org/State_supreme_court_elections,_2020#Incumbent_win_rates.

41. *Id.*

42. See Joanna M. Shepherd, "Are Appointed Judges Strategic Too?," *Duke Law Journal* 58 (2009): 1589.

43. Caleb Nelson, "A Re-Evaluation of Scholarly Explanations for the Rise of the Elective Judiciary in Antebellum America," *American Journal of Legal History* 37 (1993): 205 (quoting Charles Ruggles).

44. *Id.*, 206 (quoting David Davis, delegate to the Illinois Constitutional Convention of 1847).

45. Shepherd, "Are Appointed Judges Strategic Too?," 1591.

46. See, e.g., John W. Kingdon, *Agendas, Alternatives, and Public Policies* (Boston: Little, Brown, 1984) (describing the salience for candidates of potential voter reaction in the future).

47. See Bonneau and Hall, *In Defense of Judicial Elections*, 70–103.

48. *Id.*

49. See Melinda Gann Hall, *Attacking Judges: How Campaign Advertising Influences State Supreme Court Elections* (Redwood City: Stanford University Press, 2015); Melinda Gann Hall and Chris W. Bonneau, "Mobilizing Interest: The Effects of Money on Citizen Participation in State Supreme Court Elections," *American Journal of Political Science* 52, no. 3 (2008): 457.

50. See, e.g., Melinda Gann Hall, "State Supreme Courts in American Democracy: Probing the Myths of Judicial Reform," *The American Political Science Review* 95, no. 2 (June 2001): 315; Lawrence Baum, "Explaining the Vote in Judicial Elections: The 1984 Ohio Supreme Court Elections," *The Western Political Quarterly* 40 (1987): 361; Marie Hojnacki and Lawrence Baum, "'New-Style' Judicial Campaigns and the Voters: Economic Issues and Union Members in Ohio," *Western Political Quarterly* 45, no. 4 (December 1992): 921.

51. See generally Joanna Shepherd and Michael S. Kang, "Skewed Justice: Citizens United, Television Advertising and State Supreme Court Justices' Decisions in Criminal Cases," *American Constitution Society* (2014), https://www.acslaw.org/analysis/reports/skewed-justice/.

52. See Sara C. Benesh, "Understanding Public Confidence in American Courts," *Journal of Politics* 68, no. 3 (July 2006): 704; Melinda Gann Hall, "State Supreme Courts in American Democracy: Probing the Myths of Judicial Reform," *American Political Science Review* 95, no. 2 (2001): 322–24.

53. See Adam Skaggs, Maria da Silva, and Linda Casey, *The New Politics of Judicial Elections, 2009–10: How Special Interest "Super Spenders" Threatened Impartial Justice and Emboldened Unprecedented Legislative Attacks on America's Courts* (Washington, D.C.: Justice at Stake Campaign, 2011): 13–20; Stephen B. Bright and Patrick J. Keenan, "Judges and the Politics of Death: Deciding Between the Bill of Rights and the Next Election in Capital Cases," *Boston University Law Review* 75 (May 1995): 763; Anthony Champagne, "Television Ads in Judicial Campaigns," *Indiana Law Review* 35 (2002): 684.

54. See Shepherd and Kang, "Skewed Justice: Citizens United" (collecting examples from TV advertisements).

55. Carlos Berdejo and Noam Yuchtman, "Crime, Punishment, and Politics: An Analysis of Political Cycles in Criminal Sentencing," *The Review of Economics and Statistics* 95, no. 3 (2013): 748.

56. *Id.*, 752. See also Brandice Canes-Wrone, Tom S. Clark, and Jason P. Kelly, "Judicial Selection and Death Penalty Decisions," *American Political Science Review* 108, no. 1 (January 2014): 35.

57. Gregory A. Huber and Sanford C. Gordon, "Accountability and Coercion: Is Justice Blind When It Runs for Office?," *American Journal of Political Science* 48, no. 2 (April 2004): 248.

58. Sanford C. Gordon and Gregory A. Huber, "The Effect of Electoral Competitiveness on Incumbent Behavior," *Quarterly Journal of Political Science* 2, no. 2 (2007): 128–30.

59. Paul Brace and Melinda Gann Hall, "Studying Courts Comparatively: The View from the American States," *Political Research Quarterly* 48 (1995): 24.

60. See, e.g., Paul Brace and Brent D. Boyea, "State Public Opinion, the Death Penalty, and the Practice of Electing Judges," *American Journal of Political Science* 52 (2008): 370; Paul R. Brace and Melinda Gann Hall, "The Interplay of Preferences, Case Facts, Context, and Rules in the Politics of Judicial Choice," *The Jounral of*

Politics 59, no. 4 (November 1997): 1223; Claire S.H. Lim, "Preferences and Incentives of Appointed and Elected Public Officials: Evidence from State Trial Court Judges," *American Economic Review* 103, no. 4 (June 2013): 1361; Elisha Carol Savchak and A.J. Barghothi, "The Influence of Appointment and Retention Constituencies: Testing Strategies of Judicial Decisionmaking," *State Politics & Policy Quarterly* 7, no. 4 (Winter 2007): 406–408; Melinda Gann Hall, "Electoral Politics and Strategic Voting in State Supreme Courts," *Journal of Politics* 54 (1992): 442; Eric Helland and Alex Tabarrok, "The Effect of Electoral Institutions on Tort Awards," *American Law and Economic Review* 4, no. 2 (2002): 345–46; Alexander Tabarrok and Eric Helland, "Court Politics: The Political Economy of Tort Awards," *Journal of Law and Economics* 42, no. 1 (April 1999): 158.

61. Huber and Gordon, "Accountability and Coercion," 249.

62. *Id.*, 258 ("Our finding is not attributable to bidirectional convergence with a preponderance of lenient judges."); Herbert M. Kritzer, *Justices on the Ballot* (Cambridge University Press, 2015), 63 ("The overall pattern here strongly suggests that judges facing reelection are attuned to the risks of being labeled soft on crime by a potential opponent.").

63. Huber and Gordon, "Accountability and Coercion," 258.

64. Shepherd and Kang, "Skewed Justice: Citizens United," 2–4. The following several pages draw from findings in our ACS report.

65. Citizens United v. Federal Election Comm'n, 558 U.S. 310 (2010).

66. See Melinda Gann Hall, *Attacking Judges*, 74.

67. See *Id.*, 75.

68. See *Id.*, 79.

69. See Michael S. Kang and Joanna M. Shepherd, "Judging Judicial Elections," *Michigan Law Review* 114, no. 6 (2016): 929 (reviewing Melinda Gann Hall, *Attacking Judges*).

70. Melvin I. Urofsky, *Money and Free Speech: Campaign Finance Reform and the Courts* (University Press of Kansas, 2005), 3 (quoting Mark Hanna).

71. Sue Bell Cobb, "I Was Alabama's Top Judge. I'm Ashamed by What I Had to Do to Get There," *Politico*, March–April 2015, 1, https://www.politico.com/magazine/story/2015/03/judicial-elections-fundraising-115503/.

72. Melody Luetkehans, "Dark Money and the Future of Judicial Elections," *The National Judicial College*, October 13, 2015 (quoting Sue Bell Cobb), https://www.judges.org/dark-money-and-the-future-of-judicial-elections/.

73. See Cobb, "I Was Alabama's Top Judge."

74. Brennan Center for Justice, "New Poll: Vast Majority of Voters Fear Campaign Cash Skews Judges' Decisions," October 29, 2013, https://www.brennancenter.org/our-work/analysis-opinion/new-poll-vast-majority-voters-fear-campaign-cash-skews-judges-decisions.

75. *Id.*

76. Greenberg Quinlan Rosner Research Inc., "Justice at Stake—State Judges Frequency Questionnaire November 5 2001–January 2, 2002," *BrennanCenter.org*, January 31, 2002, 3–4, http://www.gqrr.com/articles/ 1617/1411_JAS_judges.pdf.

77. *Id.*, 9.

78. *Id.*, 5.

79. Luetkehans, "Dark Money and the Future" (quoting Sue Bell Cob).

80. *Id.*

81. See James Sample, Lauren Jones, and Rachel Weiss, *The New Politics of Judicial Elections 2006: How 2006 Was the Most Threatening Year Yet to the Fairness and Impartiality of Our Courts—and How Americans are Fighting Back*, (Washington, D.C.: Justice at Stake Campaign, 2007).

82. See Scott Greytak, Alicia Bannon, Allyse Falce, and Linda Casey, *Bankrolling the Bench: The New Politics of Judicial Elections, 2013–14* (Washington, D.C.: Justice at Stake Campaign, 2015), 31.

83. See Alicia Bannon, Cathleen Lisk, and Peter Hardin, *The Politics of Judicial Elections 2015–2016: Who Pays for Judicial Races?* (New York: Brennan Center for Justice, 2017): 11.

84. See *Id.*, 7–10.

85. See Kang and Shepherd, "The Partisan Price of Justice." The following results are drawn from this *NYU Law Review* article.

86. *Id.*

87. See generally George L. Priest and Benjamin Klein, "The Selection of Disputes for Litigation," *Journal of Legal Studies* 13 (January 1984): 17–19.

88. See Bannon et al., *Who Pays for Judicial Races?*, 4.

89. Kang and Shepherd, "The Partisan Price of Justice."

90. *Id.*

91. See, e.g., Thomas L. Brunnell, "The Relationship Between Political Parties and Interest Groups: Explaining Patterns of PAC Contributions to Candidates for Congress," *Political Research Quarterly* 58, no. 4 (December 2005): 681 (concluding that most significant PACs favor one party or the other).

92. Marty Cohen, David Karol, Hans Noel, and John Zaller, *The Party Decides: Presidential Nominations Before and After Reform* (University of Chicago Press, 2008), 34.

93. Conservative single-issue groups included pro-life, anti-gun control, Christian Coalition and religious right, limited government, school choice, and Republican Party–affiliated groups that are not formal party committees.

94. Liberal single-issue groups included pro-choice, animal rights, LGBTQ, racial minority and women's, pro-environmental, public-school advocacy, and Democratic Party–affiliated groups that are not formal party committees.

95. Michael S. Kang and Joanna M. Shepherd, "The Partisan Foundations of Judicial Campaign Finance," *Southern California Law Review* 86 (2013): 1243. The following results are drawn from this article.

96. Bush v. Gore, 531 U.S. 1046 (2000).

97. See Richard L. Hasen, "Election Law's Path in the Roberts Court's First Decade: A Sharp Right Turn but with Speed Bumps and Surprising Twists," *Stanford Law Review* 68 (2016): 1603.

98. See, e.g., Ariz. Democratic Party v. Hobbs, 976 F.3d 1081 (9th Cir. 2020).

99. See Michael S. Kang and Joanna M. Shepherd, "The Long Shadow of *Bush v. Gore*," *Stanford Law Review* 68 (2016): 1411 (describing the dataset). The results in this section are drawn from this article.

Chapter 4

1. See Russell Mokhiber, "The Price of Justice: Greed, Corruption and Big Coal," *Common Dreams*, June 18, 2013, https://www.commondreams.org/views/2013/06/18/price-justice-greed-corruption-and-big-coal.
2. See Laurence Leamer, *The Price of Justice: A True Story of Greed and Corruption* (New York: St. Martin's Griffin, 2013), 211.
3. Adam Liptak, "Justices Hear Arguments on Money-Court Nexus," *The New York Times*, March 3, 2009.
4. See Toby Coleman, "'Kids' Group Still Not Charity, Organization Known for Ads Against McGraw," *Sunday Gazette & Daily Mail*, April 10, 2005, 1A.
5. Rehearing Brief of Appellee Hugh M. Caperton, Caperton v. Massey, 2008 WL 651433.
6. *Caperton*, 556 U.S. at 873.
7. See Leamer, *The Price of Justice*, 206.
8. Adam Liptak, "Case May Alter Judge Elections Across Country," *The New York Times*, February 14, 2009.
9. *Id.*
10. West Virginia Judicial Code of Conduct, 3E(1).
11. Rehearing Brief of Appellee Hugh Caperton, Caperton v. Massey, 2008 WL 651433, at *35–36.
12. See Rehearing Brief of Caperton, 2008 WL 651433, at *40; Reply Brief of Appellee Hugh Caperton to Supplemental Brief of Appellants, Caperton v. Massey, 2006 WL 5441516, at *20–22.
13. Len Boselovic, "Lawyers Cite Poll in Effort to Get W.Va. Judge Off Case," *Pittsburgh Post-Gazette*, March 29, 2008, A1.
14. Caperton v. A.T. Massey Coal Co., 679 S.E.2d 223, 302 (W.V. 2008) (Benjamin, C.J., concurring and dissenting), reviewed and remanded, 556 U.S. 868 (2009).
15. Rehearing Brief of Caperton, 2008 WL 651433, at *38.
16. *Id.*
17. *Id.*
18. See, e.g., Len Boselovic, "W.Va. Chief Justice Accused of Bias," *Pittsburgh Post-Gazette*, January 15, 2008, A1.
19. See Leamer, *The Price of Justice*, 285.
20. Adam Liptak, "Case Studies: West Virginia and Illinois," *The New York Times*, October 1, 2006 (quoting Starcher).
21. Caperton v. A.T. Massey Coal Co., 679 S.E.2d 223, 306 (W.V. 2008) (Benjamin, C.J., concurring and dissenting).
22. *Caperton*, 556 U.S. 868, 884 (2009).
23. *Id.* at 886.

24. *Id.* (quoting Aetna Life Ins. Co. v. Lavoie, 475 U.S. 813, 825 [1986], internal quotation marks and citations omitted).

25. *See* Paul N. Nyden, "They Are not Friends Dinner; Campaign Report Shows Connections between Blankenship, Benjamin," *Charleston Gazette*, February 15, 2009, 1A.

26. Liptak, "Case May Alter Judge Elections."

27. Nancy S. Rosenblum, *On the Side of the Angels* (Princeton University Press, 2008), 239 (quoting Bill Bradley).

28. Christie Thompson, "Trial by Cash," *The Atlantic*, December 11, 2014 (quoting Gary R. Wade), https://www.theatlantic.com/politics/archive/2014/12/trial-by-cash/383631/.

29. See, e.g., Michael S. Kang and Joanna M. Shepherd, "The Partisan Price of Justice: An Empirical Analysis of Campaign Contributions and Judicial Decisions," *NYU Law Review* 86, no. 1 (April 2011): 72.

30. Morgan L.W. Hazelton, Jacob Montgomery, and Brendan Nyhan, "Does Public Financing Affect Judicial Behavior? Evidence from the North Carolina Supreme Court," *American Politics Research* 44, no. 4 (2016): 587.

31. *Id.*, 587–90.

32. Damon M. Cann, "Justice for Sale? Campaign Contributions and Judicial Decision Making," *State Politics and Policy Quarterly* 7, no. 3 (August 2006): 281.

33. Damon Cann, Chris Bonneau, and Brent Boyea, "Campaign Contributions and Judicial Decisions in Partisan and Nonpartisan Elections," in *New Directions in Judicial Politics*, ed. Kevin T. McGuire (New York: Routledge, 2012), 38.

34. Madhavi McCall, "The Politics of Judicial Elections: The Influence of Campaign Contributions on the Voting Patterns of Texas Supreme Court Justices, 1994–1997," *Politics & Policy* 31, no. 2 (June 2003): 330 (showing that when two litigants contribute to justices' campaigns, Texas Supreme Court decisions tend to favor the litigant that contributed more money).

35. See, e.g., Kang and Shepherd, "The Partisan Price of Justice," 75.

36. See Kang & Shepherd, "The Partisan Price of Justice"; Michael S. Kang and Joanna M. Shepherd, "The Partisan Foundations of Judicial Campaign Finance," *Southern California Law Review* 86 (2013): 1239; Michael S. Kang and Joanna M. Shepherd, "The Long Shadow of *Bush v. Gore*," *Stanford Law Review* 68 (2016): 1411.

37. J. Christopher Heagarty, "The Changing Face of Judicial Elections," *North Carolina State Bar Journal* 7, no. 4 (Winter 2002): 20 (quoting an Ohio AFL-CIO official).

38. Bruce E. Cain, "Moralism and Realism in Campaign Finance Reform," *University of Chicago Legal Forum* 1995, no. 1 (1995): 116.

39. Kang and Shepherd, "The Partisan Price of Justice," 104; Joanna M. Shepherd, "Money, Politics, and Impartial Justice," *Duke Law Journal* 58 (2009): 664.

40. The business cases were originally collected as part of an earlier study: Joanna M. Shepherd, "Justice at Risk: An Empirical Analysis of Campaign Contributions and Judicial Decisions," *American Constitution Society* (2013). Business

cases were identified by a key search in WestLaw. Once all business cases were identified within a given state and year, twenty-five cases were randomly selected for the sample. If there were twenty-five or fewer cases in a given state and year, all available cases were coded.

41. The data on campaign contributions are collected by the National Institute on Money in State Politics, a nonpartisan, nonprofit charitable organization dedicated to accurate, comprehensive, and unbiased documentation and research on campaign finance at the state level. We follow the common empirical practice of transforming each contribution measure because of the non-linearity observed in bivariate analysis; we use log base 2 for a more straightforward interpretation of the coefficients than the natural log.

42. The margins are computed from a logit regression of pro-business votes on all explanatory variables discussed above.

43. See Melinda Gann Hall, "Electoral Politics and Strategic Voting in State Supreme Courts," *Journal of Politics* 54, no. 2 (May 1992): 427; Melinda Gann Hall, "Constituent Influence in State Supreme Courts: Conceptual Notes and a Case Study," *Journal of Politics* 49, no. 4 (November 1987): 1117; Paul Brace and Melinda Gann Hall, "Studying Courts Comparatively: The View from the American States," *Political Research Quarterly* 48, no. 1 (1995): 24.

44. The margins are computed from a logit regression of pro-business votes on all explanatory variables discussed above.

45. The average contributions raised from business groups in the most recent election was $119,000 for judges in their mandatory last term and $173,000 for judges not facing mandatory retirement.

46. For simplicity we include a "*" to indicate statistical significance at the .05 level and a "+" to indicate statistical significance at the .10 level. If a coefficient is statistically insignificant, that means that there is not a statistically reliable relationship between the explanatory variable (e.g., campaign contributions) and the dependent variable (in our case, judges' pro-business votes) in the data.

47. These estimations measure the marginal impact of business contributions on all judges, including judges who receive no contributions and judges in states without any sort of retention election. When we limit the analysis to only judges in states that use competitive elections for the retention of judges—either partisan or nonpartisan elections—the difference in the likelihood of voting for business litigants between lame duck judges and non–lame duck judges is even greater. For judges in competitive elections systems, a doubling of business contributions is associated with a 36 percent increase in the likelihood of a non–lame duck judge casting a pro-business vote, but only a 16.8 percent increase in the likelihood of a lame duck judge voting for the business litigant. A doubling of non-business contributions is associated with a 21.4 percent decrease in the likelihood of a non–lame duck judge casting a pro-business vote, but only a 6.2 percent decrease in the likelihood of a lame duck judge casting a pro-business vote. The larger difference between the pro-business voting of lame duck judges compared to non–lame duck judges in

competitive election systems is consistent with there being a stronger biasing effect in states that use competitive elections for retention.

48. In our data, judges in their mandatory last term range in age from fifty-six to seventy-nine, and judges not in their last term range in age from thirty-seven to eighty-nine.

49. The same pattern still holds when, instead of restricting our analysis to judges over sixty, we restrict it to judges over fifty-five, or to judges over sixty-five. In other words, there is nothing anomalous about age sixty as a cutoff. Regardless of how we limit our sample, the older age of lame duck judges does not explain the weaker influence of money on their votes.

Chapter 5

1. Rick Hasen, "Justice Kennedy Heed Justice Kennedy: Money Buys Influence," *National Law Journal*, October 30, 2015 (quoting Blankenship).

2. Caperton v. A.T. Massey Coal Co. Inc., 556 U.S. 868, 872 (2009) (quoting Withrow v. Larkin, 421 U.S. 35, 47 [1975]).

3. *Caperton*, 556 U.S. at 876 (quoting "The Federalist No. 10").

4. Tumey v. Ohio, 273 U.S. 510, 535 (1927).

5. *Id.* at 532.

6. *Caperton*, 556 U.S. at 882.

7. *Caperton*, 556 U.S. at 886 (quoting Aetna Life Ins. Co. V. Lavoie, 475 U.S. 813, 825 [1986]) (internal quotation marks omitted).

8. *Caperton*, 556 U.S. at 884.

9. Joan Biskupic, "Supreme Court Case with the Feel of a Best Seller," *USA Today*, February 17, 2009.

10. *Caperton*, 556 U.S. at 882.

11. *Id.*

12. See, e.g., Alvin W. Gouldner, "The Norm of Reciprocity: A Preliminary Statement," *The American Sociological Review* 25 (1960): 171 (arguing that reciprocity is a universal human norm and a "principal component" in the development of moral codes); Andreas Diekmann, "The Power of Reciprocity," *Journal of Conflict Resolution* 48 (2004): 487–88 (finding that study participates continue to adhere to the reciprocity norm even as the cost of reciprocating increases).

13. Kevin Townsend, "A Supreme Court Impeachment Fight That's Already Under Way," *The Atlantic*, October 31, 2018 (quoting Richard Neely, former West Virginia Supreme Court Chief Justice).

14. Martin H. Redish, *Judicial Independence and the American Constitution: A Democratic Paradox* (Redwood City: Stanford University Press, 2017), 110.

15. Adam Liptak, "Case May Alter Judge Elections Across Country," *The New York Times*, February 14, 2009 (quoting Blankenship).

16. *Caperton*, 556 U.S.

17. Redish, *Judicial Independence*, 112.

18. *Id.*

19. Ronald Rotunda and Michael Dimino, Amicus Brief in Caperton v. Massey, 20.

20. *Caperton*, 556 U.S. at 891 (Roberts, C.J., dissenting).

21. *Caperton*, 556 U.S. at 900.

22. Amam McLeod, "*Caperton v. A.T. Massey Coal Co.:* A Ten-Year Retrospective on Its Impact on Law and the Judiciary," *West Virginia Law Review* 124, no. 1 (2021).

23. See William Glaberson, "New York Takes Step on Money in Judicial Elections," *The New York Times*, February 13, 2011.

24. Allyse Falce, "On Anniversary of Caperton v. Massey, Recusal Rules Still an Issue," *Brennan Center for Justice*, June 6, 2014, https://www.brennancenter.org/our-work/analysis-opinion/anniversary-caperton-v-massey-recusal-rules-still-issue.

25. See, e.g., Cmt to New Mexico Rule 21.211 (2012).

26. See, e.g., Andrew Adams, "After the Partisan Fight, Lawmakers Approve Bill Limiting Donations in Judicial Election," St. J. Reg. (April 8, 2022) (discussing Illinois's adoption of new judicial campaign finance rules).

27. See, e.g., Michael S. Kang, "The Brave New World of Party Campaign Finance Law," *Cornell Law Review* 101 (2016): 531; Michael S. Kang, "The Year of the Super PAC," *The George Washington Law Review* 81, no. 6 (November 2013): 1902; Michael S. Kang, "The End of Campaign Finance Law," *Virginia Law Review* 98, no. 1 (March 2012): 1.

28. See Kang, "End of Campaign Finance Law."

29. State Bar of Wisconsin, "Judicial Task Force Report and Recommendations" (2013): 13.

30. See, e.g., Leamer, *The Price of Justice*, 219–20.

31. See Andrea Lannom, "WV Supreme Court: Massey Shareholders Lacked Standing," *WV State News Journal*, September 13, 2013.

32. Pema Levy, "This Election Inspired a John Grisham Novel. Now It Just Got Even Weirder," *Mother Jones*, May 9, 2016 (quoting attorney Anthony Majestro).

33. Chris Dickerson, "WV CALA Says Benjamin's Record Is 'Cause for Concern'," *W.Va. Record*, May 3, 2016 (quoting CALA executive director Roman Stauffer).

34. Rick Hasen, "Justice Kennedy Heed Justice Kennedy: Money Buys Influence," *National Law Journal*, October 30, 2015 (quoting Benjamin); Billy Corriher, "The Million Dollar Judges of 2015–16: Independent Spending and Secret Money," *Center for American Progress*, December 19, 2016, https://www.americanprogress.org/article/the-million-dollar-judges-of-2015-16-independent-spending-and-secret-money/.

35. Shauna Johnson, "On the Campaign Trail: Justice Brent Benjamin, State Supreme Court Candidate," *WV MetroNews*, April 19, 2016 (quoting Benjamin).

36. See Kevin Townsend, "A Supreme Court Impeachment Fight That's Already Under Way," *The Atlantic*, October 31, 2018.

37. See Alex Kotch, "Outside Money Wins Big in West Virginia Supreme Court Election," *Institute of Southern Studies*, May 13, 2016.

38. Editorial, "Robed Politicians: Justice O'Connor Cites the Judicial Election Problem," *Pittsburgh Post-Gazette*, June 19, 2013.

39. Karen Chadra, "Justice Sandra Day O'Connor Speaks to Packed House at Elmhurst College," *Patch.com*, June 1, 2013 (quoting O'Connor).

40. *Id.*

41. James Podgers, "O'Connor on Judicial Elections: 'They're Awful. I Hate Them,'" *ABA Journal*, May 9, 2009 (quoting O'Connor).

42. American Bar Association, "Justice in Jeopardy: Report of the American Bar Association Commission on the 21st Century Judiciary" (2003): viii.

43. Joan Biskupic, "Supreme Court Case with the Feel of a Best Seller," *USA Today*, February 17, 2009.

44. See, e.g., Annenberg Public Policy Center, "Americans Overwhelmingly Favor Election of Judges but Disapprove of Judicial Campaign Fund-Raising, Fearing It Affects Fairness," May 23, 2007 (citing results of a national survey of 1,002 respondents in August 2006); Justice at Stake Campaign survey, October 2001.

45. See Raymond J. McKoski, "Living with Judicial Elections," *University of Arkansas at Little Rock Review* 39, no. 4 (2017): 494 ("Even staunch supporters of merit selection, however, admit that the overwhelming majority of Americans prefer an elected judiciary. Polling data consistently illustrates that preference. For example, a poll in Alabama disclosed that 85% of respondents chose judicial elections as the best method of judicial selection. In a poll of 500 registered voters in Oklahoma, 74% preferred electing judges and 22% preferred appointing judges. Eighty percent of Ohioans support elections. A survey in 2002 revealed that 78.5 % of Illinois voters supported the election of judges. A national survey conducted by Justice at Stake found that 76% of voters favored the election of judges while 20% supported judicial appointments. A Harris Interactive Poll conducted for the ABA in 2002 disclosed that 75% of respondents were of the opinion that judges voted into office are more likely to be fair and impartial than judges appointed to office. In 2008, Harris Interactive found that 55% of Americans favored electing judges and only 19% favored appointing judges.").

46. High Point University Survey, May 18, 2018; Elon University Survey, November 20, 2009.

47. Public Opinion Strategies Survey, December 11, 2007.

48. ABA, "Justice in Jeopardy," 98.

49. Redish, *Judicial Independence*, 111.

50. See, e.g., Joshua Eaton, Ilana Marcus, and Ed Timms, "Federal Judges: From Political Players to Lifetime Appointments," *Roll Call*, March 20, 2020.

51. Joshua Eaton, Ilana Marcus, and Ed Timms, "Cashing In On Justice," *Roll Call*, March 30, 2020.

52. *Id.*

53. John M. Walker, Jr., "The Unfortunate Politicization of Judicial Confirmation Hearings," *The Atlantic*, July 9, 2012.

54. See Seung Min Kim, "McConnell's Historic Judge Blockade," *Politico*, July 14, 2016.

55. See Roxanne Roberts, "Merrick Garland Was Historically Snubbed—But He's Emerged More Respected than Ever," *Washington Post*, October 10, 2020.

56. See generally Charles M. Cameron, Cody Gray, Jonathan P. Kastellec, and Jee-Kwang Park, "From Textbook Pluralism to Modern Hyperpluralism: Interest Groups and Supreme Court Nominations, 1930–2017," *Journal of Law and Courts* 8, no. 2 (Fall 2020): 1 (documenting the modern shift to election-style mobilization, spending, and public campaigning in interest group advocacy on federal judicial appointments).

57. See Travis Gettys, "Secretive Group who Bankrolled Brett Kavanaugh Confirmation Is Now Backing Amy Coney Barrett: Report," *Salon.com*, September 30, 2020.

58. See Jeremy W. Peters, "Conservative Groups Unify to Push Neil Gorsuch's Confirmation," *The New York Times*, February 1, 2017; Pete Tucker, "Backed by $10 Million in 'Dark Money,' Gorsuch Claims He's Apolitical," *Huffington Post*, March 25, 2017.

59. See David Sirota and Andrew Perez, "Group that Led Kavanaugh Confirmation Got $15.9 Million from One Mystery Donor," *Daily Poster*, July 16, 2020; Robert O'Harrow, Jr., and Shawn Boburg, "A Conservative Activist's Behind-the-Scenes Campaign to Remake the Nation's Courts," *Washington Post*, May 21, 2019; Brian Schwartz, "Schumer, Democrats Claim Outside Trump Advisor Helps Rig the Judicial Nomination Process," *CNBC*, July 2, 2020.

60. See Michael Biesecker, "Barrett Ads Tied to Interest Groups Funded by Unnamed Donors," *WNEP*, October 26, 2020.

61. See Marianne Levine, "Judicial Crisis Network Launches $3 Million Ad Campaign for Barrett," *Politico*, September 26, 2020; Inyoung Choi, "Koch-Backed Advocacy Group Launched a 'Full-Scale' Campaign to Push Amy Coney Barrett's Supreme Court Confirmation," *Business Insider*, September 28, 2020; Alex Gangitano, "Barrett Ad War Exceeds Kavanagh Fight," *The Hill*, September 30, 2020.

62. See, e.g., Carrie Johnson, "Koch-Funded Group Focuses on Lifetime Appointments of Judges," *NPR*, March 14, 2018; Brian Schwartz, "Conservative Dark Money Groups Gear Up for Battle over DC Circuit Court that Once Included Brett Kavanaugh," CNBC, April 3, 2020; Rachel Frazin, "Giffords, Demand Justice to Pressure GOP Senators to Reject Trump Judicial Pick," *The Hill*, May 12, 2019.

63. ABA, "Justice in Jeopardy," 96.

64. *Id.*

65. Redish, *Judicial Independence*, 138.

66. See Elliott Ash and W. Bentley MacLeod, "Intrinsic Motivation in Public Service: Theory and Evidence from State Supreme Courts," *The Journal of Law and Economics* 58, no. 4 (2015): 881.

67. See *Id.*

68. See *Id.* (reporting that roughly 90 percent of state supreme court justices retired, died, or resigned from their position, with just 10 percent of justices getting promotions or losing re-election).

69. See, e.g., John M. Carey, Richard G. Niemi, Lynda W. Powell, and Gary F. Moncrief, "The Effects of Term Limits on State Legislatures: A New Survey of the 50 States," *Legislative Studies Quarterly* 31, no. 1 (2006): 105.

70. See *Id.*, 897.

71. See Brent D. Boyea, "Does Seniority Matter? The Conditional Influence of State Methods of Judicial Retention," *Social Science Quarterly* 91, no. 1 (March 2010): 209.

72. See Paul Brace, Jeff Yates, and Brent D. Boyea, "Judges, Litigants, and the Design of Courts," *Law & Society Review* 46, no. 3 (September 2012): 497.

73. See ABA, "Justice in Jeopardy," 96.

74. Jed H. Shugerman, "The Twist of Long Terms: Judicial Elections, Role Fidelity, and American Tort Law," *Georgetown Law Journal* 98, no. 5 (June 2010): 1349.

75. See Paul Brace and Melinda Gann Hall, "The Interplay of Preferences, Case Facts, Context, and the Rules in the Politics of Judicial Choice," *The Journal of Politics* 59, no. 4 (November 1997): 1206.

76. See Carey et al., "Effects of Term Limits," 105.

77. See, e.g., Susan M. Miller, Jill Nicholson-Crotty, and Sean Nicholson-Crotty, "The Consequences of Legislative Term Limits for Policy Diffusion," *Political Research Quarterly* 71 (January 2018): 573; David R. Berman, "Legislative Climate," in *Institutional Change in American Politics: The Case of Term Limits*, eds. Karl T. Kurtz, Bruce Cain, and Richard G. Niemi (University of Michigan Press, 2007), 107; Daniel C. Lewis, "Legislative Term Limits and Fiscal Policy Performance," *Legislative Studies Quarterly* 37, no. 3 (2012): 305.

78. See Gary Moncrief and Joel A. Thompson, "On the Outside Looking In: Lobbyists' Perspectives on the Effects of State Legislative Term Limits," *State Politics and Policy Quarterly* 1, no. 4 (Winter 2001): 400.

79. See Dorie Apollonio and Ray La Raja, "Term Limits, Campaign Contributions, and the Distribution of Power in State Legislatures," *Legislative Studies Quarterly* 31, no. 2 (May 2006): 259.

80. U.S. Supreme Court Justice Samuel Alito described that his life as a federal judge "consisted of driving to the office, walking up to my chambers, reading and writing, talking to no human beings except my assistants and my law clerks, getting back in my car, driving home, and doing the same thing the next day." Margaret Talbot, "The Last Word," *The New Yorker*, September 5, 2022, 24, 31.

81. Carey et al., "Effects of Term Limits," 123.

82. See Charles Wood, "Term Limits for Justices Are Rejected," *Montana Lawyer* 28, no. 6 (February 2003); Ballotpedia, "Colorado Term Limits for Supreme Court and Court of Appeals Judges, Initiative 40 (2006)."

83. State Bar of Wisconsin, "Judicial Task Force Report and Recommendation" (September 2013): 3, 10–11.

84. Arkansas Bar Association Task Force on Maintaining a Fair and Impartial Judiciary, "Report and Recommendations of the Task Force on Maintaining a Fair and Impartial Judiciary" (June 1, 2016): 5. Along similar lines, the Pennsylvania House Judiciary Committee has passed Pennsylvania House Bill 1880 in December 2021, which would limit its state supreme court justices to two ten-year terms. See Pennsylvania House Republican Caucus, "Bill to Impose Term Limits on Judges, Justices Passes Committee," December 13, 2021, https://www.pahousegop.com/News/22971/Latest-News/Bill-to-Impose-Term-Limits-on-Judges,-Justices-Passes-Committee-.

85. "The Federalist No. 78."

86. John D. Feerick, "Impeaching Federal Judges: A Study of the Constitutional Provisions," *Fordham Law Review* 39, no. 1 (October 1970): 13.

87. "The Declaration of Independence," para. 11 (U.S. 1776).

88. "The Federalist No. 78."

89. Steven G. Calabresi and James Lindgren, "Term Limits for the Supreme Court: Life Tenure Reconsidered," *Harvard Journal of Law and Public Policy* 29 (2006): 772.

90. Calabresi and Lindgren, "Life Tenure Reconsidered," 813.

91. See *Id.*, 779.

92. See *Id.*, 786.

93. See *Id.*

94. See generally *Id.* (advocating for U.S. Supreme Court term limits and outlining scholarly support for their position).

95. Victor Morton, "Democrats to Introduce 'Supreme Court Term Limits' Bill," *Washington Times*, September 24, 2020.

96. See "Final Report of the Presidential Commission on the Supreme Court of the United States," December 2021. In the spirit of full disclosure, one of us (Michael Kang) served on the Presidential Commission. The Commission itself was not charged with reaching a formal recommendation regarding term limits, but its report presented a persuasive case for a single-term limit applied to the U.S. Supreme Court, as well as the relevant counterarguments.

97. See Seung Min Kim and Robert Barnes, "Supreme Court Term Limits Are Popular and Appear to Be Going Nowhere," *Washington Post*, December 28, 2021.

98. See, e.g., Mary Ellen Klas, "Should Florida Be First State to Impose Term Limits on Justices," *Miami Herald*, February 9, 2017.

Appendix

1. Our measure of non-business contributions aggregates the contributions from several different sectors that are generally not strong supporters of business interests: labor unions, education, tribal governments, nonprofit institutions, clergy, lawyers (most of whom are members of the plaintiffs' bar), candidate contributions, political party contributions, and single-issue groups.

2. Party affiliation was compiled from The American Bench, a directory with biographical information on over 18,000 judges. In situations in which no party

information was available for a judge, but the judge was initially appointed to the high court by a governor, the party of the judge was inferred to be the same as that of the appointing governor.

3. We use the Pacific Research Institute's U.S. Tort Liability Index, which evaluates the tort litigation risks and liability costs across states, as it's a measure of the state law's underlying partiality to business interests.

4. We use the Berry measure of citizen and government ideology. William D. Berry, Evan J. Ringquist, Richard C. Fording, and Russell L. Hanson, "Measuring Citizen and Government Ideology in the American States, 1960–93," *American Journal of Political Science* 42, no. 1 (January 1998): 327.

5. Theodore Eisenberg and Geoffrey P. Miller, "Reversal, Dissent, and Variability in State Supreme Courts: The Centrality of Jurisdictional Source," *Boston University Law Review* 89, no. 5 (December 2009): 1470–72.

Index

527 organizations, 98, 143

abortion, 6, 187n94
"act of God" clause, 97
AFA Action Inc., 3
age, 125–27, 191n49
Alabama, 36, 43, 82, 153
Albright, Joseph, 98
Alito, Samuel, 195n80
American Bar Association (ABA): First Amendment rights and, 43; growing state court influence and, 41–43; Harris Interactive Poll and, 193n45; Model Code of, 434; opposition to judicial elections, 5, 55, 146–47, 152; reform and, 146–47, 152, 155, 193n45; retention and, 66; term limits and, 155
American Bench, The, 196n2
American College of Trial Lawyers, 146
American Constitution Society (ACS), 77, *78*
"And for the Sake of the Kids" group, 48, 93
animal rights, 187n94
appointed judges: big money and, 6, 101, 114, 128–29, 132; governors and, 20–21, 28–29, 61, 64, 71–72, 148, 159; judicial elections and, 20–21, 27–30, 33; reappointment and, 39, 67–73, 128–29, 135, 140, 146–47, 154, 159, 184n37; reform and, 135, 140, 143–51, 158–61, 193n45, 194n56; research methodology and, 196n2; retention and, 59, 61, 64–73, 184n37; rise of judicial elections and, 26–32, 35–39
Arkansas, 56, 196n84
Atlantic magazine, 149
A.T. Massey Coal Company Inc., 97, 135
attack ads: Blankenship and, 49, 99; Brennan Center for Justice and, 79; Campaign Media Analysis Group and, 79–80; crime and, 73–82; Democrats and, 81–82; inflammatory, 44, 48, 50, 60, 73, 79, 99; influence of, 73–82; Justice at Stake and, 79; McCormack and, 60; National Institute on Money in State Politics and, 79–80; re-election and, 73–82, 94; Republicans and, 81–82; retention and, 69, 75–76, 79–82, 94; rise

attack ads (*continued*)
of judicial elections and, 48, *49*, *51*; television and, 5, 48, *49*, *51–52*, 69, 75–76, 79–82, 94, 103; as voter education, 47–48; weaponized decisions and, 73–74

Baker, Justice, 3
bankruptcy, 97
Barrett, Amy Coney, 149–50
Barrow, Clyde, 35
Beckley Register-Herald, 99
Benjamin, Brent: bias and, 99–103, 137; big money and, 8–10, 96–104; Blankenship and, 8–9, 96, 98–103, 135–39, 143, 189n25; *Caperton v. Massey* and, 8–10, 96–103, 136–44; public opinion on, 99–100; recusal and, 8, 99–102, 136, 143–44; reform and, 135–45; subsequent career of, 143–45
Berdejo, Carlos, 75
bias: Benjamin and, 99–103, 137; big money and, 3, 7–18, 25, 56, 63, 66, 76, 83, 85, 100–24, 131–42, 150–52, 161–62, 190n41, 190n47; business cases and, 84–87; campaign finance and, 7–9, 12–17, 25, 56, 63, 66, 76, 83–87, 100–16, 120, 123–24, 131–34, 137–42, 150–52, 161–62, 190n41; *Caperton v. Massey* and, 9–10, 14, 16, 99–104, 136–42; criminal law and, 75–76; endogeneity and, 106–7; gender, 10; good faith and, 109; ideology and, 17, 108, 111; lame ducks and, 14–15, 17, 107, 111–19, 123–24, 131, 138–39, 151–52; last-term judges and, 129–31; probability of, 16; racial, 10; re-election and, 10–18, 56, 63, 66, 76, 104–15, 121, 124, 131, 138–39, 150–52, 161–62; reform and, 133–52, 161–62; retention and, 58–59, 63, 66, 76, 83, 85; retrospective gratitude and, 138–39; rise of judicial elections and, 25, 28, 39, 48, 55, 56; Roberts and, 16; selection effects and, 13–14, 17, 103–4, 107–15, 120–21; statistical analysis of, 104, 107–8, 112, 118–28
Biden, Joe, 160
big money: appointed judges and, 6, 101, 114, 128–29, 132; attack ads and, 5, 48, *49*, *51*, 69, 75–76, 79–82, 94, 103; Benjamin and, 8–10, 96–104; bias and, 3, 7–18, 25, 56, 63, 66, 76, 83, 85, 100–24, 131–42, 150–52, 161–62, 190n41, 190n47; Blankenship and, 8–9, 48, 96–103, 135–39, 143; business cases and, 84–87, 89, 112, 116–20, 189n40; campaign finance and, 1, 4–17, 98–114, 117, 119, 121–24, 131, 190n41; *Caperton v. Massey* and, 8–10, 14, 16, 96–103, 136–39, 143; *Citizens United vs. Federal Election Commission* and, 14, 105; conservatives and, 3, 6, 96–97; corruption and, 15–16; court effects of, 8–12; death penalty and, 121; Democrats and, 3, 87–90, 97–98, 112–13, *120*; donors and, 5–8, 11–17, 96, 105–7, 110–17, 131–32; election cases and, 12–15, 90–94; fundraising and, 2–3, 7, 16, 106–15, 121, 123, 131; governors and, 3; ideologies and, 87–90; incumbents and, 8, 96, 111; interest groups and, 2, 5–7, 12, 103, 117; Iowa Supreme Court and, 1–4; lame ducks and, 14–15, 17, 107, 111–19, 123–32, 190n47, 191n49; last-term judges and, 129–31; lawyers and, 3, 7–8, 109; liberals and, 98; McCormack and, 106; partisanship and, 2, 6, 11, 16, 97, 112–14, 120, 127–28, 190n47; re-election and, 1–2, 5, 10, 12–18, 98, 104–25, 128–32; reform and, 12, 15–18, 114, 117, 119, 132; Republicans and, 87–90, 96–99, 112–13, *120*; retention and,

1–4, 17, *120*, 121, *122*, 127–30, 174n37, 190n47; statistics and, 10, 13–14, 104, 107–8, 112, 118–28, 190n46; Super PACs and, 44, 98, 179n88; television and, 117; tenure and, 107, *128*; Ternus and, 1–5, 12, 14; West Virginia Supreme Court and, 96–102
Birch, Justice, 24, 175n15
Blackmun, Harry, 20
Blankenship, Don: A.T. Massey Coal Company, Inc. and, 97, 135; attack ads and, 49, 99; Benjamin and, 8–9, 96, 98–103, 135–39, 143, 189n25; big money and, 8–9, 48, 96–103, 135–39, 143; *Caperton v. Massey* and, 8, 96–103, 136–39, 143; imprisonment of, 135; McGraw and, 8, 96, 98–99; Maynard and, 97–103; Steptoe & Johnson and, 98
Bolivia, 26–27
Bonneau, Chris, 108
Boyea, Brent, 108
Brace, Paul, 76
Bradley, Bill, 105
Brennan Center for Justice, 44, *49*, 79, 141
bribery, 102
Bush v. Gore, 90–91, *93*
business cases: big money and, 84–87, 89, 112, 116–20, 189n40; interest groups and, 117; retention and, 84–87, 89

Cady, Mark, 3
Calabresi, Steve, 159–60
California, 5, 34–36, 53–54, 64
campaign finance: 527 organizations and, 98, 143; attack ads and, 5, 48, *49*, *51*, 69, 73–82, 94, 103; bias and, 7–9, 12–17, 25, 56, 63, 66, 76, 83–87, 100–16, 120, 123–24, 131–34, 137–42, 150–52, 161–62, 190n41; big money and, 1, 4–17, 98–114, 117, 119, 121–24, 131, 190n41; Blankenship and, 8–9, 48, 96–103, 135–39, 143; business cases and, 84–87; *Citizens United v. Federal Election Commission* and, 14, 44–45, 78, 105; court effects of, 8–12; dark money and, 44, 59; election cases and, 90–94; fundraising and, 2–3 (*see also* fundraising); ideologies and, 87–90; increasing costs of, 39–43, 173n12; influence of, 67, 82–94, 105–11; interest groups and, 2 (*see also* interest groups); Justice at Stake and, 79; lawyers and, 196n1; McCormack and, 59; Michigan Campaign Finance Network and, 59–60; National Institute on Money in State Politics and, 80; new-style judicial elections and, 43–53; qualitative evidence and, 62–63; re-election and, 12–15, 82–94; reform and, 15–18 (*see also* reform); research methodology and, 163–66, *167–71*; retention and, 59–62, 78–79, 82–94; rise of judicial elections and, 19, 44–45, 53–54; Roberts and, 16; role of, 82–94; Scalia on, 4, 6; selection effects and, 13–14, 17, 103–4, 107–15, 120–21; Super PACs and, 44, 98, 179n88; television and, 5; Ternus and, 1–5, 12, 14, 109; understanding influence of, 12–15
Campaign for Working Families, 3
Campaign Media Analysis Group, 79–80
Cann, Damon, 108
Canon 3E(1), 99, 101
Caperton v. Massey: "act of God" clause and, 97; Benjamin and, 8–10, 96–103, 136–44; Benjamin and, 8–10, 96–103, 136–44; bias and, 9–10, 14, 16, 99–104, 136–42; big money and, 8–9, 96–103, 136–39, 143; Blankenship and, 8, 96–103, 136–39, 143;

Caperton v. Massey (*continued*)
Canon 3E(1) and, 99, 101; Democrats and, 97–98, 112–13, *120*; donor influence and, 8, 96–103, 136–39, 143; due process and, 8–9, 96, 102, 136–40; Grisham and, 8, 96, 100; Maynard and, 97–103; post-trial actions since, 140–45; recusal and, 8–10, 99–102, 136, 140–44; reform and, 8, 16–17, 96–97, 135–45; Republicans and, 96–99, 112–13, *120*; Roberts and, 140–42; U.S. Supreme Court and, 8–10, 14, 16, 96–103, 135–44; West Virginia Supreme Court and, 8–9, 48, 96–102, 135–38, 142, 144
Charleston Gazette, 99
Chemerinsky, Erwin, 4
Cherokee Nation, 30
Citizens United vs. Federal Election Commission: big money and, 14, 105; reform and, 142; retention and, 78–79, 84; rise of judicial elections and, 44–46
Clean Courts Committee, 48, *49*
Clement, Elizabeth, 61–62
Cobb, Sue Bell, 82–83
Cold War, 36
Commonwealth Club of California, 34
Conference of Chief Justices, 146
Congressional Record, 73–74
conservatives: big money and, 3, 6, 96–97; reform and, 143, 149; research methodology and, 164; retention and, 79–82, 87, 91–94, 187n93; rise of judicial elections and, 22–25; Tennessee and, 22–25
corruption: big money and, 15–16; recusal and, 8–10, 99–102, 136, 140–44; reform and, 136, 150–51, 159, 161; retention and, 67; rise of judicial elections and, 29–34, 38; scandal and, 29; sports and, 7
CQ Roll Call, 148–49
crime: attack ads and, 73–82; being soft on, 17, 25, 50, 66, 76–77, 79, 186n62; Bonnie and Clyde, 35; children and, 48; *Citizens United v. Federal Election Commission* and, 78–79; Curb Crime movement, 34–36; gender and, 50; liberals and, 25, 76; longer sentences and, 75–76; murder, 22–24, 36, 77; organized, 34; "Pretty Boy" Floyd, 35; rape, 22–23, *49*, 77; Uniform Crime Reporting Program and, 77; Warren and, 34–35; waves of, 34–36; White and, 22–25, 36, 66
criminal law: bias and, 75–76; death penalty and, 22–24, 75, 121, 156, 183n28; retention and, 68, 75–76; state courts and, 6
Curb Crime movement, 34–36

dark money, 44, 59
Davis, Robin, 98, 101
death penalty: big money and, 121; reform and, 156; retention and, 75, 183n28; White and, 22–24
Democrats: attack ads and, 59–60, 81–82; Biden, 160; big money and, 3, 87–90, 97–98, 112–13, *120*; business cases and, 87; *Caperton v. Massey* and, 97–98, 112–13, *120*; election cases and, 90–94; ideological influence and, 87–90; liberal, 81, 87, 91–92, 98, 187n94; Obama, 60–61, 148–49; reform and, 148–49, 160; research methodology and, 164, *167–71*; retention and, 58–61, 81, 87–93, 187n94
Diaconis, Persi, 183n16
disclosure, 5, 44, 100, 196n96
donors: big money and, 5–8, 11–17, 96, 105–7, 110–17, 131–32; *Caperton v. Massey* and, 8, 96–103, 136–39, 143; reform and, 15–18, 133–34, 145,

151, 153, 161; retention and, 58–59, 64–67, 74, 82, 84–87, 95; rise of judicial elections and, 32, 44, 53–56
due process: *Caperton v. Massey* and, 8–9, 96, 102, 136–40; reform and, 136–40; *Tumey v. Ohio* and, 136

École Nationale de la Magistrature, 26
election systems: big money and, 8, 12–15; competitive, 16–21, 26, 40, 53, 55, 59, 65–68, 74, 77–82, 86, 94, 114, 132, 140, 145, 148, 156, 164, 190n47; McCormack and, 57–58; merit-based, 56, 147–48, 181n29 (*see also* merit); party sponsorship and, 61; reform and, 134, 147; retention and, 57–58, 61
endogeneity, 106–7
ethics, 2

Facebook, *51*
Fair Courts for Us, 3
FBI, 77
federalism, 41
Federalist Papers, 159
Federalists, 29
First Amendment, 43, 55, 142
Florida, 36–37
Floyd, "Pretty Boy", 35
France, 26, 101
Frank, Barney, 67
French, Judith, 52
fundraising: big money and, 2–3, 7, 16, 106–15, 121, 123, 131; dark money and, 44, 59; reform and, 134, 145, 149–52; retention and, 62, 67, 82–83, 86, 88; rise of judicial elections and, 34, 46, 53–54

Garland, Merrick, 149
gender, 10, 48, 50
Georgia, 29, 108, 153
Ginsberg, Tom, 160
Ginsburg, Ruth Bader, 149
good faith, 109
Gordon, Sanford, 75–76
Gorsuch, Neil, 149
governors: appointed judges and, 20–21, 28–29, 61, 64, 71–72, 148, 159; big money and, 3; currying favor with, 70–71; reform and, 146, 148, 159, 196n2; retention and, 61, 67–73, 94; rise of judicial elections and, 20–22, 28–39, 42, 56; self-interest and, 70–71
Great Depression, 34
Grisham, John, 8, 96, 100

Hall, Melinda Gann, 76
Hamilton, Alexander, 159
Hardberger, Phil, 42–43
Harman Mining, 97
Harris Interactive Poll, 193n45
Hazelton, Morgan, 107
health care, 7, 119
Holder, Eric, *51*
Holmes, Susan, 183n16
honesty, 26, 67, 134
Huber, Gregory, 75–76
Huntington Herald-Dispatch, 99

Idaho, 153
Illinois, 48, 53
impartiality. *See* bias
incumbents: big money and, 8, 96, 111; re-election campaign rates of, 184n34; reform and, 151; retention and, 65, 68, 74–75, 81, 184n37; rise of judicial elections and, 28, 48
Independents, 81
Indiana, 37
inflammatory ads, 44, 48, 50, 60, 73, 79, 99
Instagram, 50
insurance, 42, 87, 119, 178n73

interest groups: attack ads and, 5, 48, *49*, *51*, 69, 75–76, 79–82, 94, 103; big money and, 2, 5–7, 12, 103, 117; business cases and, 117; dark money and, 44, 59; disclosure and, 5, 44, 100, 196n96; growing involvement of, 40–41; labor unions, 25, 28, 44, 78–79, 87, 114, 196n1; reform and, 146, 149, 194n56; retention and, 61, 83, 87, 93, 95; rise of judicial elections and, 40–50, 53–55, 179n88; shaping legal decisions and, 6; Super PACs and, 44, 98, 179n88
Iowa Supreme Court, 1–4

Jacksonian Era, 30
Japan, 26
John F. Kennedy Profile in Courage Award, 3–4
Judicial Crisis Network, 60, 149–50
judicial elections: ABA opposition to, 5, 55, 146–47, 152; alarm over, 53–56; appointed judges and, 20–21, 27–30, 33; attack ads and, 5, 48, *49*, *51*, 69, 73–82, 94, 103; Bolivia and, 26–27; disclosure and, 5, 44, 100, 196n96; election incentives and, 94–95; France and, 26; historical perspective on, 28–39, 63–67; hybrid, 58; increasing costs of, 39–43; Japan and, 26; labor unions and, 25, 28, 44, 78–79, 87, 114, 196n1; Lasser on, 27; modern era of, 1–18; new-style, 43–53; politicization of, 39–43; reform and, 133–62; retention and, 63–67; rise of, 19–56; self-interest and, 70–71; Switzerland and, 26
Justice at Stake, 79
Just Say No campaign, 21–22

Kansas, 76
Karofsky, Jill, *51*
Kavanaugh, Brett, 149
Kelly, Daniel, *51*
Kelly, Mary, *52*
Kennedy, Caroline, 3–4
Kennedy, Sharon, *52*
Kentucky, 29, 31–32

labor unions, 25, 28, 44, 78–79, 87, 114, 196n1
lame ducks: age and, 125–27; bias and, 14–15, 17, 107, 111–19, 123–24, 131, 138–39, 151–52; big money and, 14–15, 17, 107, 111–19, 123–32, 190n47, 191n49; counter-explanations on, 124–25; ideology and, 17, 108, 111–12, 125; last term and, 129–31; re-election and, 13–17, 75, 107, 111–19, 124, 129, 131–34, 138–39, 151–52; reform and, 133–34, 138–39, 151–52; research methodology and, 115–19, 131–32, 166, *168–70*; retention and, 75; retirement and, 14, 111–12, 115, 117, 119, 123–31, 151
Lasser, Mitchel, 27
last-term judges, 129–31
lawyers: big money and, 3, 7–8, 109; campaign finance and, 196n1; reform and, 141, 143–46, 156; retention and, 82, 84, 87; rise of judicial elections and, 20, 25, 33, 35, 48, 53
leniency, 50, 76, 186n62
Lessig, Lawrence, 67
Lewis, Michael, 7
LGBTQ community, 187n94
liberals: big money and, 98; crime and, 25, 76; Democrats and, 81, 87, 91–92, 98, 187n94; press and, 25; retention and, 76, 81, 87, 91–92
Lindgren, Jim, 159–60
lobbyists, 53, 84, 157
Louisiana, 147

Madison, James, 66–67
Maine, 37
Massachusetts, 38–39

Mayhew, David, 66
Maynard, Elliot "Spike", 97–103
McCall, Madhavi, 108
McCormack, Bridget: attack ads against, 59–60; background of, 57–58; big money and, 106; campaign finance and, 59; retention and, 57–62, 94; on role of judge, 58; *West Wing* and, 60
McCormack, Mary, 60
McGraw, Warren, 8, 96–99
McWherter, Ned, 20–22
merit: American Bar Association (ABA) and, 55; big money and, 127, *128*; France and, 26; historical perspective on, 27, 34–37; individual cases and, 70, 78, 91, 144; reform and, 147–48; state courts and, 27, 34–37, 55–56, 181; Warren and, 34–35
Michigan Bar Association, 146
Michigan Campaign Finance Network, 59–60
Michigan Supreme Court, 57–61, 94, 108
Minnesota, 147, 153
Mississippi, 29–31, 39, 56
Missouri Plan, 21, 35–36
Model Code, 434
Moneyball (Lewis), 7
Montgomery, Jacob, 107
Montgomery, Richard, 183n16
Morales, Evo, 176n32
murder, 22–24, 36, 77

Natchez Aristocrats, 30
National Center for State Courts, *116*, 181n129
National Institute of Money in State Politics, 80, 190n41
National Organization for Marriage, 3
Native Americans, 30
Nevada, 147, 153
New Hampshire, 39
New Jersey, 37
New York, 29–31, 39, 141
New York Court of Appeals, 154
New York State Bar Association for American Progress, 146
New York Times, 98, 101, 138
North Carolina, 37, 56, 107, 142, 147
Nyhan, Brendan, 107
N.Y. State Board of Elections v. Lopez Torres, 55

Obama, Barack, 60–61, 148, 149
Obergefell v. Hodges, 3
O'Connor, Sandra Day, 5, 55, 145–46, 174n14, 181n121
Odom, Richard, 23–24
Ohio, 29, 33–34, 52, 153
OpenSecrets, 44
Oregon, 153
Overstreet, David, 48

Pacific Research Institute, 197n3
Parker, Bonnie, 35
partisanship: big money and, 2, 6, 11, 16, 97, 112–14, 120, 127–28, 190n47; election cases and, 90–94; reform and, 133, 145, 147–49; research methodology and, 164, *167–71*; retention and, 58, 60, 64–65, 69, 71, 76, 81, 84, 86–93; rise of judicial elections and, 19, 21, 25, 27, 32–39, 44, 56, 177n53
Pennsylvania, 31, 75–76, 85
Pennsylvania Republicans, 29
Pittsburgh Post-Gazette, 99
polls, 54, 82, 193n45
Presidential Commission on the Supreme Court of the United States, 160
pro choice, 187n94
Progressive Era, 33
Prohibition, 34

public opinion: anecdotal evidence and, 62–63; attack ads and, 73–82 (*see also* attack ads); Benjamin and, 99–100; re-election and, 67; reform and, 147, 149, 156, 158; retention and, 62–63, 67, 74, 94; rule of law and, 4; U.S. Supreme Court and, 58, 62
public schools, 187n94

quid quo pro, 9–10, 25, 102, 136–37

race, 10, 35–36, 187n94
rape, 22–23, 48, *49*, 77
recusal: Benjamin and, 8, 99–102, 136, 143–44; *Caperton v. Massey* and, 8–10, 99–102, 136, 140–44; Judicial Code of Conduct and, 99, 101; Starcher and, 101; U.S. Constitution and, 8; U.S. Supreme Court and, 102
Redish, Marty, 139–40, 148, 152
re-election: attack ads and, 73–82, 94; bias and, 10–18, 56, 63, 66, 76, 104–15, 121, 124, 131, 138–39, 150–52, 161–62; big money and, 1–2, 5, 10–18, 98, 104–25, 128–32; campaign finance and, 12–15, 59–62, 78–79, 82–94; crime and, 73–82; election incentives and, 94–95; Iowa Supreme Court and, 1–4; lame ducks and, 13–17, 75, 107, 111–19, 124, 129, 131–34, 138–39, 151–52; longer sentences and, 75–76; methods of, 68–73; modern changes in, 1–18; pressures of, 73–82; public opinion and, 67; reform and, 17, 134–40, 143–46, 150–57, 161–62, 195n68; removing, 150–53; research methodology and, *167–71*; retention and, 57, 61–82, 94, 184n34; rise of judicial elections and, 19, 21, 27–28, 32, 38–39, 54, 56; Scalia on, 4; self-interest and, 70–71; term limits and, 12, 17, 39; Ternus and, 1–5, 12, 14, 68; U.S. Constitution and, 140; weaponized decisions and, 73–74; White and, 19–25, 36
reform: American Bar Association (ABA) and, 146–47, 152, 155, 193n45; appointed judges and, 135, 140, 143–51, 158–61, 193n45, 194n56; Benjamin and, 135–45; bias and, 133–52, 161–62; big money and, 5, 12, 15–18, 114, 117, 119, 132; *Caperton v. Massey* and, 8, 16–17, 96–97, 135–45; *Citizens United vs. Federal Election Commission* and, 142; conservatives and, 143, 149; corruption and, 136, 150–51, 159, 161; *CQ Roll Call* and, 148–49; death penalty and, 156; Democrats and, 148–49, 160; donors and, 15–18, 133–34, 145, 151, 153, 161; due process and, 136–40; election system and, 147; fundraising and, 134, 145, 149–52; governors and, 146, 148, 159; incumbents and, 151; interest groups and, 146, 149, 194n56; Judicial Crisis Network and, 149–50; lame ducks and, 133–34, 138–39, 151–52; lawyers and, 141, 143–46, 156; Louisiana and, 147; merit and, 147–48; Minnesota and, 147; Missouri Plan and, 21, 35–36; Nevada and, 147; New York and, 141; North Carolina and, 142, 147; O'Connor on, 5, 145–46; partisanship and, 133, 145, 147–49; public opinion and, 147, 149, 156, 158; re-election and, 17, 134–40, 143–46, 150–57, 161–62, 195n68; Republicans and, 142–44, 148–49; retention and, 60; rise of judicial elections and, 21, 27–28, 31–37, 42–44, 56; solutions for, 134–35, 142, 145–47, 160–63; South Dakota and, 147; state courts and, 147; television and, 150; tenure and, 148, 151, 154–61; term limits and, 153–61, 196n94, 196n96; Texas and, 147; *Tumey v. Ohio* and, 136;

U.S. Chamber Institute for Legal Reform and, 146; U.S. Constitution and, 140, 146, 148; U.S. Supreme Court and, 149–50; Washington and, 147; way forward for, 15–18; West Virginia Supreme Court and, 142, 144, 153; Wisconsin and, 142

Republican Party of Minnesota v. White, 43

Republicans: attack ads and, 60, 81–82; Benjamin, 8–10, 96–104, 135–45, 189n25; big money and, 87–90, 96–99, 112–13, *120*; business cases and, 87; *Caperton v. Massey* and, 96–99, 112–13, *120*; election cases and, 90–94; ideological influence and, 87–90; Pennsylvania, 29; reform and, 142–44, 148–49; research methodology and, 164, *167–71*; retention and, 58–62, 81–82, 86–93, 187n93; rise of judicial elections and, 19, 22–23, 29, 43; same-sex marriage and, 3; Tennessee, 22; Trump, 148–49

research methodology: appointed judges and, 196n2; campaign finance and, 163–66, *167–71*; conservatives and, 164; control variables for, 164–65; Democrats and, 164, *167–71*; lame ducks and, 115–19, 131–32, 166, *168–70*; odds ratios and, 165–66; partisanship and, 164, *167–71*; party affiliation and, 164, 196n2; re-election and, *167–71*; Republicans and, 164, *167–71*; retention and, 72–73, 163–65, *167–71*; statistics, 10 (*see also* statistics)

resigning, 146, 154, 195n68

retention: appointed judges and, 59, 61, 64–73, 184n37; attack ads and, 69, 73–82, 94; bias and, 58–59, 63, 66, 76, 83, 85; big money and, 1–4, 17, 117, *120*, 121, *122*, 127–30, 174n37, 190n47; business cases and, 84–87, 89; campaign finance and, 59–62, 78–79, 82–94; *Citizens United vs. Federal Election Commission* and, 78–79, 84; conservatives and, 79–82, 87, 91–94, 187n93; corruption and, 67; criminal law and, 68, 75–76; death penalty and, 75, 183n28; Democrats and, 58–61, 81, 87–93, 187n94; donors and, 58–59, 64–67, 74, 82, 84–87, 95; election incentives and, 94–95; fundraising and, 62, 67, 82–83, 86, 88; governors and, 61, 67, 68–73, 94; historical perspective on, 63–67; incumbents and, 65, 68, 74–75, 81, 184n37; interest groups and, 61, 83, 87, 93, 95; Iowa Supreme Court and, 1–4; judicial selection and, 63–67; lame ducks and, 75; lawyers and, 82, 84, 87; liberals and, 76, 81, 87, 91–92; McCormack and, 57–62, 94; methods for, 68–73; Missouri Plan and, 21, 35–36; modern changes in, 1–18; partisanship and, 58, 60, 64–65, 69, 71, 76, 81, 84–93; pressures of, 73–82; public opinion and, 62–63, 67, 74, 94; re-election and, 57, 61–82, 94, 184n34; reform and, 60; Republicans and, 58–62, 81–82, 86–93, 187n93; research methodology and, 163–65, 72–73, *167–71*; rise of judicial elections and, 21–28, 35–40, 55–56; self-interest and, 70–71; solutions for, 140, 147, 154–55, 158; state courts and, 87; statistics and, 69–72, 77–80, 84–85, 89, 92, 183n16; television and, 59, 69, 74–82; Tennessee Supreme Court and, 58, 60, 64–65, 69, 71, 76, 81, 84–93; tenure and, 71; voting patterns and, 183n28; White and, 21

retirement, 68; cross-state analysis of, 115–19, 127–29; lame ducks and, 14, 111–12, 115–19, 123–31, 151; mandatory, 115, 127–29, 191n48; term limits and, 20, 27, 151, 153, 155

Rhode Island, 39
rise of judicial elections: appointed judges and, 26–32, 35–39; attack ads and, 48, *49*, *51*; bias and, 25, 28, 39, 48, 55–56; campaign finance and, 19, 44–45, 53–54; *Citizens United vs. Federal Election Commission* and, 44–46; conservatives and, 22–25; corruption and, 29–34, 38; donors and, 32, 44, 53–56; fundraising and, 34, 46, 53–54; governors and, 20–22, 28–39, 42, 56; incumbents and, 28, 48; interest groups and, 40–50, 53–55, 179n88; lawyers and, 20, 25, 33, 35, 48, 53; partisanship and, 19, 21, 25, 27, 32–39, 44, 56, 177n53; re-election and, 19, 21, 27–28, 32, 38–39, 54, 56; reform and, 21, 27–28, 31–37, 42–44, 56; Republicans and, 19, 22–23, 29, 43; retention and, 21–28, 35–40, 55–56; state courts and, 19, 28, 40–42; tenure and, 26–27, 29, 37–39
Roberts, John, 14, 16, 140–42

same-sex marriage, 1–4
Scalia, Antonin, 4, 6, 20, 139, 145
scandal, 29
self-interest, 70–71
Senate Judiciary Committee, 149
Shugerman, Jed, 29, 156
social media, 46, 50
Souter, David, 55
South Carolina, 37
South Dakota, 147
Stabenow, Debbie, 61
Starcher, Larry, 98, 101
state courts: big money and, 6; business cases and, 84–87; case loads of, 40–41; criminal law and, 6; growing influence of, 41–43; historical perspective on, 28–39; increased caseloads of, 40–41; merit-based selection and, 27, 34–37, 55–56, 181; National Center for State Courts and, *116*, 181n129; reform and, 147; retention and, 87; rise of judicial elections and, 19, 28, 40–42; term limits and, 153–58. *See also* specific state
State v. Odom, 22–24
statistics, 6; big money and, 10, 13–14, 104, 107–8, 112, 118–28, 190n46; Bonneau and, 108; Boyea and, 108; Cann and, 108; chi-squared, *167–71*; data-driven society and, 7; finding bias and, 104, 107–8, 112, 118–28; Hazelton and, 107; McCall and, 108; Montgomery and, 107; Nyhan and, 107; p-value and, 166; retention and, 69–72, 77–80, 84–85, 89, 92, 183n16
Steptoe & Johnson, 98
Stevens, John Paul, 25, 55
Streit, Justice, 3
Sundquist, Don, 22
Super PACs, 44, 98, 179n88
Supreme Court Term Limits and Regular Appointments Act, 160
Switzerland, 26

television: advertising costs and, 46–48, 59–60, 69; attack ads and, 5, 48, *49*, *51–52*, 69, 73–82, 94, 103; big money and, 117; Campaign Media Analysis Group and, 79–80; crime and, 73–82; inflammatory ads and, 44, 48, 50, 60, 73, 79, 99; influence of, 73–82; interest groups and, 5; reform and, 150; retention and, 59, 69, 74–82; spending on, 5; *West Wing* and, 60
Tennessee Code of Judicial Conduct, 25
Tennessee Conservative Union, 22–25
Tennessee Court of Criminal Appeals, 20–21

Tennessee First Judicial Circuit, 20
Tennessee Republican Party, 22
Tennessee Supreme Court, 54; big money and, 106; *State v. Odom*, 22–24; term limits and, 20; White and, 19–25, 36
tenure: big money and, 107, *128*; Calabresi on, 159–60; lifetime, 6, 17, 27, 71, 148, 151, 158–61; Lindgren on, 159–60; reform and, 148, 151, 154–61; retention and, 71; rise of judicial elections and, 26–27, 29, 37–39
term limits: legislative, 156–57; long single, 153–58; re-election and, 12, 17, 39; reform and, 153–61, 196n94, 196n96; retirement and, 20, 27, 151, 153, 155; state courts and, 153–58; Supreme Court Term Limits and Regular Appointments Act, 160; Tennessee Supreme Court and, 20; tenure and, 6, 17, 39, 151, 154, 156, 158; U.S. Supreme Court and, 39, 135, 153–61, 196n94, 196n96
Ternus, Marsha: bias and, 109; campaign finance and, 1–5, 12, 14, 109; re-election and, 1–5, 12, 14, 68; same-sex marriage and, 1–4
terrorists, 60
Texas, 42–43, 108, 147, 153
Thomas, Gregory Alan, 98, 143
TikTok, 50
Trump, Donald, 148–49
Tumey v. Ohio, 136
Twitter, 50

UC Berkeley Law School, 4
underwriting, 178n73
Uniform Crime Reporting Program, 77
United States v. Windsor, 3
University of Michigan Law School, 57, 60
University of Virginia Law School, 144
U.S. Chamber Institute for Legal Reform, 146
U.S. Chamber of Commerce, 43
U.S. Congress, 66–67, 69, 73, 160
U.S. Constitution: American Bar Association (ABA) and, 42; American Constitution Society (ACS) and, 77, *78*; Article III, 146, 148, 160; court independence and, 159; *Federalist Papers* and, 159; First Amendment, 43, 55, 142; oath to, 61; recusal and, 8; re-election and, 140; reform and, 140, 146, 148; unwise laws and, 55
U.S. Declaration of Independence, 159
U.S. Supreme Court: abortion and, 6; Alito, 195n80; big money and, 8–10, 14, 16, 96–103; Blackmun, 20; *Caperton v. Massey* and, 8–10, 14, 16, 96–103, 135–44; caseload of, 6, 101–2; *Citizens United v. Federal Election Commission*, 14, 44–46, 78–79, 84, 105, 142; Ginsburg, 149; influence of, 149; Judicial Crisis Network and, 149–50; Kavanaugh, 149; McGraw and, 96–99; *N.Y. State Board of Elections v. Lopez Torres*, 55; O'Connor, 5, 55, 145–46, 174n14, 181n121; Presidential Commission on the Supreme Court, 160; public opinion and, 58, 62; recusal and, 102; reform and, 149–50; *Republican Party of Minnesota v. White*, 43; Roberts, 14, 16, 140–42; same-sex marriage and, 3; Scalia, 4, 6, 20, 139, 145; Souter, 55; special role of judges and, 58; Stevens, 25, 55; Supreme Court Term Limits and Regular Appointments Act, 160; term limits and, 39, 135, 153–61, 196n94, 196n96; *Tumey v. Ohio*, 136; White and, 20, 25; *Worcester v. Georgia*, 30
U.S. Tort Liability Index, 197n3

Varnum v. Brien, 1–3
Vermont, 29
Virginia, 153

Walker, Beth, 144
Warren, Earl, 34–36
Washington, 147, 153
West Virginia Citizens Against Lawsuit Abuse, 144
West Virginia Supreme Court: Benjamin and, 8–9, 96–103, 135–39, 143, 189n25; big money and, 96–102; Canon 3E(1) and, 99, 101; *Caperton v. Massey* and, 8–9, 48, 96–102, 135–38, 142, 144; Davis and, 98, 101; Judicial Code of Conduct and, 99, 101; McGraw and, 8, 96–99; Maynard and, 97–103; reform and, 135–38, 142, 144, 153; Starcher and, 98, 101; term limits and, 153
West Wing, The (TV show), 60
White, Penny, 54, 68, 175n15; background of, 20; conservatives' campaign against, 22–25; crime and, 22–25, 36, 66; death penalty and, 22–24; First Judicial Circuit and, 20; Just Say No campaign against, 21–22; McWherter and, 20–22; on women as targets, 48, 50; *State v. Odom* and, 22–24; Sundquist and, 22; talents of, 20; Tennessee Supreme Court and, 19–25, 36
Whole Hogs, 30
Wisconsin, 142
Wisconsin Manufacturers and Commerce, 48
Worcester v. Georgia, 30

YouTube, 60
Yuchtman, Noam, 75